WILHELM MARR

STUDIES IN JEWISH HISTORY

Jehuda Reinharz, General Editor

Moshe Zimmermann
Wilhelm Marr: The Patriarch of Anti-Semitism

Other Volumes Are In Preparation

WILHELM MARR
The Patriarch of Anti-Semitism

Moshe Zimmermann

New York   Oxford
OXFORD UNIVERSITY PRESS
1986

Oxford University Press

Oxford   New York   Toronto
Delhi   Bombay   Calcutta   Madras   Karachi
Petaling Jaya   Singapore   Hong Kong   Tokyo
Nairobi   Dar es Salaam   Cape Town
Melbourne   Auckland

and associated companies in
Beirut   Berlin   Ibadan   Nicosia

Published by Oxford University Press, Inc.,
200 Madison Avenue, New York, New York 10016

Oxford is a registered trademark of Oxford University Press

Library of Congress Cataloging-in-Publication Data

Zimmermann, Moshe.
    Wilhelm Marr, the patriarch of Anti-Semitism.

    Translation of: Vilhelm Mar, "ha-patri arkh shel ha-
Antishemiyut."
    Includes index.
    1. Marr, Wilhelm, 1818–1904. 2. Anti-Semitism—
Germany—History—19th century. 3. Politicians—
Germany—Biography. 4. Germany—Ethnic relations.
I. Title.
DS146.G4M37913   1986   943.07'092'4 [B]   86–8349
ISBN 0–19–504005–8

9 8 7 6 5 4 3 2 1

Printed in the United States of America
on acid-free paper

Contents

Introduction, vii

Prologue: Germany in the Nineteenth Century, 3

1. The Man and His Origins, 8
2. From the Commercial Academy to the Revolutionary School, 14
3. The Radical in the Revolution of 1848, 20
4. From Politics to Business and Back: 1852–1862, 35
5. *The Mirror of the Jews,* 42
6. The "German Mazzini," 53
7. *The Victory of Judaism over Germanism,* 70
8. The "Business of Anti-Semitism" Syndrome, 96

Epilogue: The Decline of the Term "Anti-Semitism," 112
Appendix, 116
   The "Bremen Letter," 116
   "Within Philo-Semitism" (1887), 118
   "The Testament of an Anti-Semite" (1891), 133

Notes, 157

List of Marr's Writings, 173

Index, 175

Introduction

Historians, psychologists, sociologists, and publicists have invested a great deal of effort in the study and evaluation of the phenomenon of anti-Semitism, without paying much attention to the anti-Semites. Were it not for Hitler, Wagner, and a few other "chosen," it is doubtful whether we would have gained any insight into the working of the minds and the frame of reference of those for whom anti-Semitism was the be all and end all, the raison d'être. It would not be hard to surmise how far the study of the sources of Hitler's anti-Semitism would have reached had its subject been a "regular" anti-Semite and not the demon that brought all Europe to its knees. Here is proof: Streicher, the prototype of the most vulgar kind of anti-Semitism, earned the right to a serious biography only in 1974, and little more has been written about him since. Works dealing with Eichmann focused more on the key to the problem of the human automaton than on the question of the man's anti-Semitic motivation. By the same token, the prominent nineteenth-century anti-Semites who did not excel in anything but their "chosen vocation" were never honored with biographies. And so it happened that the personality of Wilhelm Marr, the man who rightly called himself the "patriarch of anti-Semitism," was never given any biographical coverage. Paradoxically enough, the Hebrew version of Marr's biography appeared at the same time as G. Field's biography of H. S. Chamberlain who, despite his renown as a racist and an anti-Semite, had not been given the appropriate scientific attention before.

Several explanations suggest themselves for the relatively wide interest in anti-Semitism and the limited interest in anti-Semites. First, political, social, and cultural anti-Semitism was, and still is, considered symptomatic of fundamental phenomena in human society and history such as nationalism, fascism, or racism. Consequently, it is only natural that the research and analysis that focus on these important historical phenomena should concentrate on these symptoms. Furthermore, because social scientists are aware of the existence of these phenomena and processes, they have developed tools for their analysis. Thus it has been possible to analyze and to relate to the specific phenomenon of anti-Semitism on the general level. This awareness has developed, as could be expected, mainly after the Second World War, in the wake of the holocaust of European Jewry, and therefore the historical research has been carried out in the special mood characteristic of that period.

Concerning the research produced in Germany, the problem is even more complicated: Until the beginning of the 1960's, anti-Semitism was a concept whose study was overshadowed by the collective bad conscience; more than that, it was a dirty word. Since that time, anti-Semitism has received systematic conceptual treatment, and yet one cannot quite ignore the suspicion that some of the German social scientists are using the research in a surreptitious attempt to clear the collective conscience. While striving to achieve this aim, they often obscure the importance of anti-Semitism by associating it with more general sociological and psychological terms, such as those mentioned previously, or by subordinating it to phenomenological classifications such as "minorities" or "prejudices."

Focus on anti-Semitism as a phenomenon or as a symptom implies lack of interest in the individual anti-Semites, and thus the specific interest in anti-Semitic activities or in anti-Semites becomes marginal. The prevailing attitude is that the social scientist aiming at a high level of generalization has no use for private careers of single anti-Semites. Moreover, if the purpose of the research is to treat anti-Semitism as a collective issue, and if the historians commit themselves to the sociopsychological classifications, then the study of the lives of individual anti-Semites—as long as they do not add up to a group profile—is of doubtful value at best.

There are, of course, also prosaic explanations for the scarcity of biographical studies of this sort: in contrast to anti-Semitism, which was considered an important social and ideological manifestation, the anti-Semites appeared only as the scum of the earth. There was obvious reluctance to write biographies of worthless anti-Semites, and even nowadays, in the era of the revival of great historical biographies, historians prefer writing about "great" men, usually men who caused great damage to mankind—such as Hitler, Wallenstein, or Bismarck—rather than writing about "small fry" or people who were usually only potential murderers. However, historians writing dissertations usually prefer biographies of "lesser" but "respectable" men; a socialist of secondary importance is certainly better than an anti-Semite.

There is also the question of sources. It is quite difficult to find sufficient material on people who were not meant to leave much documentation behind them, and the truth should be told: had I not found the papers of Wilhelm Marr—the anti-Semite who is the subject of this book—it would not have occurred to me to write his biography. Nevertheless, it is surprising that his huge *Nachlass* has lain in the Archives of Hamburg for seventy-five years, without challenging even those who made use of it to initiate a study of the personality of the man who is considered the originator of the term "anti-Semitism."

At first sight one could claim that, after all, the study of anti-Semitism has dealt with the biographical aspect at least from two points of view. On the one hand, we find the psychoanalytic study of anti-Semitism: the relation between the Oedipus complex and anti-Semitism, between the inhibition of the lust for patricide and anti-Semitism, or between fear of castration and anti-Semitism. However, the scientific psychohistoric literature on the subject (except for the kind dealing with the man Hitler) remains on the level of generalization. The application of those theories rests with the biography writer who, like myself, has the unenviable task of reconstructing the facts to prove their accuracy. On the other hand, we find the historical study of anti-Semitism, which in itself is not as extensive as we would like to think. This form of research uses biographical elements in an attempt to deduct from them to the general level. Nonetheless, biographical glimpses of this sort serve only as an insignificant background to "anti-Semitism per se." In those instances when there is no biographical study available, the historical study mainly contents itself with flashes of insight, lacking in relevancy and accuracy. Wilhelm Marr the man, who is our concern, is neither relevant nor revealing in most instances where his name was mentioned. His contribution to the development of anti-Semitism descends on the researcher and his reader mainly as a case of deus ex machina, leaving the riddle unsolved.

There is no doubt in my mind that biographical studies, including this one, aid in the analysis of anti-Semitism as a historical phenomenon. The study of Marr's personality serves to illuminate anti-Semitism from a biographical perspective, and the starting point of this biographical study— in contrast to those mentioned previously—is the concept of anti-Semitism as defined and expounded by this figure. It will become apparent to the reader that the biographical details mentioned until now in historical literature in connection with Marr the man and his well-known book *Sieg des Judenthums über das Germanenthum* reveal very little of the complex personality hidden behind a complex problem. The abundant material on the man who was usually characterized as a minor figure reveals the broad sphere of influence within which anti-Semitism worked. Wilhelm Marr is a figure standing at an important crossroad in German history: he was a prominent activist in the revolutionary movement during the restoration regime in the 1840's and a friend of the father of German socialism, Wilhelm Weitling; a known politician in the revolution of 1848 and one of Mazzini's circle, he corresponded with Bismarck and waged a personal war against the leader of the movement for Jewish emancipation, Gabriel Riesser. Here is a man who experienced the old order and the new, who was involved in the world of artists and writers, and made a name for himself as a politician. His biography is not of secondary importance; it throws light on the complexity of relationships within which anti-Semitism evolved and developed. The context, the connection, these are the key-words: anti-Semitism and its patriarch are no longer limited to the inferiority complex developed by a man through his conflict with Jews, but are part and parcel of the complexity of German and European history of the nineteenth century, in the broadest sense of the word. A biography of this kind also proves the futility of attempting to distinguish between Jewish history and "general" history, and clearly demonstrates the unity of these histories.

But because only the widest sphere of reference lends significance to the anti-Semite, I have resorted, though sometimes indirectly, to the methods used by modern social history. Fundamental in the composition of this biography are the guidelines and terminology of sociologists and psychologists. I show, for instance, that the prejudice in this specific case is actually linked to downward social mobility, or that Marr's criticism of the Jews is a projection of his personal failures and inclinations, or a symptom of his paranoia. But I will not indulge in these explanations at every step, to avoid closing the door on a variety of potential interpretations or lapsing into dilettantism, and especially not to disrupt the flow of the story. Suffice it to say that the facts have been put together in such a way as to suit any person following any of these paths in search of an explanation for the evolution of anti-Semitism and the shaping of the anti-Semite.

In this book I deal not only with the basic question in the study of anti-Semitism—how and why it emerges and works—but also with a more specific question: how was the term "anti-Semitism" coined and circulated until it became the sine qua non of the international vocabulary. It is the study of Wilhelm Marr—the man who spread this term on the waters of propaganda—which will make possible the semantic and historical analysis of the development of anti-Semitism. We shall examine in detail the influence of the term "anti-Semitism" on the phenomenon called before Marr's time simply "hatred of the Jews," while refuting some of the conventional clichés on the subject. Another matter I would like to clarify at this point is that a man like Marr does not necessarily justify a detailed biographical study unless it is certain that his personality is worth studying. References made to Marr in works written so far seem to exclude an examination of his personality. But this is a false impression. Despite his failings and his failures, Marr has earned the right to be examined. Here is a man who is intelligent, analytical, universal, and learned, a man who fought fanatically for his opinions. This is apparent not only in his writings but, according to the graphologist I consulted, in his handwriting as well. Marr was deeply involved in the events of his day, and even his anti-Semitism is interspersed with systematic criticism of the world he lived in. His anti-Semitism is permeated with a pessimism that is not a cheap propagandistic trick, as generally assumed by his readers, but a pessimism resulting from a developed Weltanschauung. There is real originality in his opinions, and this fact alone entitles him to close examination. But above all, the contradiction between the anti-Semitism and the "repentance" of the sworn anti-Semite throws new light on the history of anti-Semitism, at least in Germany. Paradoxically, a biography intended to deal with the man as an anti-Semite thus turns into a biography of a man to whom anti-Semitism was only one aspect of his personality and activity, as was the case with people like Wagner, Schoenerer, Drumont, and others.

This biography is based on a large selection of sources by an individual whom we could consider "the man of the nineteenth century," as Marr's life nearly overlapped the years of that century (1819–1904). During his long life he published many papers and articles on various subjects, the greater part in newspapers and journals by which he was employed. These papers and articles alone provide ample information to the historian, but later in life Marr also wrote several works that have never been published—memoirs (in six volumes), a quasi-political testament, and other shorter compositions—which supply important additional information about the man and his times. The wide sphere of his activities is revealed also in his correspondence with some three hundred people, which Marr carefully saved and later left to the State Archives of Hamburg. Such sources therefore grant us insight into the society within which he acted, and hence they are of great importance.

I have selected for inclusion at the end of this study three of Marr's works that are representative of the man and his times. The first is an early shorter essay, Marr's first anti-Jewish writing, dating back to 1862. It was published as a letter to the journal *Courier an der Weser*. The second essay, entitled "Within Philo-Semitism," was written in 1887 by a 68-year-old Marr who was deeply disappointed with the anti-Semitic movement. This work, which has never seen light, is of particular interest for those who look for the connection between the boy, the youth, the adult, and the old anti-Semite; between events connected with his adolescence and those of a later period. But the quest for this connection will certainly be an arduous task. The last, and maybe also the most impressive work, is "The Testament of an Anti-Semite" written in 1891. Like the others, this essay accumulated dust in the files of the archives and was never published. It is a rigorous settling of accounts on the part of the "patriarch of anti-Semitism" with what he calls "business-of-anti-Semitism" (*Geschäftsantisemitimus*). Beyond this, it is judgment passed by a nineteenth-century man, aware of the problems of his day, on the answers supplied to those problems by his contemporaries. No other document could grant us such insight into the role played by anti-Semitism in the complexity of conflicts, ideologies, and political moves of the century. These three essays provide a complex and interesting answer to the question of the sources and the role of anti-Semitism in Germany and Europe in the overall social process, and hence their importance.

I wish to note that deciphering Marr's handwriting was no easy matter. In several of the letters addressed to him we find the comment, "Please write more legibly," or "hire a secretary." If his handwriting presented problems during his life, it presented even more difficulty after his death. Marr's German handwriting was so illegible that it put off publishers in his day and historians after his death. This could easily be one of the reasons why his memoirs and his later works were never published. If it were not for my mother, Hanna Zimmermann, who helped me decipher Marr's handwriting, which worsened towards the end of his life owing to an arthritic disease, I think these documents would have gone on gathering dust, and an important chapter in the history of anti-Semitism would have remained fragmentary.

WILHELM MARR

PROLOGUE

Germany in the Nineteenth Century

The value of a biography as historical research can be measured by the weight given to the relationship between the subject of the biography and the historical period—the individual as a mirror, and fashioner, of the period, and the period as the context for the actions of the individual and as the object of his actions. This chapter attempts to clarify this relationship by briefly outlining the significant events in nineteenth-century Germany—the Germany between the Napoleonic Wars and World War I—the context in which Wilhelm Marr's activities took place, a context that explains Marr's actions, and which, in turn, was clarified by Marr.

The concept "Germany" was of limited political significance in 1819, the year Wilhelm Marr was born. Four years earlier, the peace treaty of the Congress of Vienna had concluded the wars that Napoleon had waged against Germany and Europe, and had created the German Confederation (Bund) on the ruins of the First German Reich, which Napoleon had abolished. The Confederation consisted of thirty-nine German states without a leader (i.e., without a kaiser). The two largest states in the Confederation—Austria and Prussia—were also its strongest states and expressed, in the clearest possible fashion, German particularism. Each state zealously guarded its sovereignty. The German Bund had no uniform foreign policy, no army, and no modern national message. The only issue on which the Bund could agree was that of "restoration" (i.e., the reaction against the concepts of liberalism and nationalism). In 1819, after a radical student assassinated a reactionary poet, the representatives of the member states of the Bund agreed to a string of matching censorship laws that were directed mainly against the press and the universities, with the aim of suppressing any expression of democratic nationalism. Thus the term "German Bund," which had been synonymous with the political term "Germany," became clearly identified at this time with the reaction—the antidemocratic, antiliberal, and, mainly, antinational tradition.

The reaction was felt throughout Germany in 1819. The Austria of Metternich set the pace, but its rival, Prussia, was also clearly headed on the path of reaction. The attempts at reform that had begun in Prussia in 1807 were now blocked by King Friedrich Wilhelm III and his advisors, and the restrictions placed in that same year on the democratic and innovative element of the Prussian army, the Landwehr, marked a clear turning point in the transition from reform to reaction. In the smaller German states there was also a general reactionary trend, albeit not one that proceeded at a uniform pace. In twenty years' time, Hannover in the north would become more reactionary, while Baden in the south would become much less reactionary. The city-state of Hamburg, Germany's largest port and the city in which Marr would take citizenship, exhibited a clearly reactionary stance in 1819, when it deferred the attempts to reform its obsolete constitution. The year 1819 therefore encapsuled the political message of Germany during the first half of the nineteenth century: the struggle between the unequal forces of reaction and political innovation, with reaction holding the upper hand.

The year 1819 also sharply expressed the dialectic between reactionary politics and a changing society: economic reorganization was a central mission for the German states in the economic crisis following the Napoleonic Wars; the Restoration had no role to play here. In this same year Prussia consolidated its customs policy for all its provinces, thus becoming a monolithic unit concerning financial management and placing itself in a position to take control of additional German states. The German Customs Union that Prussia formed fifteen years later was based on the steps taken towards internal consolidation in 1818–1819. Also in 1819, the German manufacturers informed the Bund of the need for economic expression of the constitutional structure (the Bund), and requested a reduction in customs between the German states and an increase in customs vis-à-vis other countries with economic advantages, particularly England. This request did not win any response in 1819. With the beginning of the Industrial Revolution, however, Germany gradually became aware of the need for a radical change in the commercial and economic policies of the German states. This awareness opened the way for a basic change in the general policy of these states.

The Jews also noted 1819 as a significant year in which the "Hep! Hep!" riots against the Jews broke out all over Germany, from the south to the north (with the exception of Austria and Prussia). These riots were also an expression of the dialectical relationship between the Restoration, or reaction, and the change in the social infrastructure. In places where there was fear of change, and where the Jews were seen as the bearers of change, those who had been hurt by the crisis, or who felt threatened by constitutional changes, gave vent to their fears by staging riots. This connection was evident in Hamburg, Marr's city: riots against the Jews broke out during the discussions concerning a change in the status quo of the guilds. The riots' message was clear: the Restoration had to be complete. The Hamburg authorities acted accordingly: to maintain quiet, they froze both the proposed changes in the area of economic reorganization and the constitutional reforms for changing the status of the Jews. The reaction was complete, and order was restored.

Ludwig Börne wrote in 1826 that "the ministers in Germany would have wanted to wrap every shell in the war in cotton batting, so as not to hear them when they landed. . . . Quiet is the citizen's first responsibility." It was as if quiet was a guarantee for order, as it had been in pre-revolutionary times. Under the conditions which had developed in Germany and in Europe as early as the 1820's and 1830's, it was impossible to halt the shell in flight or to stop politics in its place. Börne, like Heine and Marr, belonged to the revolutionary "Young Germany" movement, which had indeed acted vigorously, both openly and secretly, to achieve a Germany that would be different both politically and socially. The consciousness of liberal, democratic, and national ideals among the intellectual bourgeoisie joined with the discontent of the initiators at the head of the Industrial Revolution—the artisans, farmers, and others—to form a German revolutionary potential. In the 1830's, groups for political reforms were poised for radical action (Marr belonged to such a group); in the early 1840's, the weavers in Silesia revolted; and in 1847–1848, Germany suffered a severe economic crisis.

Finally, in 1848 the shell exploded in Germany: revolutions erupted—or constitutional changes were implemented to allay fears of revolution—in all the German states. The concept of German unification was expressed in the establishment of an All-German Parliament in Frankfurt, which also enacted a new constitution for all of Germany. All the forces that had been actively undermining quiet and order for the past thirty years burst forth during this revolution. The year 1848 was a great year for anyone who actively participated in it, and it was especially significant for Marr, a revolutionary democrat, who viewed it until his dying day more than half a century later as a climax in his life. His political and social actions and thought would revolve around this axis until his old age. Marr was not alone in this: 1848 was also an instructive and decisive year for the famous Bismarck, Marr's senior by four years, and it guided him in making far-reaching decisions. To cite only one example: in 1848 it seemed that the entire issue of German unity depended upon what would occur in the duchies of Schleswig and Holstein in the north. These two duchies, with a large German population, which were under the rule of the Danish king, but not part of Denmark, served as the touchstone of German nationalism. Marr, living in Hamburg on the border of these duchies, as well as Bismarck, in nearby Prussia, viewed this as a decisive issue. Both Hamburg and Prussia were involved in the war for the annexation of the two duchies that broke out during the revolution—a war that ended in disgrace for Germany, Prussia, and the proponents of German national unification. The war's outcome was engraved, in a traumatic manner, on the consciousness of the 48'ers; both Marr and Bismarck were to be involved again in this issue fifteen years later. The outbreak in 1864 of the "Danish War" over these two duchies, with Bismarck now the chancellor of Prussia, as well as the reaction of the state of Hamburg and of Marr the journalist to that war, can be understood only if one realizes the traumatic significance of a seemingly marginal incident that occurred in 1848.

In the eyes of the following generation that had not experienced the revolution, the impression the revolution had made on its generation was exaggerated. Many historians share this opinion; in the final analysis, the revolution had failed, and it did not receive political legitimization or sympathy in the official German histories. In this book, however, the revolution occupies a central position, with Marr's biography accordingly reflecting the period.

During the second half of the nineteenth century, Germany was characterized by the renewed political organization which had led, with the help of three wars, to what was termed "German unification" under Prussia in 1871. At the same time, the nature of Germany had changed as the Industrial Revolution had progressed. These developments left their mark—direct or indirect, conscious or unconscious—on the people who had participated in them, and Marr is most representative of this. The discrepancy between reality and expectations, between the battles that had been and the battles that were taking shape, a discrepancy that explains the conduct and reactions of individuals and masses, was openly expressed in Marr's writings and actions. The hope of 1848 was followed by a decade of frustrating political reaction, which in turn was followed by another decade of hope and political and economic progress. And then came the 1870's, the years following the establishment of the Bismarckian Second German Reich, which also brought frustration to many who had hoped and had been disappointed. The year 1871 had brought Germany not only "unification" but also a seemingly democratic-liberal regime and emancipation for the Jews. Many wanted to find a connection between these events and their frustration, making use of all manner of explanations. Anti-Semitism, with Marr as one of its pioneers during those years, was one of these explanations. An examination of the path that Marr followed during those years will provide a concise understanding of this explanation within the historical context.

Just as many of the people of 1871 had not understood the significance of 1848, there were many people in 1890—the year Bismarck was removed from Germany's political leadership—who did not understand the significance of 1871. The Germany of the end of the nineteenth century and the beginning of the twentieth was a society and state that not only accelerated and continued previously existing trends but which also underwent a radical change—large-scale and organized capitalism with a large and organized social democracy, imperialistic nationalism, militarism for its own sake, and cowed liberalism. This generation no longer understood what they had fought for in 1871 or in 1848. The alienation felt at the end of the nineteenth century by those born at the beginning of the century finds its expression in Marr's autobiography and in Bismarck's memoirs, which were written during the same years that Marr wrote his memoirs. These memoirs emphasize the chasm that separated the beginning and end of the century.

Marr died in 1904, a citizen of the German Reich for about a generation. One of the founders of modern anti-Semitism, he died in the same year as Theodor Herzl, the founder of Zionism, and six years after the death of Bismarck, the symbol of German nationalism. In 1904, the Germans were the subjects of Kaiser Wilhelm II, and Germany competed against France, Russia, and England for the rule of Europe and the world. This was a Germany that was modern economically but "half-baked" politically. The image of strength was faced by a reality of discontent. In 1903, a year before Marr died, the Social Democratic party, which was antimilitaristic, antinationalist, and anticapitalist, won an unprecedented victory: 32 percent of the vote. Along with the 9 percent of the left liberals (the regime's traditional critics) and the 9 percent of the national minorities, they joined together into a large bloc of the discontented. German society was not a united and monolithic one, as anyone who peered beyond the horizons of his own class could see. This is the reason why Marr, like other critics of German society, viewed the future with great trepidation. The chasm that opened in fin-de-siècle Germany between the conservative-bourgeois regime and the lower class revolutionary workers' movements was reminiscent—for anyone capable of remembering—of what had preceded 1848, but on a larger scale. It is possible that, from this perspective, Marr was indeed exceptional—he did not view the future with tranquility and security, but was profoundly afraid of a catastrophe. If Marr had lived another ten years, World War I and the revolutions which it spawned would have come as no surprise to him.

1
The Man and His Origins

Despite being the man who coined the term "anti-Semitism" and founded the "Anti-Semitic League," Marr did not occupy a central position in the history of anti-Semitism. Stoecker, Treitschke, and Chamberlain are better known than Marr as the pivots of the first wave of modern anti-Semitism. But what is even more surprising is that wherever his name was mentioned it was automatically associated with the claim—raised immediately on his appearance on the anti-Semitic scene—that Marr was of Jewish origin.[1] This claim was unfounded and was only one in a chain of pathetic attempts to strike at famous anti-Semites by denouncing them as Jews, as men whose special psychological background made them prone to self-hatred. It is a well-known fact that Richard Wagner, Marr's contemporary, and Theodor Fritsch, Marr's heir in the anti-Semitic movement, were "accused" of being of Jewish origin, and no efforts were spared to prove that Jewish blood was flowing in Hitler's veins. Still, in light of events in contemporary history, we should not condemn these attempts altogether, because there have been cases of converted Jews turned into haters of Jews and thereby doing real service to the cause of non-Jewish anti-Semitism. To cite only a few: Jacob Brafman, Aaron Briman, Joseph Lehmann, and Arthur Trebitsch. A book published in 1941 by Freienwald, presenting a self-portrait of the Jews, includes Wilhelm Marr on that list.[2]

The official confirmation of Marr's "purity of blood" was issued during the Second World War, at his grandson's request, who needed the notorious "Aryan certificate." A racist German researcher even published an article[3] defending Marr against the accusation of being of Jewish origin, a fact which had even caused his name to be erased from the official list of the fathers of anti-Semitism. This article, based on church registers and official documents, and supplemented by testimonies, indeed certified Marr's "pure Aryan" origin. But should we really act on the basis of this article?

The Lexicon of Hamburg Writers, published since the fifth decade of the nineteenth century, makes no distinction between great writers and second-rate journalists. This publication cites the name of almost anybody who ever indulged in writing in the city of Hamburg. So it happens that we have a detailed description of Wilhelm Marr, his father, and his grandfather.

Marr's grandfather, Johann Wilhelm, was born in 1770 in Eisenhammer on the Zwick to non-Jewish parents, married a non-Jewish woman in church and became a Hamburg citizen in 1796. From 1819 he ran the inn "King of England" and was a member of the butchers' guild, to which of course no Jew belonged. His literary activity was connected with the opposition to the French occupation of Hamburg, but beyond that he tried his hand at writing a play, "Wanderings of a Butcher," probably based on autobiographic elements. He died in 1837, when his grandson was eighteen years old.[4] Wilhelm Marr mentioned him several times in his memoirs and also in the preface to the eleventh edition of his book *The Victory of Judaism over Germanism*. No wonder he did: a significant part of his childhood was spent in Hamburg under the supervision of his grandfather.

Wilhelm Marr's father, Heinrich, was one of the most famous actors in Germany,[5] the first protagonist of Goethe's *Mefisto*. He was born in Hamburg in 1797 and took active part, alongside his father, in the liberation wars of 1813 and 1815 against Napoleon. In 1815 he began his career as an actor, first in Hamburg and then in Lübeck, Braunschweig, Kassel, Magdeburg (where his son Wilhelm was born), Hannover, again Braunschweig, Vienna, Leipzig, Weimar, and back to Hamburg. His frequent moves forced his son to change schools often. From 1857 on he became the first director of the Thalia Theater in Hamburg and was considered until his death one of the prominent figures in the German theatrical world. Heinrich Marr was the man who discovered and promoted Hebbel's career. His first wife, Katharina Henriette Becherer from Braunschweig, whom he married in her hometown on March 21, 1819, was not Jewish, nor of Jewish origin. After divorcing his first wife, Heinrich Marr married Elizabeth Sanghelli, a well-known writer. She wrote one of the first novels dealing with the working class, *Rich and Poor*, published in Leipzig in 1849. Among Heinrich Marr's writings we should mention a drama, *The Stockmarket Swindle* (*Börsenschwindel*), based on Balzac's *Mercadet* and written in 1851. It is only to be assumed that the title of this drama left an impression on his son, who was active in the first wave of anti-Semitism which swept the country after the shock of the "stockmarket swindle" in the 1870's.[6]

According to this information there is no reason to doubt Marr's racial "purity": he was 100 percent Aryan. However, after going carefully into the matter, I found that there might be a flaw in this theory. In the birth register of the Johannes Church of Magdeburg,[7] Wilhelm Friedrich Adolf Marr's birth was entered on November 16, 1819 (the same date mentioned by Marr in his memoirs and in *The Lexicon of Hamburg Writers*). Wilhelm Marr was christened on December 5 of that year, so there is no doubt that young Marr was—as his father before him—a Christian Evangelist and not converted. Yet the catch is to be found on the list of godparents at the ceremony, all of whom were Heinrich Marr's colleagues in the theater. Among the godfathers we find the words "the child's father," and it is not clear whether this refers to Heinrich Marr (who was in that case both the father and the godfather of his son) or to someone else, the actor Heinrich Buchholz, whose name is mentioned just before the words "the child's father." Since it is improbable that somebody would be father and godfather at the same time, I assume that Buchholz was indeed Wilhelm's natural father. Does that mean that Marr had a *Geier* of his own, like Wagner? A careful examination of the dates seems to support this assumption: Wilhelm was born five to six weeks prematurely, if one is to count the days from his parents' wedding. It could well be that Marr was a premature baby, or, more probably, that the pregnancy started before the wedding, but it is also possible that the wedding took place when Miss Becherer was already carrying the fruit of her relationship with the actor Buchholz. Nevertheless, I am inclined to think the last alternative as probable, although there is no allusion in Marr's writings to his doubtful parentage. I have found only one reference to Marr's birth certificate, in a letter from 1843: his father seems to have urged the 24-year-old Wilhelm to get married, and asked him if he should want his "christening certificate." The son refused to think of marriage until he found "his millionaire."[8] One could, of course, speculate that the father feared the discovery his son might make upon receiving the certificate, but as there is no other supporting evidence for this theory, I am inclined to discard it. Moreover, even supposing that Buchholz was Marr's natural father, it is nonetheless obvious that the man was Evangelist, and there is no evidence to point to the fact that he was not Aryan, so that Marr's German origin remains unshaken. Besides, in those cases where Marr was accused of being of Jewish origin, no mention was made of his Christening certificate, and therefore *it is not this document* from which the rumors originated.

Where, then, did the idea of Marr's Jewishness spring from? In 1862, with the publication of his first anti-Jewish book *Der Judenspiegel* (*The Jewish Mirror*), Marr's renown did not reach beyond the boundaries of Hamburg. The reactions to the book were indignant, yet no one voiced the suspicion that Marr could be Jewish. There are two explanations for this. The least important one is that there were no clear racial elements in his anti-Jewish attack, and therefore any claim to his Jewish origin would have been irrelevant to the discussion. But the main reason was that his opponents, citizens of Hamburg like himself, knew who Wilhelm Marr was, and also knew his father, Heinrich Marr, and therefore they did not raise this claim.

The claim was first made in 1879, after Marr published his anti-Semitic book, *The Victory of Judaism over Germanism*. This book found an echo throughout Germany, but first and foremost in Berlin. No wonder, therefore, that the favorite weapon was used here: "Marr never denied the claim that his grandfather was Jewish." This random accusation was published in a Berlin newspaper and was quoted in a magazine published by a Jew in July of the same year.[9] Marr felt obliged to reject it in the eleventh edition of his book. Another newspaper, the *Börsen-Courier* of Berlin, sustained that Marr's Jewishness reached as far as his father, Heinrich Marr. There was no proof to support these accusations. Marr publicized the genealogy of his family (back to the time of the Reformation) and stressed that his grandfather, who was suspected of being Jewish, raised pigs in the backyard of his inn and that his father wrote an unpublished article entitled "The Jewification of the German Theatre."[10] For a long time following this reaction, no more claims about Marr's Jewishness were raised. And during Marr's years of activity as an anti-Semite, there was no reminder of this accusation among his anti-Semitic friends, except for one incident in Austria in 1886, which is reported in the encyclopedia *Sigila Veri*.[11] The encyclopedia states that Glagau, one of the sworn anti-Semites of 1873 and after, believed that Marr was Jewish. But the encyclopedia did not accept this asumption and described Marr as a pure Aryan.

It might well be that some of Marr's articles in an Austrian paper *Österreichischer Volksfreund* (*Friend of the Austrian People*) of 1891 and 1892,[12] in which he attacked his anti-Semitic colleagues, were the reasons for the renewed interest in Wilhelm Marr and his origin, and I suspect this to be the reason for the connection made between his "Jewish origin" and his repentance for being anti-Semitic, as we shall see later. And indeed, the renewed claim about Marr's Jewishness reappeared one year after Marr's public condemnation of the *Geschäftsantisemitimus*, "business-of-anti-Semitism," at the time the newspapers were announcing his retirement from anti-Semitic activities (1893).[13] In his book published in 1941, von Freienwald based his conclusion on a newspaper article published by Rabbi Adolf Jellinek in 1893,[14] the last year of his life. The article appeared on the eve of the New Jewish Year 5654 under the title "For the Sin of anti-Semitism." As with the well-known prayer "For the Sin," it listed alphabetically all the sins of anti-Semitism from "Anti-Semitism" and "Ahlwart" to "Xanten" and "Zunftwesen" (the blood libel of 1891 in Xanten and the interdiction of Jewish membership in the guilds). Under the letter *M*, Marr appears for the following sin:

> Wilhelm Marr is a veteran anti-Semite who sinned greatly against the Jews, but who has lately retired from the anti-Semitic market while promising to disclose shattering facts about the ways of the anti-Semites. He is the son of the Jewish actor Marr, who performed with great success in Leipzig in the forties. Once he [Heinrich] appeared in the play *The*

Jews by Cumberland and I gave him a very elogious critic in the paper I
was editing, the *Sabbath-Blatt.* Thereby he called on me to express his
gratitude. In his opinion, his son couldn't possibly act against the Jews.

This quotation actually proves that Jellinek, who was living in
Vienna, recalled who Marr was after reading his articles in *The Friend
of the Austrian People,* in which he hinted at disclosures about the "business anti-Semites." (We shall deal with those articles later.) It also explains Dubnow's decision to refer to Marr as a convert:[15] it is only logical
to assume that if Heinrich Marr was Jewish his son could only become
non-Jewish by converting. It is also possible that this conclusion was
reached in an associative manner. Adolf Jellinek's son, Georg, was a convert, and Dubnow might unconsciously have assigned the fate of the
Jellineks to the Marrs. And how could Jellinek know that Heinrich Marr
was Jewish? Marr himself, in his unpublished memoirs[16] sustained that his
father's playing Jewish characters who were not an object of scorn
aroused in the hearts of Viennese Jews the feeling that the actor himself
was Jewish. Old Jellinek remembered correctly that Heinrich Marr performed in "his town Leipzig" in the 1840's (in 1844–1846, to be exact)
and remembered his impression of the character played by Heinrich Marr.
No wonder that at the ripe age of seventy-three, about fifty years after the
event, there was some confusion in his mind between the man and the part,
between stage and reality, and hence the wrong conclusion. (By the
way: By 1845 Marr senior was already first director at the Leipzig Theater and not a common actor.) This theme seems to have preyed a lot on
Jellinek's mind, because, in the same article, when reaching the F-Sin,
Theodor Fritsch, he wrote: "Unfortunately, he gained notoriety among
his competitors for being Jewish or of Jewish origin," a totally unfounded
claim.

In any case, it is Jellinek's last sentence in the paragraph about Marr
that arouses the greatest surprise. Why should Marr senior have put the
young rabbi's mind at ease by promising that his son would not act against
the Jews? This conversation took place at the time young Marr was known
to be involved in politics in Switzerland, and it is possible that his revolutionary tendencies awoke fears lest he direct his activities against the Jews
in the way of socialists of that time. If the conversation took place in
1846 it would be reasonable to assume that young Jellinek already knew
his contemporary Marr from the autobiographical book published by the
latter, *Young Germany in Switzerland* (*Das junge Deutschland in der
Schweiz*). But all this is irrelevant to Marr's origin. It is also possible that
Marr senior was reacting to Jellinek's inquiries about the younger Marr's
experience in Vienna: as we shall see later, Wilhelm Marr came into close
contact with the Jewish business world in Vienna in the years 1839–1841,
and he was not granted the best treatment there. Still, his memoirs state

quite clearly that the only way he could have acted against or among the Jews would have been as the blond *Goy* (gentile), not as a fellow Jew.[17]

There is also a roundabout explanation for the search for Marr's "Jewish" origin, and this is the matrimonial connection. When he finally married at the age of thirty-five, he married a Jewish woman, and after her he had two more wives of Jewish origin. There is certainly nothing in this to prove anything about his origin, but only his attitude, and to that we shall refer later. But his matrimonial preferences might have started the rumors that not only Marr's wives but also Marr himself might be "tainted" with Jewish blood.

2

From the Commercial Academy to the Revolutionary School

Marr's course of study did not herald his political and journalistic career, and pointed only obliquely at his joining the anti-Semitic movement. He went to elementary school in Hannover (1825) and to grammar school and the commercial academy in Braunschweig, Hamburg, and Bremen. Marr does not mention any particular problem in having to move from place to place owing to his father's theatrical activity. Also his encounters with the Jewish problem, mentioned in his unpublished book "Within Philo-Semitism"[1] could not have been very traumatic or extraordinary. Marr confesses that he almost took the wrong way, but thanks to the "Spartanic education" he received, he avoided the pitfall and completed his studies in Bremen.[2] The last two years of study (1837–1839), following the death of his grandfather in Hamburg and marked by long separations from his father, turned Marr against Bremen and what it stood for. He mentions, for example, the twenty-fifth anniversary of the "battle of the nations" in Leipzig (on October 18): both the fact that Bremen did not follow Hamburg's lead in the fight for independence from the French and the fact that the festivities were imbued with hatred towards the French after the fashion of a "Jewish Purim" made him swim against the current: he began to sympathize with Napoleon I,[3] turning a willing ear to the echoes of the French Revolution. In his memoirs, Marr strives to find more "method in his madness" than we would credit him with. It is doubtful whether it was his stay in Bremen that led him straight into the revolutionary camp, or whether his visit to Prague in 1839 and his encounter with the Slavic-German interrelation caused his awareness of the subject of race,[4] or whether his years in "Judified" Vienna brought about his anti-Semitism. But in his memoirs we find an attempt to reconstruct the past that does not present the facts in their true light. I assume that the events just mentioned, including his experience among the Viennese Jews, left only a fleeting impression on Marr. It was only at a later stage that he recalled them and used the facts in the service of his cause.

Finishing his studies, Marr moved to Vienna, where his father had been employed since 1831. His father used his connections with Jewish businessmen to get his son Wilhelm employed as a beginning clerk in two consecutive Jewish enterprises. Young Marr described in detail this experience and especially the atmosphere in these Jewish firms in his unpublished book "Within Philo-Semitism." His description calls to mind Gustav Freitag's *Soll und Haben,* but it seems that the atmosphere did not depress young Marr at the time. On the contrary, together with Jews and Christians he developed a semi-revolutionary activity. Talks with his friends brought forth republican ideas on the lines of the French Revolution, not an uncommon phenomenon in the Germany of the 1830's, especially after the Hambach Festival of 1832. Marr states that the group he belonged to used to sing the "Marseillese" at their meetings, although they did not go beyond that.[5] The strange combination of "France-Liberty-Napoleon" failed to inspire those strange young men to any remarkable action.

In 1841 Marr decided to try his professional luck in neighboring Switzerland, and this was indeed the starting point of his political biography. Marr put on paper the story of his years in Switzerland under the title *Young Germany in Switzerland.*[6]

"Young Germany in Switzerland" was a secret revolutionary association affiliated both with Mazzini's "Young Europe" and the movement "Young Germany," in which Gutzkow, Heine, Börne, and others were active, and whose headquarters-in-exile was in France. This association became active in Switzerland in the mid-1830's, after several political refugees from Germany came together. A radical movement, generally republican, and with a very lazy ideology; the declared enemy of this movement was the authoritarian monarchy; the real foe, though, was the communism of that time. Marr estimated that the leaders of the association had "a personal grudge against the rulers of Germany, but not a critical eye for the German society."[7] They were first and foremost revolutionaries who despised liberalism for its weakness and its lack of character. But their concern for the role of the individual in society as well as their German patriotism restrained them from cooperating with the rival movement, the communists. It is sometimes difficult to distinguish between these two ideologies that had so much in common: revolutionary aspirations, the concern for the people, for the working classes. Not everyone was aware of the liberal stress on the value of the individual (which Marr insists upon repeatedly) when comparing "Young Germany" with the communists. Also the fact that "Young Germany" did not develop a crystallized programme only aided to confuse the issue. This and more: in spite of the stress on individual freedom, Marr himself used quasi-communistic language when addressing the issue of classes and estates.

He was convinced that the only true opposition to the system in power is the productive class of the workers and that in the end the bourgeois-liberal will cooperate with the real opposition. He believed, like Marx, in polarization: "There are only aristocrats and democrats," nothing in between.[8] So the only desired policy is "a socialistic policy."[9] Nevertheless, it may be seen already at this stage of Marr's political activity that his conclusions are not only a matter of principle but to a great extent the outcome of personal grudges. This is clearly demonstrated in his article about "The Character of German Liberalism" that appeared on the eve of the 1848 revolutions.[10]

Wilhelm Marr joined "Young Germany in Switzerland" shortly upon his arrival in Switzerland. The first self-written document in Marr's archives is the letter he wrote to his father on June 27, 1843. In this letter, which was meant to report to his father the progress made in his business education, he had to admit that he had become entangled in political activities that had brought the police down on him. The closing sentences disclose that Marr's main concern was that this would hurt his mother. We also learn from this letter that at that time Marr was looking for a new job and was busy writing "an impressive essay of socialist character."[11] This, so it appears, did not arouse suspicions. But "my friend, a tailor apprentice by the name of Weitling, the writer of great communist books, was arrested and his papers were confiscated." (This event took place on June 9, 1843, and Weitling was arrested on accusations of "communism.") "He had in his possession letters from me, totally unimportant, in which I thanked him for books he lent me." Three years later, when he no longer feared his father's reaction (and the censor), Marr disclosed the truth: in his correspondence with Weitling they exchanged opinions about the latter's ideas—the same Wilhelm Weitling who is considered even today as one of the fathers of German Socialism.[12] The book Marr mentions in the letter, *Qu'est ce que la Propriété,* was published by Proudhon in 1840 and defines property as robbery. "An interesting book" Marr commented, "but not ripe enough." Referring to his father's situation in Bremen, where the latter had been refused the appointment of director at the local theater, Wilhelm Marr seizes the opportunity to air some of his social theory and here we finally find the Jew, Rothschild of course: "The time is ripe to share Rothschild's property among 3 333 333.3 poor weavers, which will feed them during a whole year." Indeed, the misery of the weavers even before the outbreak of riots in the province of Silesia (June 1844) was a focal topic for discussions among radicals.

In support of his ideas Marr published in 1843 a pamphlet entitled *Present and Future* (which was seized and confiscated by the Saxonian authorities) and another brochure on the petition of the inhabitants of Cologne to the king of Prussia.[13] From December 1844 until July 1845 he published a newspaper by the name *Blätter der Gegenwart* (*Pages of the Present*). Marr's foes, the communists, claimed that Marr could finance his enterprise only with government money paid for his services as an anticommunist agent. This accusation, which will repeat itself *mutatis mutandis* in later stages of Marr's activity, was unfounded, first of all, because Marr was supported by his father, and secondly because he made profits from the sale of a popularized version of Feuerbach's book *The Religion of the Future*.[14] It is not by chance that he dealt with this book, which shaped Marr's anti-Christian attitude both as a radical-democrat and as an anti-Semite. To understand Marr's career we should keep in mind that the years in which he embarked upon his activity were years in which various ideologies joined together in an attempt to break Christianity, the Christian society, and the conservative social order. These were the times when people like David Strauss, Bruno Bauer, and Ludwig Feuerbach, whose book young Marr abridged and simplified, were active. Another of Feuerbach's books, *The Essence of Christianism* (1840) attacked Judaism along with Christianity and named materialism and egoism as the main flaws of the former—two characteristics which were to play a critical role in Marr's anti-Jewish and anti-Semitic writings forty years later. This book also mentioned the anti-Jewish "opus magnum," *Unmasked Judaism* (*Entdecktes Judenthum*) published by Eisenmenger in 1700, and even though this mention might not have influenced Marr at the time, it supplied him with a piece of information for later use. A year later another important book saw light: *Die Judenfrage* (*To the Jewish Question*) by Bruno Bauer, and after two more years the *Unmasked Christianism* was published and confiscated immediately. The latter book was also abridged by Wilhelm Marr![15] The arguments raised in the book against the emancipation of the Jews would find their protagonist in Marr in the hour of his first anti-Jewish battle, in twenty years' time!

It is obvious, that in those years the foundation was laid on which Marr was to conduct his battle against Jewish emancipation. One could argue that Marr's attacks against the Jews in the 1860's, on the lines of the radical views of Marx and Bruno Bauer in 1843, were only a "delayed reaction" brought about by the realization of Jewish emancipation. But for the time being, Marr's critical attitude toward Christianity reflected only his disagreement with Weitling on Christian elements within communism. He rejected those elements as part of his sweeping opposition to the role played by religion in European society.[16]

In the years 1843–1845 Marr was therefore up to his neck in revolutionary activities. Although he admitted (as early as 1846) that some of those activities were ridiculous, he did not differ in that respect from the majority of German revolutionaries of his time, with the possible exception of Moses Hess and Karl Marx, both of whom he mentioned in his book *Young Germany in Switzerland* in a caustic footnote.[17]

Already at this stage Marr took a stand of absolute opposition to the communists both because of their *Glaubenstyranei* (intolerant attitude to-

wards other beliefs) and because of their cosmopolitan views. In reality
Marr was not very consistent: he represented himself as a cosmopolite, as
a fighter for the cause of humanity (for whom the term *"Volk,"* people,
meant the oppressed people, the oppressed classes), but within this cosmopolitan context the national motif appears again and again. This theme
continued to preoccupy Marr in 1848 as well as in the 1860's and 1870's,
when the problem of unifying Germany became acute.

Marr's sharp retort to the communists' claim that they were the true
"universalists" was that "Young Germany" was also universal in its
orientation but that it could not ignore the existence of peoples and nations: "The idea moves the world, the language is its instrument, and the
peoples (nations) are the objects of its activity."[18] And from his awareness of the importance of nationhood in general grew his belief in a new
Germany.

In those days the term "Germany" evoked negative connotations
owing to its political regime: "Germany" symbolized tyranny and oppression. But the "Young Germans" acknowledged the existence of nations
and therefore developed a new German vision: "the present time praised
patriotism more than ever! The skies of German politics were again
colored black-red-gold [the colors of republican Germany, dating back to
the Napoleonic Wars or even to the German medieval history]. No wonder therefore that its citizens reflected those colours."[19]

In Marr's case the "black-red-gold" ideology was accompanied by
an extreme radicalism. Beyond his quest for a republican Germany lay
the aspiration for "democracy in its fullest sense." We encounter here the
same polarization between democrats and aristocrats with no room in
between: even the liberal bourgeoisie will have to turn, according to
Marr's prognosis, into a camp follower of the democrats (i.e., of the
lower classes).[20]

Marr's opinions were considered as too extreme in Switzerland and
so he was expelled from Zurich in 1843, thus putting an end to his business career. To earn his bread he now had to do manual work: cutting
trees. On July 25, 1845, Marr was expelled from Canton Waadt, which
lies in the French-speaking part of Switzerland and was governed by a
radical group that could not agree with Marr's brand of radicalism.[21]
Two recollections from that time stayed with Marr and were to play an
important, though indirect, role in his life as an anti-Semite: on the one
hand, it was in Switzerland that he learned to use the racial distinction to
understand nationalism; the various races and the one nationality characteristic of Switzerland aroused Marr's doubts.[22] On the other hand, his
enemies stamped him as a friend of the Jews. On August 15, 1845, the
following piece of news appeared in the *Wochenzeitung* of Zurich: "The
atheist Marr, who was banned by the ultra-radical authorities of Canton
Waadt, has found shelter with the friends of Jews and other non-Christians
in our city."[23]

Marr was forced to leave Zurich and Switzerland and joined his father in Leipzig, Saxony. But it was not long before he got in trouble again because of his radical activities. He sat in prison (which he described as a joke: one of his fellow prisoners possessed a key to the prison),[24] and after his release he moved to Altenburg, then returned to Leipzig, only to be banned again. His book *Young Germany in Switzerland* was published in Leipzig by Turani, while Marr was living against his will in Hamburg, the city of his forefathers. Later he would mention with bitterness that the thirty-eight German states, the members of the German Bund, dealt with him as if he were a roulette ball, forced to slip from one square to another until he landed on the "null"—the free Hansa city of Hamburg, his father's hometown.[25] At that time, however, he did not consider Hamburg as "nil." On the contrary, he assumed that by being a republic, it would deal kindly with him. Moreover, he knew that it had much more to offer economically.[26]

The book *Young Germany in Switzerland, the History of Secret Associations in Our Days* enjoyed great publicity and Marr became a personality not only in Hamburg but all over Europe. It was the most popular book he ever wrote, *The Victory of Judaism over Germanism* included. According to Marr himself, this book was intended as a memorial to "Young Germany in Switzerland." Before the Union was dissolved, its members requested—according to Marr's version—to disclose the truth about its activities and to blunt the teeth of its critics. Lots were drawn for the man to write the book and Marr won the honor.[27] According to another version of the story, Marr betrayed the secrets of the association by writing this book. There is no clear evidence to support either version, but the second one, citing Marr as a traitor, was used against him as late as 1879, at the time when he attempted to become the leader of the Anti-Semitic League.

I could not conclude this chapter of Marr's life—a chapter of great importance for the understanding of Marr's self-contradictory attitude to the Jewish issue—without stressing that from Marr's book and his numerous articles it appears that his idols were not only Bruno Bauer and Feuerbach, the "Christians-eaters," but especially two Jews who led "Young Germany"—Heine and Börne. His admiration for these two did not dwindle over the years. Quite the opposite, it only increased! In his memoirs, written fifty years after the events mentioned in this chapter, he repeatedly praised the two forgotten idols as writers, revolutionaries, and above all as social reformers. To the end of his life, Marr was to live under the shadow of the contrast between the rival camps of his idols. His anti-Semitism reflected this paradox but could not find a solution to it.[28]

3

The Radical in the Revolution of 1848

When Marr arrived in Hamburg, he was already a "professional" revolutionary who was active along with a number of other vocal radicals. The radicals, or democrats, were the collective political spokesmen of the classes which had not been treated well by the liberals. These classes included, on the one hand, artisans whose means of livelihood were endangered, and, on the other, workers in new factories, or in works connected with Hamburg's large port. The leading democrats/radicals came from among the writers and intellectuals, such as Marr or the like-thinking Jew, Anton Rée, the principal of the *Freischule,* the free Jewish school for those of limited means. (He would later become a German Reichstag deputy, representing the Progressive Party.) Although the democrats and liberals had largely agreed with each other before 1848, mainly on the need to do away with the old regime and its constitution, the two camps, which differed ideologically and represented different social classes, were hostile and competed with each other. Even before 1848, this conflict was more striking in a city-state such as Hamburg, which was not headed by an absolute ruler. A moderate sort of liberalism was not foreign to the city-state's government, and accordingly the liberals were not so unequivocally opposed to the existing regime as were the democrats.

Marr formulated his disgust with liberalism in a very strong manner in his essay "The Nature of German Liberalism." In his opinion, cowardice, hypocrisy, and degradation were characteristic of liberalism, and therefore had no future in Germany. There was nothing new in the radicals (including Marr) viewing the liberals' abandonment of the working classes as a serious shortcoming. For Marr, however, the confrontation with the liberals was also a personal one. Marr responded to the liberals' many attacks on him by stating, "I would be happy to bury the Liberal Party; I would prefer to live under the iron rod of a despot, even that of

Nero, than under the rule of money and the bourgeoisie." This was a potentially dangerous threat; like many other radicals, Marr would carry out his threat some years later.[1]

As soon as Marr arrived in Hamburg, a problem arose to which the democrats and liberals reacted differently: the problem of Schleswig-Holstein. Moreover, when Wilhelm Marr took part in the debate, he clashed for the first time—in theory then—with an important Jewish personage, the Hamburg liberal Gabriel Riesser. Riesser was considered to be the mainstay of the Jewish struggle for emancipation during the years 1830–1848. In the future, this rivalry would expand to giant proportions for Marr and profoundly influence his position on the connection between the Jewish question and liberalism until his last years.

The problem of whether the duchies of Schleswig and Holstein belonged to Denmark or Germany had intensified since 1840.[2] This was a central issue for Hamburg, which bordered on Holstein and which until recently had itself been connected to the Danish monarchy. In 1846, the liberal Gabriel Riesser viewed the problem as one of freedom and nationalism: was it preferable for Holstein to receive more freedoms from the Danish king or to join the German alliance, even though the latter had not progressed sufficiently towards a liberal constitution? Riesser did not oppose a German Holstein, but he wanted to stress the dilemma—the same dilemma facing the liberal German Jew considering his Germanness—of living in an illiberal Germany. In contrast to Riesser, Marr saw this simply as a problem of monarchy versus democracy: "Anyone not wishing to bend his back must break. . . . A king speaks about the problem of Schleswig-Holstein. Arise German people! Give him his answer!"[3] The fight against monarchy was more relevant than the question of the current character of the other parts of Germany.

In January 1847, Marr finally succeeded in fulfilling his desire to start a newspaper, *Mephistopheles*. This was an opposition newspaper (within the limits afforded by the censor), directed against both the conservatives and the liberals; its publication was made financially possible by a partnership with an investor and journalist, a Danish doctor by the name of Peine. But Marr was forced to close the newspaper—which apparently was popular and a commercial success—in May 1847, in its first year of publication, when the Prussian government complained about an attack made on it by Marr. In accordance with the Carlsbad Decrees concerning censorship (1819), Prussia could exert influence upon the Hamburg censor's office and request the closure of the newspaper.[4] The official charges against the newspaper were formulated in a vague manner: "a crime against earthly and Divine law." Closing the newspaper was not sufficient: Marr was sent to prison for four weeks—one more stretch in jail, neither the first nor the last during his lifetime.

The paper was reopened only on April 2, 1848, with the outbreak of the German revolution and the cancellation of censorship. But the manner in which the newspaper was closed influenced Marr's future thinking about Germany, and he later became an opponent of the "Little Germany" policy. In light of Hamburg's submission to Prussian pressure to close his newspaper, Marr felt that the conservative and impotent Hamburg republic should merge with Prussia;[5] actually, he was angrier at the instrument than at its users, but as long as Prussia remained unreformed, Marr could not reconcile this idea of merger with his democratic republicanism. This explains why he acted with such vigor in 1848, as did other radicals, to nullify all the German states and replace them with the German republic. This early position (together with events connected to the 1848 revolution) also paradoxically explains why he was willing under new conditions in 1851 and 1864 to adopt a strikingly pro-Prussian stance, "Borussomanic," in his words, on the future of his city and that of Germany in general.

A perusal of *Mephistopheles* reveals a sharp pen, biting satire, and superb writing ability. This newspaper served as a school for satire for the noted Jewish satirist Julius Stettenheim, who began his career as an apprentice of Marr's and eventually thanked him for this opportunity. The bitterness that surfaces in Marr's writings prevented him from expressing himself in the refined manner of Heine and Börne, his political and literary idols, but it cannot be denied that his writing seemed to assure him a career as a man of letters from that time on. However, the bitter fact that Marr was not recognized as a respected journalist or writer caused him to become deeply frustrated, a frustration that lies at the base of his future anti-Semitic outbursts and his anti-Semitic *Weltanschauung*. A question that bothered Marr until the end of his days was why he, who had preceded the Berlin journal, the *Kladderadatsch,* had not succeeded in attaining the respected position which the latter enjoyed among the German satiric press.

But to return to the years before 1848, Marr dreamed of the coming revolution, giving first priority to the "universal European republic," while according a lesser position to the "indivisible German republic." Those were the days in which he swore to mercilessly fight the nondemocratic Hamburg republic, whose insignificance he senses at every step. Marr's ambivalent attitude towards the city of his forefathers, on the one hand, and to the Prussia in which he had been born, on the other, overshadowed to a great extent his attitude towards Germany in general, not to mention his attitude towards European universalism.

Marr's hostile attitude towards the various municipal authorities to which he had vainly appealed in an attempt to reduce his punishment for his published attack on Prussia may explain his future support for the struggle for Jewish emancipation in Hamburg. These were the same institutions, conservative to the point of extremism, which withheld emancipation from the Jews as well. The Senate, and even more so the Oberalten (the leaders of the representatives of the bourgeoisie), stood in his

way, just as they stood in the way of the Jews. The alliance between Marr
and the Jewish liberals or revolutionaries was self-understood. Marr, as a
radical, did not find it difficult to find allies in pre-1848 Hamburg; he
testified that most of the citizens had firmly opposed tyranny—and had
even favored a German republic. He stated, however, in a description
sounding like a paraphrase of Stettenheim and Thomas Mann ("Bring us
another republic . . ."), that the same public living in the Hamburg republic that wanted a German republic also desired a German kaiser. He,
himself, and his comrades saw the solution in the spirit of Louis Blanc,[6]
believing that only a *social revolution* would bring the Messiah. This idea,
in different guises, would guide him until his dying day—both into anti-
Semitism and away from it. Blancism led him to question all the founda-
tions of society, including marriage and the family. Marr's main essay of
that period, *The Man and Marriage,* which appeared in 1848 completely
rejected this institution. This essay gave expression to an additional aspect
of his war against any kind of partial emancipation, in this instance the
emancipation of women. For emancipation to be attained, the *entire* society would have to be liberated—the same hypothesis which was proposed
for the emancipation of the Jews. According to Marr, these two emanci-
pations were examples of man's liberation from things (*Sachen*), from
possessions. "Haggling [*Schacher*] is our method, and the woman [and, as
we shall see later on, the Jew also] is part of this method. Marriage is the
sale of a woman to a single man; prostitution—to all." Woman's emancipation meant liberation from the relationship of haggling and possessions.
Marr, like Marx, would eventually arrive at the conclusion that the
emancipation of the Jews would be their liberation from the spirit of
haggling, or the liberation of the world from this spirit. The path from this
to the next stage—equating the emancipation of the world from enslave-
ment to haggling with freeing the world from Jewish rule—would not have
to be very long. It is of interest, however, that *here* Marr speaks of
Schacher as a problem of the entire world, *not* as one particularly connected with the Jews. Marr used this term in its common associative context, the Jewish context, only at a much later stage.[7]

Marr later termed all his activity during this period, including his activity during the 1848 revolution, as "the folly of youth." The attempt to
explain away this activity with a wave of his hand apparently stemmed
from the need to free himself from his past support of German republicanism, at a time when he already supported Prussian conservatism. Even
when he changed camps, his "youthful ideas" still guided him.

Marr learned about the outbreak of the revolution from a Jewish
friend from Breslau by the name of Fischel. When the tidings spread
throughout Hamburg, most citizens turned into revolutionaries, thus
breaking the monopoly on revolution enjoyed until then by Marr and
his comrades. As a radical, but also in opposition to the majority, Marr
wore a *red* cockade on his hat, in contrast to most people, who wore the

black-red-golden cockade, the symbol of German liberal nationalism. We have already mentioned that Marr had championed the black-red-gold when he was a follower of "Young Germany in Switzerland," but now he changed direction, becoming more extreme. The reason which he gives for this change does not, in my opinion, explain his real, personal motive for opposing the black-red-gold, but his explanation was consistent and logical from the republican viewpoint. Marr explained that these were the old colors of the Reich, Barbarossa's colors, under the auspices of which Barbarossa had set forth on adventures in Italy and Palestine that were of no benefit to Germany. So what did a German revolutionary have to do with these colors? Now, in 1848, Marr chose the opposite of this tricolor—the red! Within twenty-two years he would choose quite another opposite: the colors of Prussian Germany, black-white-red. This symbolic act distinguished Marr's radical path from that of the radical Richard Wagner, whose character invites comparison with that of Marr. Wagner, who also changed from radical to anti-Semite, was a proponent of the black-red-gold before 1848, in the same sense that Marr related to it. The Middle Ages had a positive meaning for Wagner that led him directly to national romanticism and anti-Semitism. Marr's path was much longer and complicated.

The leaders of the merchants in Hamburg, stock exchange people, had mounted the horse of the revolution, the horse upon which Marr wished to ride from the very beginning. A revolutionary council, from which Marr and his circle were excluded, had already been elected at the first revolutionary assembly. The first issue that the revolution in Hamburg addressed was the question of Schleswig-Holstein. A large gathering, headed by Heckscher, Baumeister, and Riesser—the representatives of the liberal bourgeoisie—organized a petition on the issue. Marr and his associates, who demanded action (i.e., sending the army) instead of a petition, remained in opposition once again. The opponents of the frustrated Marr were also the winners of the following battles. From now on, Riesser, the Jew, would emerge as a target for Marr's attacks (we will elaborate on this later). The outstanding personage since the first days of the revolution was Moritz Heckscher, a converted Jew, who Marr occasionally attacked sharply.[8] Yet Marr never mentioned Heckscher's origin; he apparently did not think it was relevant.

It should be mentioned that Marr's personal disappointments and frustrations explain, to a great degree, his political positions and actions, as well as the sharp transitions and changes in attitude observed in his political thinking. There is no doubt that we are dealing with an extremely sensitive person who knowingly and inadvertently revealed his personal weaknesses. His attitude towards the events of the 1848 revolution clearly illustrates the impact of his frustrations.

Marr was not a great success during the revolution, and even though he was, according to Stettenheim, one of the most popular democrats at the beginning, his popularity did not bring him any real gains. A sober examination reveals that even those who appeared to him as successful (at his expense) did not gather any garlands. Riesser and Baumeister, the representatives of the learned bourgeoisie (*Bildungsbürgertum*) and the professions, were not successful in being elected from Hamburg to the German Parliament of Frankfurt. The "aristocracy of money," the "stock exchange," not the learned bourgeoisie, was victorious in Hamburg at the crucial hour. This aristocracy sent two of its outstanding representatives to Frankfurt, as well as the two-faced Heckscher, who was both a merchant and intellectual. This same Heckscher also became the justice minister and foreign minister in the government formed by the National Assembly in Frankfurt. Marr's wrath was aroused by this success: Marr the radical hated this aristocracy; in his opinion, it rested on the backs of the middle and lower classes.[9] Marr would later claim that Heckscher had "sold" the German interest, a claim for which he was sued by Heckscher.[10] It is questionable whether Heckscher's political success was a fitting reason for such an unbridled attack.

As for Riesser, the person who became a thorn in Marr's flesh, after failing in his attempt to be elected as a Hamburg representative to the Frankfurt Parliament, he tried his luck in the nearby state of Lauenburg. An indirect system of voting was in effect there, and a majority of the electors voted for him, in spite of the fact that thousands of those voting for the electors did not know who Riesser was and would probably not have chosen him, since Jews were not allowed to reside in this state.

Marr was severely disappointed by the election of the liberals to the Frankfurt Parliament and by the atmosphere in Hamburg, and even in Berlin, which he had visited in June as a representative of the Revolutionary Club in Hamburg.[11] About a month after the Parliament convened in Frankfurt, he reached the conclusion that it would be better for a republican like himself to fight for a model republic in Hamburg than for a weak German republic. He reported to those sharing his beliefs that "nothing can be expected from the Constituent Assembly in Frankfurt."

He also began to study Machiavelli's writings. He centered his attention on the *Discorsi,* since the concept "people" interested him. He later admitted that it was from Machiavelli that he learned to regard a "people" not as a collection of individuals but as a universe with its own pace and character, with its own natural laws. This conclusion did not blunt Marr's radicalism, but at this stage greatly eliminated the individualistic-liberal element, which had remained with him from the conflict with the communists during the "Young Germany in Switzerland" period. Marr and his radical friends made practical use of the rules they had learned from Machiavelli in the elections to the Hamburg Constituent Assembly (which will be discussed later), and succeeded: "Not democratic logic, but the lack of logic, raised us up, and I saw what success can be achieved during revolutionary times by means of the masses' base and illogical senti-

ments."[12] This position also becomes important later in his attitude towards the Jews within the conceptual context of "people."

Marr was initially more successful than his rival Riesser in his activity within the Hamburg republic. His radical-democratic party defined
its extremist goals in an assembly held on August 7, 1848: to abolish the
conservative Senate and Citizen's Assembly, since they were not constitutional, and not to pay taxes "as long as the will of the people would not
be realized." Marr was one of the three heads of the Provisional Democratic Committee, and was accordingly arrested on August 12. He was
released after he promised not to incite riots. In October, Marr was
elected to the Hamburg Constituent Assembly as a radical. The bloc to
which Marr and the democrats-radicals belonged was indeed called "liberal," represented the lower and learned bourgeoisie, and fought against
the "patriotic" party (which in practice represented the higher, merchant
bourgeoisie, which also was liberal in outlook). Marr belonged to the
left wing of the "Liberals"; his rivals even warned the electorate not to
vote for him because of his extreme atheism.[13] He nevertheless received
1,629 votes in his electoral district, District 6, in which he tied for twenty-
fourth place with another candidate. Since this district was supposed to
send twenty-four representatives to the Hamburg Constituent Assembly,
a lottery was held between the two candidates and Marr was sent to the
Assembly. Riesser did not run for election at this time, but ran in the
by-elections in March 1849, in which he received only 308 votes in his
district, far behind the winning candidate.

Marr's success in Hamburg at that time was not only due to luck,
but was mainly a result of the radicalization of the city's mood.[14] This
radicalization was largely a reaction to what had happened in the Frankfurt Parliament, and explains to a great degree the success of radical candidates such as Marr, and the failure of liberal candidates such as Riesser,
in the local elections.

Marr's electoral district was greatly dependent upon the Jewish vote
in the elections which were held on October 16, 1848. The Jewish question was obviously a central issue in such an area, and Marr did not
adopt an anti-Jewish position, despite the fact that such a position existed
in the radical camp as well. We can accept Marr's later claim that at that
stage he was among those fighting for Jewish emancipation. In his newspaper *Mephistopheles,* which reappeared in April 1848, he even attacked
the rival "Patriotic" party for lack of honesty in the presentation of its
pro-Jewish stand: the Jews had suddenly become their "brothers."[15] It
is clear, however, that he had to do this for tactical reasons as well (the
Reform rabbi Naphtali Frankfurter came in third in Marr's electoral district, with 2,898 votes—almost twice as many as Marr received). Marr,
however, in a satirical pamphlet which he published anonymously, *Die
Jacobiner in Hamburg,* settled accounts in an unsympathetic manner not
only with the radicals in Hamburg but also, explicitly, with the Jews

among them and with the supporters of Jewish emancipation.[16] And this was not all: along with his attack on the "Patriots," he also attempted to attack Isaac Wolffson, one of the leading Jews in the struggle for emancipation, who belonged to the "Patriots."[17]

We can learn something of the nature of his spontaneous attitude at that time to the Jewish fighter for emancipation from a caricature that appeared in *Mephistopheles,* in which the fighter for emancipation is portrayed as a person with a top hat, a wispy beard, and a hooked nose intent on achieving his goals without regard for the struggle between reaction and republic. This political hypothesis would become within two years the central lesson which Marr learned from the 1848 revolution, and it would assume an important position in his attacks against the Jews in the year 1862. It is therefore not surprising, considering Marr's comment about Rothschild in 1843 and Marr's radical past, that *Mephistopheles* criticized Rothschild as an extreme example of a Jew who was indifferent to the revolution, collaborated with the reaction, and won in the power struggle in Europe.[18]

It was Marr's radicalism and republicanism that lay at the base of this negative image of the Jews. His frustration was not only personal: the hoped-for German republic did not come into being, the Parliament in Frankfurt was immersed in endless debates, and a regent was appointed from among the family of the Austrian emperors in July 1848. During the next half a year, the Parliament in Frankfurt formulated the liberal constitution, which did not radically do away with the old regime and the old states. Marr declared in the radical Hamburg Constituent Assembly that "German unity has become Germany's disgrace."[19] This disgrace redoubled from the very moment that the crown of the German empire was offered to Prussia: a Germany with a monarch such as Frederick William IV, the Prussian king, had no raison d'être—this would be a monarchical-barbaric Germany. Marr believed that "our nationalism is republicanism," and therefore a republic not embracing all Germany, but including only Hamburg, would be preferable to a Germany without a republic.[20]

Marr, who at any rate was active only in the Hamburg arena, thus became one of the supporters of Hamburg particularism, as a result of his devotion to its radical republicanism.[21] Marr was not a fool and realized that this was an apparent contradiction. He had earlier explained that in principle "there is only one cure for Germany: unity which will stand against the particularism of the German states." But "German unity, as it is perceived today [in the Frankfurt Parliament] is the cheese with which the rats of the revolution are drawn to the trap, so that they will gnaw at the bonds holding the wild beasts of tyranny." While it still had some chance, Marr wanted to guard the republic from this trap, and this led him to temporary particularism.[22]

During this time of soul-searching, which for Marr lasted from the beginning of the revolution to the middle of 1849, the representatives of the German bourgeoisie, in general, and those of Hamburg in particular, committed acts which aroused the ire of the radicals to the point of revolt, with the liberal bourgeoisie siding with the existing regimes against the radicals. Marr did not take to the barricades, as did his comrade Wagner, but he bitterly attacked with his pen the liberals he knew, the liberals of Hamburg, who had—in his opinion—betrayed the revolution. It is at this point that his Jewish rival, Riesser, begins to occupy center stage: he is the person who represents, for Marr, the shortcomings of the liberal revolutionaries. (It should be noted, on Marr's behalf, that there was quite a bit of truth in his claims.)

Riesser fought for the constitution of the Frankfurt Parliament and supported the Prussian king as German emperor. All of this was abominable to Marr, but logical and desirable according to the liberals' philosophy. When the Prussian king rejected the crown offered him by the German Parliament, however, Riesser joined the large "Gotha group" that supported the idea of a Prussian empire *not* based on the Frankfurt constitution and Parliament. Its plans included sacrificing "the very core" of German unity, the annexation of Schleswig-Holstein, a plan not in accordance with the intentions of the radicals in the Hamburg Constituent Assembly. In fact, the citizens of Hamburg, angered by the history of Prussian policy on Schleswig-Holstein, provoked the soldiers of the Prussian army encamped in the city. Reactionary Prussia immediately sent an additional army to Hamburg on August 13, 1849, and suppressed the revolution there before eliminating it in the rest of Germany. The Prussian army thereby served the reactionary circles in Hamburg. The hopes of Marr and his comrades for a "model republic" were shattered; Marr's anger was directed against Riesser, who only halfheartedly protested against the steps taken by the Prussian military governor and chose the evil of royal tyranny over the tyranny of the democrats.[23]

An extremely important fact, which also sheds light on Marr's opinion and later criticism of the events of 1848, explains Riesser's changing course. Riesser's main interest was Jewish emancipation. He fought for it in the Frankfurt Parliament and was successful. On the basis of the clause in the constitution of the German Parliament in Frankfurt dealing with equality of rights, a "provisional ordinance" was adopted by the Hamburg authorities in February 1849 concerning equality for the Jews. Riesser and the fighters for Jewish emancipation in Hamburg had won! Also, in the period of the reaction, which began in the middle of 1849 and continued in Hamburg after the entry of the Prussians (and the Austrians after them), all the gains of the revolution were wiped out, save one—the "provisional ordinance" (i.e., equal rights for the Jews). Marr understood this only ten years later, but when he did come to understand it, he concluded that the Jews had used the revolution for their own purposes, betraying it when they no longer needed it!

This conclusion requires a perspective that was still missing in the two or three years after the outbreak of the revolution. In September 1849, a month after the Prussian army took control of Hamburg, Marr committed an act that apparently contradicted everything he had previously preached. In his newspaper he began to call for the absorption of Hamburg into Prussia, to turn the de facto situation into one in which Hamburg would not just suffer from the obligations imposed by Prussia but would also enjoy the rights of Prussia's citizens.[24] There is a dual explanation for this paradox:

1. *Consistent radicalism:* When the dream of the German republic failed in April 1848, Marr retreated to particularism, to the model republic in Hamburg. When it became clear, however, that the radical republican constitution in Hamburg would not be ratified, Marr was prepared—at least in theory—to sacrifice the small republic on the Prussian altar, if this would provide salvation, not only for Hamburg but for *Germany.*[25] A week before the Prussian army entered Hamburg, Marr raised his voice against the Hamburg Senate's intention to join the Alliance of the Three Kings, ignoring Hamburg's pending democratic constitution.[26] The invasion of the Prussian army obviously put an end to the democratic constitution, leaving, in his opinion, only one hope for the idea of a republic: Prussia. In actuality, Marr took the path which he had already announced at the beginning of 1849: "Anyone wishing to turn Germany into one, undivided republic will be able to achieve this only through Prussia."[27] Now, when the possibility of a German or Hamburg revolutionary republic had been lost, he returned to Prussia, with the hope that *it* would advance the idea of the republic. "The republic is dead! Long live the republic! . . . It is better that the small republic disapppear, so that it would come to life at the hour of redemption within a large republic." And, to further complicate the already complicated picture, Marr made this statement in direct response to the decision of the Hamburg Senate to enter the Alliance of the Three Kings (Prussia, Hannover, Saxony), which was federal and not republican, and which had a policy of protective tariffs that Marr strongly opposed on ideological grounds. Marr thought it would be preferable for Hamburg to be *part* of Prussia, not an ally suffering from customs barriers. At the same time, however, he was a party to the sharp criticism leveled at reactionary Prussia during the years 1848–1849,[28] especially after the Constituent Assembly in Hamburg was dispersed on June 13, 1850.

It is quite clear that Marr's later attempts in the 1860's and 1870's to represent himself as having been consistently pro-Prussian since 1849, or even since May 1847, are apologetics or rationalizations. In 1849 and 1850, during the time of the Gotha and Erfurt plan to unite "little Germany" under the Prussian crown, Prussia represented the antithesis of Marr's democratic opinions, and he was forced, despite everything, to oppose Prussia. But there was some truth to what he stated in 1869 in an attempt to resolve the contradiction: "I hated the Prussian *government* then, and for some time afterwards. . . . But I was already determined at the end of August 1847 to act in politics only with *forces,* and not with phrases or doctrines, against the policy of small states."

2. *Settling personal accounts:* Marr's rivals, the victors in the 1849 struggle in Hamburg (including Riesser and Wolffson), represented bourgeois conservatism or moderate liberalism. Prussian rule, while attacking the "sacred" Hamburg particularism, attacked its institutions, parties, and its leaders, whom Marr hated. Marr was willing to pay the price of this attack on his rivals, albeit hesitantly and with soul-searching.

It should also be remembered that Marr knew that since 1849 he had been under surveillance by the Hamburg criminal police for his radical activity.

It was apparently a personal affront which once again unequivocally tipped the scales: Austria and Prussia clashed during 1850–1851. Prussia conceded without a struggle at Olmütz, and the Austrian army replaced the Prussian army in Hamburg. Austrian soldiers attacked Marr and other Hamburg residents on May 1, 1851, killing several dozen Hamburg citizens on this Pentecost holiday; by contrast, the Prussians suddenly appeared to be saints. This incident led to Marr's decision to wage "war against the Austrians by every means"[29]—and who would wage this war if not Prussia? In August 1851, Marr was on vacation on the island of Helgoland with, among others, the democratic minister Dulon, who introduced Marr at Ostende to someone whose name Marr did not want to mention. "This meeting was fateful for my future life. It centered on the indispensable need to sacrifice popularity, if we indeed wanted to take revenge. This conversation opened my eyes to the might concealed within Prussia for Germany." When Marr wrote his memoirs in the 1890's, he noted on the margin that the person he met on the lonely island was Giuseppe Mazzini.

Marr admitted in the 1870's that the desire to take revenge upon Austria had caused him to lose his bearings. This indeed explains his seemingly strange ponderings during the years 1849–1852, when he was still a democrat, republican, and radical: Hamburg republicanism on the one hand, support for Prussia and a German republic on the other. As he had foreseen, his indecision hurt his popularity, since this behavior certainly was not compatible with Hamburg local patriotism.

His attack on Riesser continued to be the second chord in his ponderings throughout this period. Marr's attacks on the supporters of the Gotha plan (to unify Germany under the Prussian king) were aimed mainly at Riesser. When the Alliance of the Three Kings was formed and elections were held for its parliament, the Erfurt Parliament, he termed the representatives "worse than Judas Iscariot!"[30] One of the two delegates elected by Hamburg to the Parliament was Gabriel Riesser! Marr attacked him personally, both for his election to and his participation in what Marr considered the traitorous Parliament.[31]

Riesser did not stand for this; in 1850 he published a booklet, *On the Constitutional Controversy,* in which the liberal Riesser responds point by point to the radical democrat Marr, stating that those who want a revolution at all costs are willing to cooperate with the worst reaction, in an attempt to crush the "compromisers"; the revolution and revolutionism are foreign to Germany, a harmful import from the West; the imported revolution is likely to collaborate with the reaction; one must strive for the possible, even under inconvenient conditions; "no one should aid the enemies of freedom, because of anger at powerlessness over what is taking place"; one must strive for German unity, but not fall prey into the hands of a strong Power and waive independence.[32] This was an unequivocal statement; Marr in fact saw the need to respond to it in *Mephistopheles,*[33] even though he did not mention Riesser's name, just as Riesser had not mentioned Marr's.

This war was not always nameless: Marr had already mentioned Riesser's name, quite venomously, at the beginning of 1850. Discussing the controversy over Riesser's position within the Hamburg "Patriotic League" (was Riesser a reactionary or a revolutionary, "white or red") Marr concluded in his newspaper that "the person from Gotha is not red, nor can he be purified and become white. We prefer to throw him to the dead."[34] The venom became even more personal as time passed. In Marr's eyes, Riesser was transformed into "the fulfillment of the first half of Pharaoh's dream";[35] Marr therefore turned once again to the matter of Riesser's excessive appetite. He even published a poem entitled "Fat Gabriel," in which he protested against three things: "He dreams about a set table, and he dreams about a Prussian king, thus denying the German Parliament, the one in Frankfurt."[36] The same image was presented in a caricature which portrays Riesser as a coward and traitor on the Schleswig-Holstein issue: he disappears under a table laden with food, from fear of the Prussians. He is willing to bare his chest to the Prussian sword only after it was returned to its scabbard.[37]

Only once did Marr utter a hint of a compliment to Riesser during the revolutionary period, when Riesser protested in the spring of 1851 against the decision of the Jewish community council not to bury in the Jewish cemetery a child from a mixed marriage, son of a Christian mother and a Jewish father (and who was therefore non-Jewish, according to Jewish law).[38] For the radical in Marr this was indeed an issue of internal Hamburg policy—the issue of religious freedom for which he had fought since his days in "Young Germany in Switzerland." Even three years after the outbreak of the 1848 revolution, and in spite of its outcome, it seemed that he still had a common cause with the Jewish fighters for emancipation. Only a few months passed, however, and it became clear that Marr, the consistent radical, was once again in the opposition, again on the losing end.

The specific problem which involved Marr once again in this situation was the problem of mixed, interreligious marriages. The Jews of Hamburg, as we have seen, had enjoyed equal rights since February 1849. But the problem of marriages between members of different religions had arisen because legislation had left family law within the jurisdiction of the churches (including the Jewish community) and civil marriage had not yet been introduced. Mixed couples used to solve this problem in a pragmatic manner by traveling to London and marrying in a civil ceremony. It was specifically the Jewish emancipationists and reformers, however, who pressed for an arrangement within the context of Hamburg law. And indeed, after prolonged and difficult preliminary deliberations, the Senate presented, on September 25, 1851, a "temporary order" that permitted mixed marriages between Jews and Christians. Marr, who was no longer a member of the Constituent Assembly, which had been dispersed, but only a radical journalist, naturally did not view this proposal favorably. For him, the sworn atheist, a critic of the institution of marriage, this order circumvented the two central problems—that of separation of church and state, and that of general human emancipation. Marr demanded the total abolition of church marriages; he therefore did not view the specific arrangement permitting civil marriages as a step in the right direction, but only as a Jewish attempt to avoid christening as part of the process of assimilation.[39] In contrast, Riesser, one of the enthusiastic supporters of the "temporary order," saw it as a step towards equal rights for the Jews, as it made it possible for them to marry someone without regard for origin, while not being forced to waive the Jewish faith. This was a well-known liberal position. Marr, of course, was not convinced and carried the issue to absurd extremes: "Now every Christian will be able to marry in a civil ceremony. He must convert [to Judaism] and marry a Christian woman, or marry a Jewess."[40] In his eagerness to present the matter as absurd, Marr made a satiric proposal to the church, which is of special significance in light of his later career: "There is only one way— the Jews must be burned."[41] This was a sarcastic remark aimed at the church, not a declaration of Marr's intentions, as proved by Marr's reaction at that time to the publication in Munich of Baron Schroffenstein's pamphlet entitled "Kill the Jews" (*Schlagt die Juden todt*). Marr responded with his usual sharpness, if not out of love for the Jews, then at least out of hatred for the church fervor which initiated this brutal call.[42]

It goes without saying that Marr failed to convince either the authorities or the public, and the "temporary order" was passed.[43] In light of this event, we can, however, understand the anger that Marr later expressed against the politics of the "dark eyes." It does indeed seem that the principles of the liberals were adopted flexibly to attain practical achievements for the Jews who aspired towards emancipation, while the principles of the radicals, directed towards the emancipation of the entire society (including the Jews), were pushed aside, along with those fighting for them.

The outcome of the issue of civil marriage only confirms the story of Marr's life: The principled uncompromising radical with the vulnerable soul *could not* succeed. He always remained in the opposition, and always failed in politics. The pen was his last refuge.

The sword of the reaction descended on this last refuge too, this time from a different direction—from France. Already in 1851, on the eve of the thirty-eighth anniversary of the Battle of the Nations (*Völkerschlacht*) at Leipzig, Marr expressed his despair at the German people, in a pro-French spirit. The celebrations were to be held as usual, but Marr could not participate in them because he viewed them as an expression of the reaction and of German powerlessness, not as a real desire for freedom, and thus the celebrations were much more hypocritical after the 1848 revolution.[44] Instead of being a festival of freedom, it was one of drinking; and the Gotha people, who according to Marr had brought this disaster upon Germany, only symbolized this. Therefore, the veteran revolutionary reluctantly concluded that "only the French can bring salvation." But alas, six weeks after Marr expressed this hope, Napoleon III brought about the coup d'état. Marr, who supported the leaders of the French left—Louis Blanc and Ledru-Rollin—and who had suffered from the German revolution, the Prussians, and the Austrians—not to mention from the city of Hamburg and its government—viewed the events in France as the closing of the antidemocratic circle, and rightly so. In the beginning he had believed that this was only a passing show, but when Napoleon III received such a persuasive majority in the elections, Marr launched an attack in his newspaper. Napoleon's representatives now demanded what the Prussian government had demanded from the Hamburg censor in 1847—to muzzle Marr. The Marquis Talnay, the French representative in Hamburg, delivered a protest to the Senate. Since the censorship regulations did not permit the closure of the newspaper, Marr was sued for damages in February 1852. Marr attempted to defend himself in a paradoxical manner by claiming that, according to the accords of the 1815 Congress of Vienna, it was his *obligation* to oppose any attempt by the family of Napoleon to take control of France. The court nevertheless fined him 50 marks. The fact that due to his activity he was exposed to attacks by the Prussians, the Austrians, and now the French, without being defended by Hamburg's institutions, led him to conclude that he had to leave the city. And indeed, the newspaper closed, and Marr left Hamburg in August 1852 and headed for Central America. In the last issue of his newspaper there is a caricature depicting *Mephistopheles* boarding a ship headed for America, with all the city's newspapers shedding crocodile tears at his departure. Riesser was among those weeping.[45]

Marr never freed himself from the lessons of 1848, both on the general and the personal level. His flight after the revolution from the beliefs of the 1848 radicals was a consequence of his awareness of the failure of 1848 and of what followed. There is nothing new in the fact that, for many of the *liberals* of 1848, this failure was the cause of the reorientation which took place during the years 1862–1866. Yet it is not surprising that a radical should take the same path: Richard Wagner, Bruno Bauer, and Ludwig Feuerbach acted in this manner, and so did Marr. Powerless despair with the revolution itself, the German republic, and the lack of popular support for change was Marr's bitter lesson. Marr could never overcome this trauma, and his anti-Semitic disciple Fritsch rightly called him, in a moment of anger almost forty years later, "one of the impractical 48'ers."[46]

4

From Politics to Business and Back: 1852-1862

The fourth part of Marr's memoirs dealing with the years 1852–1860 is nothing other than his book *A Journey to Central America* (*Reise nach Central-America*), which was published in 1863.[1] Emigration in itself was not an extraordinary act for the revolutionaries of, and those disappointed by, 1848. Marr had already surmised in 1850 that America would be his next fatherland. Since migration to Central America was somewhat unusual, Marr described at length living conditions in this part of America. Although his occupations at this time remained somewhat of a mystery and provided the source of the rumors that sprang up in the Hamburg press in 1862 and again in 1879 (whenever he launched attacks on the Jews) that he was involved with the slave trade, he repeatedly denied this. Actually, Marr's journey to Central America coincided with his return to a career as a merchant. When he first went to Costa Rica, it was as a wholesale merchant. He returned to Hamburg a year later and continued his commercial dealings; it was only then that he entered a new field, settling German immigrants in Costa Rica, under conditions which were more or less accepted at that time. According to Marr's own testimony, he brought between eighty and one hundred people to Costa Rica. They committed themselves by contract to work ten hours per day for two years. Afterwards, when they fulfilled the terms of the contract, they would receive land from the government. According to Marr, there was an additional person who could confirm this,[2] the Costa Rican consul in Hamburg—the representative of a country which had become independent only five years before and wanted white workers from Europe. The conditions offered by Costa Rica apparently aroused criticism by the "Berlin Central Society for Colonialization," leading to the later accusation that Marr was a "slave trader."[3] It should be noted within this context that the later accusation that Marr had sold out to Prussia was also connected with this activity: he had formed ties with the Prussian delegation when he was in Costa Rica, and sent reports to Prussia on local trade and colonialization conditions.

Marr stayed in Costa Rica, with interruptions, until 1859. When he returned to Hamburg in August 1853, an event took place that apparently personally influenced him more than any previous occurrence in determining his stance on the Jewish question. He apparently gave up his anticonnubial ideology and married on May 21, 1854, and returned to Costa Rica less than two months later. His wife, Georgina Johanna Bertha, was the daughter of Wilhelm Callenbach, an apostate Jew. The marriage brought him wealth, but according to his own testimony, he suffered until their divorce in 1873 from an unhappy married life.[4] Just as Marr did not enter into details about his business dealings, he did not discuss his marriage and relations with his father-in-law. An analysis of his anti-Semitic writings from 1862 reveals, however, the harsh influence of his personal experience with Jews and—even more so—with half-Jews. We cannot know to what extent his marriage played a central role in his becoming a Jew-hater in 1862; it certainly played a contributory role, as we shall see later. The truth must be stated: to anyone attempting to connect Marr's acquaintance with Judaism with his presumed Jewish origin—*cherchez la femme*. As Marr testifies in his essay "Within Philo-Semitism" (see Appendix), he already had Jewish girlfriends in school, and later, during the period of his stay in Vienna, he knew a Jewish girl (who came from Poland!). In his book on his Central America trip he reports that even on the boat to Central America he courted two Jewish young women, Miss Meir and Miss Rosalie. The latter showed him a family tree "filled with Jacobs, Samuels, and Levisohns," and even one Rothschild, "to my distress, only from Lemberg."[5] After this introduction, his marriage to a "half-Jewess" was an almost natural sequence. This was not all: Wilhelm Marr married three more times—of the three, one was another "half-Jewess," and one a "full" Jewess! His mysterious attraction to Jewish women requires psychological analysis; this strange chain cannot be merely coincidental. We will return to this topic when dealing with the background to his well-known anti-Semitic activity during 1878–1879.

After five years, Marr's Costa Rican business encountered financial difficulties, and he decided to return to Hamburg, having saved a considerable amount of money. He mentioned in his memoirs that he had a Jewish partner there (who he did not name)[6] who tried to lead him astray time and again, but without success, since he was already "smart" (Marr uses the English word). He thought, as a "smart American," that he would continue in business, not in a political career, in Hamburg. He now tried to become a true capitalist. He published an advertisement in the newspaper stating that he was interested in investing money in a plant and seeking someone with ideas. The person with ideas appeared; his idea was a button factory. The raw material, mother-of-pearl, was inexpensive in Hamburg, and so was manpower. The "ideas man" was unsuccessful, however, in implementing the plan, and Marr incurred a debt of 9,000 taler before he abandoned this venture after only two months. Interestingly, the "ideas man" was a Jew from Bohemia, not a little reminiscent of Sholem Aleichem's dreamers who lived in the clouds.[7]

Marr eventually stated that this episode contributed towards opening his eyes to the Jews. It is of interest, however, that Marr was not revealed as a hater of the Jews until about two years after the incident (i.e., these events did *not* lead Marr to change his position, and he only used them retrospectively to justify or rationalize his position). Marr did not become a Jew-baiter at that stage, neither did he become poor. He lived in a villa on the outskirts of Hamburg, and resolved to return to the occupations which seemed to him to be more promising, journalism and politics.

The time was one of a liberal awakening, the *"Neue Era,"* in Hamburg as well as in Prussia. The reactionary period of the 1850's had come to an end. The trend to reform the regime in Hamburg, to change the constitution and turn the city's ruling institutions into representative bodies, took concrete shape. The deliberations which lasted less than a year bore fruit. It was decided to establish a representative, democratic, citizens' assembly (even though it still, to some degree, automatically represented certain governmental institutions). Elections were held in November 1859, and the Hamburg republic finally had a democratic parliament, with the possibility of discussing fundamental constitutional issues. The modern constitution, which had been discussed during the years 1849–1852, and which had been given the kiss of death by Prussian and Austrian threats, was discussed once again. The two camps, the moderate liberal and the radical democratic, faced each other anew, with Marr found once again in the latter camp.

Marr entered this parliament (Bürgerschaft) at a late date, after the button factory episode, in the by-elections at the beginning of 1861. His position was already well known, not only from the 1848 period but also from his activity in the local press (in the *Freischütz* newspaper).[8] Now, after Prussia had undergone a process of renewal and reform, Marr could more easily appear in support of radicalism and Prussia than he could have ten years earlier. The first major parliamentary debate in which Marr participated revolved around this issue. Once again, Marr found himself in one of the paradoxical meetings which history prepares: a head-on confrontation with Gabriel Riesser, the Jewish liberal member of the Bürgerschaft who had already aroused his ire ten years earlier.

The issue which led to the confrontation was one that had inflamed the liberals throughout Germany—the issue of the constitution of the duchy of Kur-Hessen. This constitution, which had been adopted in 1831, was suspended after the failure of the revolution in 1848 by the Kurfürst (the elector), in opposition to the stand of his parliament. The dissolution of the parliament and new elections revealed to the prince just how unpopular his stand was. To save his position, the prince, a party

to the Alliance of the Three Kings (the previously mentioned Gotha
Alliance), turned to Austria, the rival of the alliance, as head of the
German Bund, which was then considered dead. This action revived the
Bund as a tool of the reaction and led to a conflict between Austria and
Prussia, with the former emerging victorious in 1850. The question of
Kur-Hessen became a symbol of the struggle against reaction on behalf
of Prussian supremacy, and as a result of agitation within Kur-Hessen,
the issue arose once again before the Bundestag in 1859. The members
of the Bundestag (the assembly of representatives of the German Bund),
including Hamburg, had to determine their positions on the issue. A
commission of inquiry, headed by Riesser, who had been considered to be
an expert on the issue since 1850, was established by the Hamburg Bürgerschaft on May 7, 1860. The moderate liberals (Riesser's camp) were interested in a "quiet solution" and a "moral victory" for justice, not in
unleashing a fusillade.[9] The radicals, on the other hand, wanted to turn
this into a question of principle and even to use force against Austria,
against the reaction. On the basis of what we know about Marr, we
should not be surprised that he was one of the most vocal radicals in
the debate in the Hamburg parliament: "The report's author [Riesser]
once again revealed his penetrating and critical view, which always impels
him to keep out of cannon range. He is one of those people who fully
understand how to hide their heads in the sand when the bullets are
flying. When the bullet passes, however, they do not fire their bullets at
the enemy battery, but carefully pass them to the rear." Riesser did not
keep silent during the sharp debate, replying that "the members of his
[Riesser's] party . . . sincerely strive towards true freedom," while placing the blame for Kur-Hessen's inability to attain freedom even after a
century on the fact that "that party [Marr's radical one] ruled it for half
a year."[10] Marr was hurt by this comment, and interrupted with the cry
"Charles the First." Riesser replied to this with a remark about Marr that
was already well-known in Hamburg: "If Marr wants to decapitate the
Bundestag, by all means." Marr was apparently so deeply hurt by the
laughter accompanying this remark that he reconstructed the incident
in his memoirs thirty years later:

> Riesser was the one dealing with this issue. . . . He let us, the demo-
> crats, say that we were not interested in any contact with the Bundestag,
> and that the Hessen issue had to be resolved without the Bundestag (as in-
> deed happened in 1866). After the debate ended, and after the fat author
> of the report finished digesting his plum cake, the fat one got up from his
> seat and began to thunder against us, the leftists, as the party of "blood
> and filth" which is not interested in the legal way, the way which leads
> through the Bundestag. "I appeal to the party of blood and filth in the
> name of John Hampden from the Long Parliament in England, a man
> of law," the fat Jew shouted. W. Marr (incensed): "And I appeal here
> in the name of Stuart Charles I, whose decapitation was voted for by

John Hampden from the Long Parliament." I can still see today how the
fat Jewish liberal jumped to the podium and fired off a cheap shot, "If
Mr. Marr wants to decapitate the Bundestag . . ." The voice of the fat
one died in his throat. The Jewish liberal's insolence knew no bounds in
falsifying world history. . . . A typical Reform Jew, deceiving the
world with smooth talk! If this is the case, I prefer the Orthodox Jew, the
fanatic. . . . All his rhetoric is built on the ignorance of his listeners.
. . . This is the way in which Jews fight. As I have stated, I still remember to this day how Riesser twisted and turned on the podium when I
called out the name of Charles I. And so I delivered the deathblow to the
political career of the fat Reform Jew. . . . And this same fat and
superficial Jew could have played an important role in Germany for
decades![11]

"This same fat Jew" was not destroyed. He was the acting chairman
of the Hamburg Parliament, and in this capacity called Marr to order
during the debate held in October 1861 on the establishment of a war
fleet in northern Germany. Riesser and his colleagues supported the
establishment of such a war fleet, whereas Marr's support was conditional.
In Marr's opinion, the program was baseless as long as it was not founded
on an alliance with Prussia and on Prussian guarantees.[12] "If Prussia
wants, it can, whether it is monarchical, or republican, and we will be
the first to stand by its side. . . . We want Prussia to head Germany."
It was necessary, however, to receive guarantees from Prussia, which
would prevent the enthusiastic Hamburg democrats from becoming un-
witting servants of the reaction. Marr wrote in this manner in a pamphlet
entitled *To Work for the Prussian King (Travailler pour le Roi de
Prusse)*. We can see in this the continuation of the trend which had been
noticeable since the end of the revolution: Marr was against Hamburg
and German particularism, and in favor of Prussia, as long as democracy
could be maintained. This was especially true when the small state of
Hamburg did not act in accordance with Marr's wishes (and therefore
had no raison d'être), and when his rival Riesser faced him.

The forcefulness with which Riesser hurt Marr can be clearly demonstrated in the ferocity and crudeness of the prose he used in recalling
the Riesser incident thirty years later in 1892, when Marr's hatred of the
Jews had already abated, and he admitted that the Jews' conduct was
no worse than that of his anti-Semitic colleagues. Riesser served as a red
flag for Marr, not only during the actual period of conflict between them
but long after Riesser's death in 1863, as seen in Marr's writings from
1879 and in the passage from his memoirs just cited. It should not be
forgotten that, just as Marr's anti-Jewish outburst cannot be explained
without the women in his life, neither can it be explained without mentioning Gabriel Riesser, the fighter for Jewish emancipation from Hamburg. We can go so far as to state that the vocabulary of this attack on
Riesser conceals within it Marr the radical, who was influenced by his

idol from the 1840's, Feuerbach, who coined the phrase, "A person is what he eats," and who claimed that circumcision among the Jews was complemented by an act of eating. (As proof of this, Exodus 24:11: "They beheld God, and they ate and drank.")[13] When he faced Riesser, this statement was certainly present in Marr's subconscious, if not in his conscious awareness, for who knew Feuerbach's essay better than Marr, who had edited it?

The stance of Riesser and his liberal colleagues on a clearly Jewish issue, mixed marriages, also aroused Marr's ire during the same period. Like that of Kur-Hessen, the issue of mixed marriages was not new. A commission had been established on March 21, 1860, before Marr entered the Hamburg Parliament, to deal with the proposal to cancel Jewish family and inheritance law. A public debate ensued in which the camps were split according to the familiar division of liberals and radicals. There was also controversy within the Jewish camp: the Orthodox were totally opposed, while the radicals agreed completely, and the liberals only halfheartedly supported the measure. The bill to cancel Jewish family and inheritance law was introduced by Marr's Jewish fellow party member, Anton Rée. Riesser was the one who opposed the bill; just as he had ten years earlier, he favored civil marriages, but not as an obligation, as he did not want to harm the religious freedom of Jews and Christians who insisted upon religious wedding ceremonies. Marr and his Jewish colleague Rée viewed this as obviously contradictory and hypocritical. Marr remarked a short time afterwards, "A clearly 'Jewish' motif lies at the foundation of this matter! A civil marriage register? God forbid! Where would Israel remain?"[14] He added in his later memoirs, "Riesser was successful, with the help of Talmudic hairsplitting, in convincing—in the name of 'freedom of conscience'—that civil marriages had to become facultative, and our democrats fell into this trap."[15]

The issue of civil marriages was only one facet of the broader question of the change in the status of the Jewish community, however, and the debate continued, mainly among the Jews. The reform and radical circles within the community wanted to change an absurd situation, unique to Hamburg: the Jew had been a citizen of the city since the emancipation in 1849, but he could not enjoy civil rights without being registered in the Jewish community. Opposing this strange situation, a petition had been submitted on February 20, 1862, signed by 169 Jews, calling for the cancellation of the Jewish community's special, even abnormal, status. Marr supported the bill in principle, since he really wanted the radical elimination of religious differences, and of religion in general. Marr viewed it as necessary to defend the radical Reform Jewish position, and decided to write a book. "I wrote a booklet, without giving it a name, calling in it for the complete fusion of Judaism with Aryanism." The book was written during the very days in which the request of the 169 Jews was prepared, and Marr finished writing it at almost the same time as the proposal was submitted.[16] The direct link between the Jewish political act and Marr's book cannot be disputed. Marr subsequently stated that the writing of the book was an act of philo-Semitism, describing its contents as a major attack on Orthodox Judaism, in a style reminiscent of anti-Jewish writings from the period of the Enlightenment. Marr thought that the thesis upon which the book was based—that Judaism had come to a dead end, due to the Orthodox preservation of the race (by marriage), and the conclusion that the Jews must waive their special status as a nationality and community—would be accepted by his friends among the 169 Jews who favored the cancellation of the Jews' special status. He wrote in his memoirs that "in good faith, and not knowing which sacred cows I had attacked, I gave the manuscript to a Jewish lawyer with whom I was friendly [his partner from the 1850's (!), and one of the 169] Dr. Lazarus. He told me, 'It would be better to leave the manuscript unpublished; even though its writing was inspired, they won't understand you. They will suspect you of *Risches* [Jew-hatred].' I did as he advised me, and left the book on my desk for five months."

The book appeared after five months. Named *The Jewish Mirror* (*Der Judenspiegel*), it was Marr's major attack on Judaism.

5

The Mirror of the Jews

The untitled manuscript which was given to the Jew Lazarus to read, and which had gathered dust on Marr's desk for five months, underwent slight changes in an anti-Reform direction before being printed in five editions during the second half of 1862. What caused Marr to change his views and sharply attack even the Jewish Reform movement? He explained in his memoirs that "in the meantime, the struggle between Orthodox and Reform Judaism continued. . . . Reform Judaism demanded that all welfare matters be nationalized . . . and so the last religious difference would disappear." Poor Orthodox Jews had explained to him that Reform Jews were interested in the new law for an economic reason, and not as a matter of ideological principle: they wanted to rid themselves of the burden of material support for the Jewish poor borne by the wealthy members of the community (mainly members of the "Reform Society") in addition to their regular taxes. Under the new arrangement, the state would assume support of the Jewish poor, improving conditions for the rich Jews and worsening them for the poor ones. Marr realized that in this controversy he was a tool of the economic class which he hated. "The final result was that I ignored the entire question of the administration of Jewish matters, thinking to myself—in the spirit of Heine—'that the two of them stink,'[1] both the Reform and the Orthodox Jews."

These words could possibly have explained the change in Marr, if this had been a stage in a process of continuous change, but such a process did not occur. It is reasonable to assume that this change was a convulsive reaction to a specific event, but it is also possible that the cause lies in a family quarrel, frictions between his father-in-law and the Jews,[2] or in disputes within the democratic party, Marr's party. Another possibility is that he was angered once again by Riesser's personality in the Hamburg Parliament, a possibility that receives credence when we consider the proximity in his memoirs of his account of Riesser's remark about him and his comments on the Jewish Reform movement. To a certain degree, Marr's continuing defense of the goals of Reform Judaism (which were represented by Riesser) after the clash in the Parliament is more surprising than his attack in *Der Judenspiegel*. For lack of better evidence, it appears to me that Marr supported the Reform Jews in this case since in principle their affairs were close to him and since his fellow radical-democrats bore the demand for change, thereby permitting him to ignore Riesser and his circle. Psychologically speaking, he may have changed his mind when at some point he apparently became angry at a Jewish democratic member of his organization. We have already seen on several occasions how sensitive Marr was to insults and how impulsively he changed his positions; this was apparently the case here as well. Proof of this can be seen in the sharp debate which Marr conducted in the press during the months of July and August with Anton Rée, his fellow member in the democratic party and an extreme reformer among the Jews.[3] The party's activity in the Hamburg Parliament served as the background for the debate, with Marr attacking Rée for deviating from the guidelines established by the Hamburg Pre-Parliament in 1849. He demanded "constitutional change through a Parliament chosen in general elections, or the boycotting of the present Parliament, a perpetual protest by means of our empty chair." This debate was also part of the preparations for the elections meant to be held within four months. As the elections drew nearer, Marr feared that he was about to be pushed aside, as had always happened in the past. Either way, we can assume that election considerations were the catalyst for Marr's becoming a declared Jew-hater.

When *Der Judenspiegel* appeared on June 22, 1862, it did not surprise the residents of Hamburg. The book served as a confirmation and continuation of a document that had been published ten days earlier, a letter by Marr to the liberal Bremen newspaper *Courier an der Weser,* which had led to immediate angry reactions in Hamburg. Marr had received a letter from Hobelmann, his democratic friend in Bremen, at the beginning of June 1862, in which he wrote, "Marr, you must help with your skilled pen. We are currently laying the groundwork for the attainment of equal rights for the Jews in Bremen as well." Bremen, like Lübeck, was even more conservative than its sister city, the Hansa town of Hamburg, in granting rights of residence and citizenship to its Jews; in 1855, it reinstituted the restrictions on Jewish residence within the city which had been abolished in 1848. The democrat Hobelmann therefore expected the support of the democrat Marr. The reply which Marr wrote on June 4, 1862, astounded Hobelmann: "Leave me alone. The truth on the Jewish question is slowly being revealed to me. . . . I am no longer willing to cooperate on this issue." Marr requested that his reply be published in the Bremen newspaper, and Hobelmann complied. The people of Bremen, followed by the people of Hamburg, learned on June 13, 1862, of the change in Marr's stance. The letter is not long and out-

lines the main points in *Der Judenspiegel,* with the same degree of im-
maturity in defining the problem. The letter lacks, however, several of
the contradictions that resulted from the manner in which the book was
written, as we shall explain later. (The text of the Bremen letter appears
in the Appendix.)

The most interesting aspect of this letter is that it shows that the
strange change which Marr is undergoing *is based on, and is a continuation of, his radicalism.* He uses democratic principles—those of the majority and freedom of conscience—to strike at the Jews, instead of defending them. He presents the rights demanded by the Jews as coercion
of the majority by a minority, and emancipation—as he thinks it is
demanded by the Jews—as contradicting the general social emancipation
to which he aspired. His attack on the contradiction between Jewish
emancipation and that of society sounds as if he was quoting from Bruno
Bauer's 1841 and 1843 essays: "We must be free ourselves before we
think to invite others also [Jews] to participate in freedom."[4]

Marr was well aware that his definition of the concept "Jew" was
liable to become the Achilles' heel of this claim. Indeed, the entire letter
is infused with his anticlerical approach: he compared the granting of
rights to the Jews in Bremen to the granting of rights to a group of
monks; he portrayed the struggle as one against the church per se, in
favor of separation of church and state, and against Orthodoxy as Orthodoxy. There was logic in Marr's claim that, as long as religion was not
separated from the state, emancipation for the Jews would only be a
component of the distorted and unenlightened system of church-state relations. Marr was nevertheless in a dilemma. An attack on religion per
se was not sufficient to iron out the internal contradictions in his arguments. There is a discrepancy throughout the letter between the approach
that assumes the barrier between Jews and non-Jews to be on the confessional level, and which therefore invalidates confessional argumenta-
tion for or against emancipation, and the perception that this assumption
cannot sufficiently explain the dividing factor between Jews and non-
Jews. First of all, it is insufficient since the major claim of the Jewish
fighters for emancipation was that they were no longer a church, that
they were not "a state within a state," and that they did not support a
theology opposed to real social and political partnership within a modern
state. The acceptance of this claim sweeps away the basis of Marr's
assumptions and conclusions; yet Marr rejected this claim, since his in-
tuition showed him that a difference did exist between Jew and non-Jew,
and that this difference was highly significant. Second, this distinction
would have impelled Marr, the anticlerical radical, to do the work of
the Christian Church and theology in the struggle against equal rights for
the Jews. Marr did indeed recommend conversion as a solution, for its
provocative effect and as a test, but this was indisputably a tactical

maneuver. Marr accordingly revealed that he had discovered a better method for distinguishing between Jew and non-Jew, a method relating to *race*. At this stage, Marr formulated his method in a moderate fashion, and his vocabulary was still diversified: *Stamm* (tribe), *Stammeseigen-thümlichkeiten* (origin-qualities), *race*. This was a clearly regressive claim, especially after the Jews had attained recognition for their demands for equality between members of different religions concerning life in the state, and even emancipation. Marr raised here, in the wake of the attainment of emancipation by Hamburg's Jews, a clearly post-emancipatory argument. Fifteen years later, this claim characterized the general attack, both within and without Germany, against the equal rights that Jews had attained on a large scale at a *later* stage.

It must be stated that Marr's use of the concept of race underwent a process of development. The conclusion in the Bremen letter and in *Der Judenspiegel* was ambiguous. The Oriental element was indeed presented as the converse of European political and social life, but it was possible to leave the Oriental for the "light." As we shall see, this possibility was completely obliterated in 1878, when the discarding of the racial element through an act of volition—conversion, adaptation, or waiving religious customs—was negated. This would be Marr's position in his book *The Victory of Judaism over Germanism* (*Sieg des Judenthums uber das Germanenthum*). Paradoxically, this approach is not only radical in the literal meaning of the concept, but as long as it refrains from irrational and romantic statements, it can also be placed within the eighteenth-century intellectual trend which sought links between natural environmental factors and the nature of the political order, as did Montesquieu, for example. Marr could therefore deny the charge which was raised against him that his racial theory (the one presented in 1862) was a betrayal of his radical-democratic principles.[5]

The following sentence from the Bremen letter reveals the influential role played by current events: "I and several congenial friends, no longer attend the local parliament, . . . where Abraham's descendants play the role of faithful satellites of the reaction." The question of continued participation in the sessions of the Assembly was a crucial question for him; as we have noted, he even debated this question with his fellow party member, the Jew Anton Rée. We can therefore see what was really troubling Marr—Riesser, Wolffson, and others, who were participating in the Assembly with a great deal of success. The motto under which he concealed his personal problems was that of "radicalism against reaction," in which the Jews were portrayed as reactionaries who betrayed the ideas of the left for personal benefit. It should be remembered that Marr was aware of the situation in Bremen, where the Jewish leadership, with one exception, opposed the proposal of the committee in whose name Hobelmann spoke and supported the reactionary Senate. The veteran Jews actually favored a law which entailed the removal of most of the "new" Jews from Bremen.[6] In Marr's state of mind, this fact could hardly impel him to act on behalf of "the Jewish issue."

The publication of the letter caused an enormous controversy in Hamburg and a general attack on Marr. "Oh, a storm erupted then in Hamburg against me. It was a real witches' Sabbath."[7] The satirist Julius Stettenheim, Marr's former disciple, wrote a manifesto which was carried in the city streets on poles, and whose bearers shouted, "Marr the Jew-eater [*Judenfresser*]." A play was also performed in which Marr was portrayed as the evil Haman. The quickest reaction was from the "Democratic Association" and the "Association for Freedom of Conscience," two political associations that resolved, on the spot, to demand an explanation from Marr. A member of these associations, an apostate Jew named Zacharias,[8] with whom Marr had had commercial ties in America, warned him not to come to the meeting of the associations, noting, "Once again you've overshot," a sentence which indeed summed up the way in which Marr acted. Marr appeared, defended himself, and argued. The meeting, chaired by a Jew by the name of Horwitz, allowed Marr to reply to each charge; his main argument was that it was permissible for an atheist such as himself to attack Jews, and not only Christians, in the "Association for Freedom of Conscience." Marr was willing to leave the executive board of the Association; his competitor for the seat, a person named Wex, was apparently his sharpest attacker and the one who accused Marr of a "nondemocratic past" in America.

Attention should be paid to a comment that Marr made in his memoirs concerning this matter: to the best of his recollection, it was, of all people, several Jewish women who came to his defense during that meeting. This memory compelled him to relate once again to the subject of the Jewish woman. He thoroughly praised Jewish women. He thought that they "stood way above Jewish men," and did not exhibit, racially, the materialistic attributes of Jewish men.[9] He believed that Jewish women could not stand Jewish men (and who should know better than him). If this seems to contradict what was stated earlier about the influence on him of his marriage to a woman of half-Jewish origin, it will suffice to cite the continuation of his statement: his words of praise for the Jewish woman do not apply to women who are the product of mixing, the mulatto. These are the worst of all!

At the conclusion of the meeting, Marr was approached by the publisher Otto Meissner, who asked him to write out his response "in a literary manner." Marr accordingly dusted off the yet unpublished manuscript *Der Judenspiegel,* preparing it for printing within a day and a half. As we can learn from the finished product, he hastily added sentences meant to harm Reform, progressive Judaism. The book contains many internal contradictions, and its patchwork construction is clearly evident. The elderly Marr subsequently stated several times that this work was "immature." The attacks on Marr, the rewriting of the composition, and its preparation for printing all took place between June 13 and June 22; we can only admire the output of the 1862 printers. It was necessary to publish a second edition only eight days after the book appeared, and two more editions within another ten days.

Marr's original thesis opens and closes the book: the Jews are a "state within a state" and preserve their nationality by means of the ghetto, by means of religion alone, but they nevertheless want to have equal rights in a non-Jewish state. Even if the state were non-Christian, the Jewish "state within a state" would have no right to exist, since the Jewish religion could not have preferential status if there were no state religion, claims the radical atheist. The real solution was total assimilation which would bring about real emancipation. But the Jews believe that they are a racially pure people (*racenreines Volk*) and a consolidated nation (*consolidirte Nation*). They would be aliens as long as they believed this; he states explicitly[10] that this is an erroneous belief on the part of the Jews. On the other hand, he claims that a Jewish physiology has developed. The Jews are, or were, a tribe. He still does not claim that the Jews are a race: the physical appearance of the Jews is not uniform,[11] since the Jews comprise at least twelve tribes, and therefore "the Jews are a mixed people [*Mischlingsvolk*]. It is impossible to historically prove the existence of a racially pure Judaism." If there are racial characteristics, they can be ascribed to the process of degeneration which is a consequence of the Orthodox Jewish law which demands exclusivity in marriage.[12] In striking contrast to all this, however, he raises the claim which will be heard over and over during the wave of 1879:[13] "There is too great a racial difference between the Germans and the Orientals."

The proposed solution that appears at the end of the book provides striking proof of the conceptual weakness of the work and Marr's vacillation on the issue. On the one hand, influenced by the controversy among the different Jewish factions, he suggests a solution which had been proposed by Reform Jews, and which had apparently appealed to him at the time that he wrote the first draft of the book;[14] "Those people in Hamburg who demanded that you waive your community-linked citizenship, a special and particularist citizenship, and the synagogue, wanting to turn the ritual into a private matter, proposed to you a clearly humane and practical means . . . Judaism must cease, if you desire that humanity begin." The hereditary degeneration would also stop then, and the characteristics of Judaism (*Eigenthümlichkeiten*), which are the reasons for the hatred of the Jews, would vanish! This solution greatly resembles the solution that had been proposed twenty years earlier by Karl Marx and other radicals.

On the other hand, he proposes an even more radical solution: in place of the "abstract emancipation" of (and from) Judaism, he conceived of the idea of intermarriage, or, in his language, "the mixing of

flesh" (*fleischliche Vermischung*), crossbreeding,[15] all the way to complete Germanization, as the way to overcome racial differences. Baptism
would also be beneficial, not as baptism per se, but as a means of leaving the spirit of Judaism. Bruno Bauer had also prophesied in this same
spirit.

There is also an allusion to the "classical" solution of Jew-haters,
emigration, but it is not raised in a serious manner: "Our government
would simply hang a second Moses, if he were to appear." In addition,
"It is hard to believe that you would emigrate to Palestine in order to
establish a model state [*Musterstaat*] there, even if you were given all
of Syria."[16] The motif of a "model state" reappears later in Marr's works,
just as it appears in Zionism.

Either way, it is clear that emancipation for the Jews, in its present
form, would only be a hypocritical lie,[17] as long as "the Jewish essence
does not change." Regarding the reform of Judaism, Marr leaves no room
for doubt as to whether only Orthodox Judaism must be corrected. The
"Reform-Juden" (quotation marks in the original) are only caricatures[18]
for Marr. He attacks the representatives of this "caricature" in his book,
albeit without mentioning them by name. The following passage, whose
content already appeared in the Bremen letter, can only be directed at
Riesser and Wolffson: "It is an infamous fact that the Jews, most of
whom were outstanding radicals before the emancipation, went over in
masses to the camp of the reaction or the doctrinaire bourgeoisie after
the emancipation, and swarm over government positions in order to receive them. . . . When a Jew [Riesser] was chosen as Supreme Court
judge in Hamburg, a friend made an accurate remark: 'You see, Israel
was exultant; not because a qualified man was chosen, but because he is
a Jew.' . . . It is a fact that most of the Jews have left us entrapped . . .
after having obtained emancipation for themselves."[19]

Marr stated more than once, with the same hypocrisy and consistency characteristic of the prejudiced—after accusing the Jews of lazi-
ness, ambition, greediness, speculation, etc.; after claiming that Judaism
is barbarous and revengeful (the Purim holiday); after alluding to im-
morality among the Jews (David and Jonathan); after condemning "the
rich Jewess" who boasts of her wealth—that he was not raising charges
against any specific Jew, but rather against Judaism, against the abstract
concept. Why, he himself had many Jewish friends . . .[20]

This essay, in contrast to what Marr would later contend, is not so
distant from *The Victory of Judaism over Germanism*. He already agrees
here that hatred of Jews is not religious hatred, but rather hatred of the
alien possessing distinctive characteristics; the attack on Jewish emancipation and its consequences, including "the Jewish takeover of the press
in Germany" (which was the apple of his eye), is already present.

Even after the publication of this book, it was the democrats from
Marr's society, not the Jews, who raised their voice in protest. Elections

were held for the executive board of the "Democratic Association" a week after the publication of the book. Marr was the only one of the five members of the executive to be unseated. Two of the other four were Jews. One of them, Emil Wohlwill (later to become a famous chemist)—who was a stubborn adherent to the idea that the Jewish community, as a political and administrative entity, must disappear—told a friend afterwards that the society's spending of three weeks on discussions on Marr's works, instead of on "the war for human freedom," was an unexpected waste of time.[21]

New ammunition was now added to the democrats' slander about Marr's dealings in the slave trade in Costa Rica[22]—Marr's statements about the Negroes in America. His opponents recalled an article, "Towards an Understanding of the Events in North America," he had published in *Freischütz* a short time after the outbreak of the American Civil War. This article attempted to prove that the issue of slavery was not unequivocal, economically or politically. Marr's interpretation was understood by the public as a defense of slavery. It is possible that he had stated, or that they understood from what he had written, that "the Negroes are closer to beasts than to human beings."[23] These statements, combined with the sentence in *Der Judenspiegel* that Negro blood also is intermingled in the blood of the Jews,[24] and with the degrading descriptions of the inferior physical characteristics of the Jew quoted from the book of Naudh (Nordmann),[25] *The Jews and the German State*, made Marr lose the last ounce of credit he had enjoyed among the democratic-radical community in Hamburg.

It was easier for the liberals to attack Marr than it was for the radicals. One of the former pointed out the absurdity in Marr's demand that the Jews follow the *majority:* would Marr become a Mormon if there were a Mormon majority in Hamburg? They stressed an additional contradiction in Marr's thesis: an antireligious stand coupled with religious coercion against the Jews. It was this anonymous liberal who made an observation which later proved correct—that this was precisely the way in which radicalism evolved into cooperation with the reaction.[26] The racial issue raised by Marr also appeared to be extremely refutable in the eyes of this liberal: "Marr despises the 'race' of the Jews . . . just as a pure-blooded Southern Yankee despises the colored race, and any person in whose veins flows even one drop of African blood. . . . But Marr's attempt to find supporters for the American South's Yankeeism here, in Germany, is doomed to failure. Thank God, we have already gone beyond the stage of fine distinctions between humans on the basis of 'races' and religions."[27] This was the self-confident German liberal of the 1860's. He did not fear backward opinions that belonged to the past or to a backward country such as the United States . . .

The relevant criticism of Marr's book became part of the political battle being waged by the established political blocs before the elections to the Hamburg Parliament, which were to be held within one hundred days. The democratic newspaper *Freischütz,* for which Marr wrote, and whose Jewish editor Lenz now disassociated himself from Marr, devoted two lead articles to the issue.[28] The non-Jewish radical who wrote the articles discussed the internal contradictions within the work, labelling it "a confused mixture of radical and conservative ideas." The author of the articles, who could not be suspected of sympathy for the Jewish religion, and certainly not for Jewish Orthodoxy (which he termed "an obstacle to free human life"), was aware of the fact that the ruling principle in the book was the racial principle, allegedly logical, and founded on "the methodology of the natural sciences!" He peels off the scientific-ideological wrapping from Marr's essay with a critical eye, positioning it within the personal plane, the plane of local politics. The contradiction between an antireligious stance and demands which are no longer connected to religion is thoroughly explored. The writer does not mention Riesser by name, but the object of his statements is clear:

> If they [the Jews] rub their hands in pleasure at the evidence of the acknowledgment of their equal rights [the election of Riesser as Supreme Court judge], they are not different from any other group in a similar situation. . . . Reaction appears among a small group, the Jews, only as a clear reflection of what is happening among the entire nation. . . . If he [Marr] does not want to look beyond Hamburg, he must at least acknowledge that the Jewish satellites of the reaction in Hamburg to whom he refers . . . never were ultraradicals, as everyone knows [!]."

The radical author, who was not comfortable with any religion, reminds Marr that the Purim holiday, against which Marr had sent his arrows, was not unique to the Jews: the Catholics in France celebrated St. Bartholomew's Eve.

A written response by Riesser or Wolffson, the people to whom Marr referred, is not to be found. They considered it beneath their dignity and totally useless to enter into a debate with Marr. In addition, the mood among the Jews forestalled the need for an immediate response. As strange as this may seem to us, *Der Judenspiegel* was read by Hamburg Jews within the context of the controversy between Orthodox Jews and those wishing to disband the Jewish community. Marr was right when he said that his Jewish friends understood him, and were not hurt by his position.[29] Proof of this is supplied specifically by those Jewish responses which were published. One of those in favor of disbanding the Jewish community wrote to a newspaper that "we assume that the author [Marr] seriously intended to act towards the goal of removing 'harmful Judaism.' There is no doubt that Jews must increasingly get rid of the sorry remnants of the Jewish state within the modern state." The anonymous Jewish writer believed that the pamphlet was of benefit, since it prompted the Jews to examine their actions and to change their customs, as he and his Jewish associates had demanded. He noted, with a great deal of satisfaction, that "my party is not the 'Judaism' against which the author of *Der Judenspiegel* has declared war,"[30] hoping that the existing blemishes—Jewish dietary laws, the existence of the community, and all the other things separating the Jews from their surroundings—would disappear.

An Orthodox Jew, using the same limited way of thinking, arrived at quite the opposite conclusion. In a pamphlet entitled "Hep! Hep!," he portrayed Marr as someone who only wanted to have the Jews abandon their religion. Since he thought (with some justification) that Marr acted together with the Jewish Reform movement, he concluded that it was the Reform movement which had to be changed, as it was, in its entirety, a blemish on Judaism that had to be removed.[31]

A balanced counterattack by a Jew was nevertheless published. The satirist Julius Stettenheim, editor of the journal *Wespen* (*Wasps*), who had learned his craft as a writer for Marr's newspaper, *Mephistopheles,* and later gained fame in Berlin, attacked Marr in a pamphlet bearing the title "The Jew-Eater [*Der Judenfresser*]."[32] The four-page pamphlet portrays Marr both in caricature and written text. But even Stettenheim, as a Jew, does not take *Der Judenspiegel* very seriously: "My dear Wilhelm . . . if you think that you can harm even one Jew with this weapon of yours, you've lost your marbles." This was apparently the prevalent opinion among Hamburg Jews—no real harm would come from this essay. It should be regarded as intervention in an internal Jewish controversy, as a "mirror" of that controversy to non-Jewish eyes, and no more than that. It is interesting that neither this controversy nor Marr's anti-Semitic attack in 1879 caused a break in the friendly relationship between Marr and Stettenheim.

It is therefore not surprising that this essay of Marr's was also important to his political affiliation as a democrat, arousing sharp responses specifically from the democratic party. Stettenheim also attacked him mainly within this context. The main caricature shows Marr burying his past and dropping his mask: "Devil! You're removing the mask from your face." *Democracy* is written on the mask. *The slave question* (in America) is written in large letters, and *The Jewish question* in small letters, on the Devil's tail. Marr's democratic comrades were undoubtedly more aware than the Jews of the danger posed by Marr—racism! He was expelled from their ranks for his generally racist stance, and not for his particular hatred of Jews.

Indeed, the practical consequence of the controversy surrounding Marr during those months in Hamburg was directly connected to his political activity as a democrat. Half of the members of the Hamburg Parliament had to stand for reelection, three years after the previous elections. Marr was one of those up for reelection. Since the split between Marr and the "Democratic Association" was by now total, he could not run as its candidate in the election. Yet he insisted on running; since he had no political backing, he ran as an independent candidate for the region which had previously elected him. The elections were held on October 26, 1862. Out of 111 valid votes, the representatives of the democratic party received more than half and the liberals about a third; Marr received only 10 votes.[33] Marr's political career in Hamburg suffered a blow from which he would not recover. Worst of all for Marr, this election showed him how badly he had misjudged the political state of affairs in Hamburg and the role played by the Jews. The radicals, and not the liberals or conservatives, had won consistently. Thirty-seven democrats had been reelected, as opposed to only six liberals. He had been defeated in his own district by radical voters, not by conservatives. He had been defeated—but not by Jews. The fact that his rival Riesser had been defeated in the election no less decisively than he had (Riesser received fifteen votes in his district) was no consolation, since it paradoxically proved his error: Riesser the "reactionary" had been severely attacked by Wex, Marr's rival and successor within the "Democratic Association," and had failed while opposing a *democratic* candidate. The electoral loss and its significance were apparently so embarrassing for Marr that there is no mention of this in his memoirs, which usually suffer from a surfeit of detail.

6
The "German Mazzini"

In his memoirs, Marr wrote that after the *Judenspiegel* affair he went into seclusion in his villa on the outskirts of Hamburg for a year. This is one more instance, however, where he was not accurate; he had left political activity, but not his writing. He sat in his remote villa and wrote his memoirs and his impressions from the period of his stay in Central America—a two-volume, 598-page book, which did not lack a haughty attitude towards the black and red races that he had encountered in America.[1] Of course this did not satisfy Marr, so he returned to the realm of public debate. In February 1863 he once again presented himself as a self-professed expert on American affairs in a long article entitled "Towards an Understanding of the Events in North America."[2] Once again he attacked the liberal "bleeding hearts" in Germany, who uncomprehendingly supported the North. Marr claimed that the North was so realistic that it spoke of an end to slavery while most of the slave ships embarked from the port of Boston. He claimed that the problem of slavery would be solved by the mechanization of agriculture, and not by Negrophilic ideology. He made fun of the idea of raising an army of three hundred thousand Negroes to fight the South, an army which would stir up controversy in the North and would be worthless militarily, in light of the inferiority of Negroes fighting against whites. He reemphasized his racist position: the attempts made in the North to advance the culture of the Negroes were doomed to failure; the Negroes, as Negroes, would never advance. The only method he proposed to eliminate the Negro problem was the crossbreeding of whites with Negroes. This was exactly the same solution which he had proposed half a year earlier for the Jewish problem! Once again proof for those who saw racism as Marr's main evil, even though he had still not arrived at the extreme practical conclusions that he would reach in 1878.

As soon as he finished this article he set out against a new foe, the organized proletariat. Lassalle was the object of his arrows this time. A new enemy of the radical-democrats of Hamburg had arisen from the left, while they were occupied with the election campaign and Marr's removal. The "Association for the Advancement of Working Men and Women" (*Bildungsverein*) had in fact been founded in Hamburg in 1861 under the auspices of the democratic party. When, however, workers' organizations were founded in Berlin and Leipzig, and called for the establishment of a general German workers' organization, the founding of a workers' movement in Hamburg acquired momentum from a new direction. A "Provisional Council of Hamburg Workers," in which workers sat and, for all intents and purposes, were represented, was founded in December 1862. The *Bildungsverein* saw itself as no less qualified to be represented in Leipzig, and mustered all the workers and artisans organizations to form a council of their own; the representatives of the petite bourgeoisie, who politically identified with the democratic party, were to be found here. The Association's problem was twofold: how to create a homogeneous representation for the array of bourgeoisie and workers in these councils and how to resolve ideological issues with the tenets of the democratic party. How should "worker" be defined? Were artisans and bourgeoisie also to be considered "workers" for this purpose? Assemblies of workers began to be held in Hamburg before this issue was resolved. Lassalle's brand-new "Workers' Program" was read at an assembly held in January 1863. A joint committee for the two associations was finally chosen in the large assembly which was held on January 17; most of its members were from the "Provisional Council" (i.e., the new workers' representatives), not from the bourgeoisie or the democratic party. An additional assembly was held, but it was interrupted by a noisy clash between the two camps. Marr entered the picture now. In the newspaper *Freischütz,* for which he still wrote, he defended the bourgeois-democratic wing of the organization and attacked the workers' representatives who had won the battle, calling them the "red party," which propagated communism and which had learned nothing from 1848; all this, for having "forcibly taken over" the representation of the workers to the general German assembly.

Jacob Audorf, the 27-year-old leader of the workers in the city, was the one who responded in the workers' newspaper *Nordstern.* This was the beginning of the controversy between Marr and Audorf, which developed into a typical debate over workers' affairs between a progressive and a socialist, overshadowed by the struggle in Prussia between Lassalle and the workers' party, versus the bourgeois "progressive party." On March 28, the "General Assembly of Hamburg Workers" adopted Lassalle's position as expressed in his "Public Response." The workers organized in this assembly in Hamburg participated during the next two months in the discussion over the establishment of the *Allgemeiner deut-*

scher Arbeiterverein (ADAV). Marr decided now that he had to forestall the danger.

The chronicler of the workers' movement in Hamburg relates in detail the struggles of the workers to organize. The chronicler chose to discuss Marr, out of all the rivals of this new movement. Marr was certainly not a rival of political importance, but as a journalist he aroused much interest. The leader of the Hamburg workers accordingly took pains to debate with him, and the historian of the workers' movement excitedly attacked his position fifty years later.[3]

Marr, who because of his anti-Jewish and racist stance was already on the way out of his newspaper (*Freischütz*), wanted to establish his own journal. This newspaper was meant to be satirical, but different from *Mephistopheles.* Called *Opposition,* it first appeared in June 1863. The declared goal of the newspaper and the spirit of the articles appearing in it was a "German republic" based on universal suffrage. As on previous occasions, Marr now more than ever before turned to the antiparticularist forces in Germany after the Hamburg republic turned its back on him. He did not, however, surrender his democratic-republican stance, as if to say that *Der Judenspiegel* and everything connected with it appeared to him only as a way station on the consistent path of his radical democratism. He therefore attempted, in his own way, to criticize "democracy in a nightgown," while doing everything to assist the progressives in Prussia to rid their state of reaction, so that Prussia could assume the task which he had long ago assigned to it.[4]

Announcements about the start of Marr's new journal appeared in the Hamburg newspapers for several weeks. Marr tried to draw the attention of potential readers by advertising the title of the main article that would appear in the new journal, "Mr. Lassalle and the Workers' Question." The journal appeared only three times in 64-page editions from June 1863 to the end of the year, when it ceased publication. The major attack on Lassalle was made in the spirit of the ideology of the liberal workers' associations (*Schulze-Delitsch*) and was not lacking in venom, as was customary for Marr. He accused Lassalle of "the haughtiness of a garrison lieutenant." Audorf immediately responded with a pamphlet of his own, *Wilhelm Marr and the Workers' Question,* in a style no less stinging and strong than Marr's. He attributed to Marr "the haughtiness of an assistant in a bookshop," and reminded him of his unsavory past: his desertion of "Young Germany," his stand on the issue of slavery in America, and even the Jewish question. Despite this, he portrayed the dispute between them as a "family matter": "Until now we appreciated Marr, to a certain degree, as an energetic fighter for democracy, who aspired just as we did to the same goals, even though he played the fool at times."[5] Indeed, despite *Der Judenspiegel,* even Marr's enemies placed him within the democratic camp, and all his venomous attacks were considered only as "the antics of a fool" on the way to the goal. Perhaps Audorf thought that Marr, who was forced to leave the democrats, would now lean towards the workers union, if they would only show him the way. In all truth, the Jews were not the only ones too shortsighted to see the potential danger posed by Marr in 1862. Audorf therefore attacked Marr's weak point from the democratic point of view: the democrats, specifically, were the ones who should support Lassalle's party, since both groups (and Marr, certainly) aggressively attacked the policy of the Gotha circle on the German question, as on the social question. Marr thought perhaps that the Lassallian union would induce disorder, but Audorf believed that if Lassalle failed because the democrats did not cooperate with him—if democracy refused to cooperate with the social movement—then the social movement would become a threat to the entire society, a violent threat which would not operate in a democratic manner! Audorf wondered at the so-called democrats, cooperating with the Prussian version of progressives, who proclaimed their neutrality on the Polish question in accordance with Bismarck's policy (i.e., Bismarck's cooperation with Russia, which had crushed the Polish uprising in 1863).[6] He was surprised at Marr, the radical, for suddenly posing as an advocate of the liberal Manchester School in his attitude towards the state, or at least in his criticism of Lassalle.[7]

It seems that anyone who followed the Marr of 1862, and not just Audorf, had to greatly wonder at his position. Since he had been banished by the "Democratic Association," one would have expected him to turn to the left, as was his custom, and cooperate with the workers in attacking the democratic party (or the progressive party in Prussia) as a bourgeois party (especially since one of the leaders of the workers' union affiliated with the democrats, Martens, was his personal enemy). The explanation for Marr's surprising position may lie in the Jewish context. An allusion to this can be found in the pamphlet which Marr prepared in reply to Audorf at the end of 1863, "Lassalle the Messiah and His Hamburg Disciples." This, however, is not the full explanation. Several ideological considerations enter the picture:

1. As we have seen, Marr opposed the corporate organization of the Jews (the community) on the grounds of individual freedom. In principle, he viewed the organizing of workers in a similar light.
2. In 1848, Marr had defended the principle of free trade against the Prussian tariff union.[8] He defended this principle fifteen years later, in the wider context of the individual versus the state.
3. He viewed the Lassallian union through the eyes of a member of "Young Germany" from twenty years before! He returned to his old battlefield, where he had acted within a social movement which spoke of social reform on behalf of the rights of the individual, as opposed to the communists. (Audorf also alluded to this in his pamphlet.)

4. If Marr hoped for an antireactionary Prussia, his ally would be the Prussian progressive party, and not its proletarian rival, which might strengthen Prussian reaction, i.e. the ruling aristocracy.

It was in this spirit that he formulated his argument, which is mainly a logical defense against utopianism and wild dreams:

> The Lassallian theory concerning the intervention of a state such as this on behalf of the worker is *foolishness*. . . . The state has absolutely no right to prefer these individuals over others. ⁻. . .
>
> I therefore turn to the Lassallians: Have the courage to call yourselves communists . . . I do not fear communism. . . . It is even possible that communism will return and find a role to play, like those errors which help mankind progress in a negative manner. But the individualistic feelings of freedom within me rebel against any form of guardianship. . . . It's no wonder that the people seek solace *in a world of illusions,* in the face of the lack of principles of the parliamentary masters. . . .
>
> Let us imagine the kingdom of Lassalle the Messiah! The state would be reorganized after a successful revolution. Who would rule, who would organize, who would command? Some fanatic, like the evangelist Audorf? . . . There is no other guarantee but the right of universal suffrage, *with no additional "program."* . . . It would be an abhorrent lie to turn the worker into one dependent upon the State's mercies and machinery. . . . This right [universal suffrage] is a means for Lassalle, and a goal for me. . . . After the state, in its disgraceful way . . . has intervened on behalf of the capitalists, must it now use the same disgraceful principle concerning *the workers?*[9]

This was Marr's reaction to Lassalle's most popular pamphlets, a reaction that demonstrated his consistency, despite his many aberrations. Reacting to a remark made by Audorf, Marr was again ready to elaborate on his attitude to the Jewish problem: "I cannot make friends with the political theocratism of self-ghettoed Judaism, and I cannot place the Jew above other men."[10]

This episode does not appear in Marr's memoirs, and the explanation for this—as for the omission of his failure in the October 1862 elections—is not hard to find. Marr felt within a short time that he had become involved in a battle which did not concern him. He found himself fighting on the side of the democrats and the liberals, his rivals; he fought against Lassalle, who in the final account did Bismarck's work in the struggle against the Prussian colleagues (liberals and progressives) of the Hamburg democrats; and—most importantly—this led to Marr's opposing the policy for which Bismarck stood. Since, after the conclusion of the Lassalle episode, Marr would act on behalf of Bismarck's policy and the Prussian supremacy within Germany, and since Marr—like Lassalle—put himself at Bismarck's service, he chose to omit this episode from his memoirs, even if it was not possible to expunge it from history. We do not need the memoirs to discover that Marr did indeed reverse his anti-Lassallian position. He wrote this explicitly in his newspaper on the day Lassalle died, when he requested forgiveness from the dead.[11]

While Marr was firing his last salvos against Audorf and Lassalle, the event occurred which was to effect the greatest, most fundamental, change on Germany since 1848: Frederick VII, the Danish king, died. The issue of Schleswig-Holstein, which had enflamed the revolutionaries of 1848, had once again come to the fore. There were very few people even then who understood all the complexities of the issue. A short clarification is in order here.[12] Schleswig and Holstein were two duchies that had been indivisibly linked by an agreement made in the fifteenth century. They were ruled by the Danish king (i.e., they were linked to Denmark by a personal union). The more southern of the two duchies, Holstein, was affiliated, however, with the German Bund. Since 1847, the German national movement had wanted to separate the two duchies from Denmark, while the Danish national movement wanted to annex at least Schleswig. The issue was complicated by the question of succession: the Danish king did not have a male heir. According to the Danish laws of succession, he would be succeeded by Christian IX; according to Holstein law, his heir would be a prince from the Augustenburg line. Since it was not possible to separate Holstein from Schleswig, an international agreement was reached in London in 1852, according to which Christian would be recognized as the heir to the duchies as well. The problem was that Christian signed a law annexing Schleswig to Denmark as soon as he assumed the throne. The German liberals, members of the "National Association," and many other groups, awakened to fanatic national fervor, loudly demanded the separation of Schleswig-Holstein from Denmark, the abandonment of the London agreement, and the establishment of an additional German state, Schleswig-Holstein.[13]

Marr describes in his memoirs how he was caught up in this fiery controversy. On the occasion of his forty-fourth birthday on November 16, he left his villa and went into the city, where he found an excited crowd. The news had arrived that the Danish king had died only the day before, and his heir had ascended the throne. Marr, stunned by the news, by chance met the police inspector Paulsen, who was convinced that Marr himself was one of the organizers of the demonstration. Paulsen thought that Marr, as a revolutionary, would now take part in a rerun of the 1848 revolution over the Schleswig-Holstein issue and support the Augustenburg prince.[14] The issue, however, was not so simple. The radical revolutionaries of 1848 were indeed in favor of the annexation of Schleswig-Holstein to Germany, but they did not support the policy of the Augustenburg prince. Instead, Marr reached his decision: "My republican and revolutionary illusions collapsed around me all at once. . . . Did we fight against all the princes to celebrate the multiplication of small states?"

Marr is exaggerating once again. First, when the 1848 revolution faded out, he already spoke and wrote of the elimination of the small states by Prussia, on behalf of Germany. Second, he had already opposed Augustenburg and the reaction which it represented in 1849. As we have seen, there was nothing novel in his supporting Prussian policy on Schleswig-Holstein (i.e., Prussia taking control of the duchies and supplanting the Augustenburg prince, the "people's favorite"). Third, he left the door open, at least theoretically, for a German republic, even after November 16, 1863.

His conduct starting from this period does, however, testify that Marr's republican sentiments had begun to deteriorate as of November 16. Marr became a supporter of Bismarck, thereby assigning secondary importance to the conflict between monarchy and republic. Marr revealed his soul-searching with a great degree of frankness in his memoirs. He hated Bismarck, but he hated his rivals no less. This network of hatred was finally decided in favor of the hatred which compensated him for his failure in Hamburg and which would eventually aid in the establishment of Germany.[15] Marr's support of Bismarck was unconditional. While an action committee was founded in Hamburg which demanded that the Bundestag send an army to aid the prince of Augustenburg in the liberation of Schleswig-Holstein in spite of Prussian policy, Marr made efforts in the opposite direction (it is possible that Marr was impelled by the fact that six of the ten members of the committee were Jews).[16] Either way, the Schleswig-Holstein issue in 1863 turned Marr from a conditionally pro-Prussian democratic antiparticularist to a pro-Prussian at all costs. It is possible that his friend Ruge, the former revolutionary whom he met after his return from America, and who had taken the same strange path from revolution to admiration of Bismarck, had had a delayed influence upon him. He was certainly influenced by the actions of his acquaintance Mazzini in Italy. At any rate, we find in Marr the phenomenon which was so characteristic of the 1848'ers: the shift from liberalism, democracy, or revolution to support for Bismarck, based on the conclusion that "the revolution from below is bankrupt, and the time has come for the revolution from above." Marr called this "revolutionary pessimism," accusing his revolutionary and democratic friends of being "rags!" To Marr's credit, all his writings (and, in the opinion of a graphologist, his handwriting as well) testify to the storm which as a result raged within him, and which would cause him to pay more than lip service to republicanism even in the coming years.[17]

Mazzini's influence upon Marr was not a trifling matter. Marr saw himself as the Mazzini of the German unification movement. Just as Mazzini, the brain behind Italian unification, sought someone who would wield the sword and overcame his personal revulsion to sword-wielding to bring about Italian unification, so did Marr, according to his own testimony. Marr saw himself as close to and an equal of Mazzini, not only because he had met him and been influenced by him in 1851, but also since he had belonged in his youth to the same freedom movement of "Young Europe" and "Young Germany." Marr thought that he was following in Mazzini's footsteps in the lessons he had learned from his past in "Young Germany" and from the 1848 revolution: "It was a mistake to aspire for freedom without first creating the power by which the struggle for freedom would be conducted." Mazzini, in the spirit of Machiavelli (whose writings Marr had studied in 1848), had been willing to cooperate with the traitorous Savoy royal house, "as if choosing poison in order to bring succor to the fatherland." Marr concluded, in his own words, "We are therefore now the allies of the sword of Germany [Prussia]. We will look around at the moment that the Gordian knot will be broken and see if we can still find republicans capable of wielding the sword to the same degree, and perhaps better than, the monarchy."[18] He explained in another article, "We *want* a republic, an undivided Great Germany." It was immaterial to him whether this Germany would be headed by a president or a kaiser. He declared, however, that "we *must* reinforce the power of the strongest party [i.e., Prussia]" for the purpose of unification. If a revolution would break out in such a state, it would have much more significance than a revolution in a tiny German state, such as Lippe-Detmold. Despite the enmity towards Prussia, one must "bow one's head before the mathematical data."[19] It should be stated to Marr's credit that five years later he would still utter the slogan that he would prefer a republic, if this were a realistic option.[20] It cannot be said that Marr was inconsistent: he wanted Prussia, but still dreamed of a republic. The test of the republic, however, would be a test of power, and nothing more. Any sensible person knew who would win in such a test—it was a matter of pure mathematics. Marr was so convinced that political romanticism had already been pushed aside by *realpolitik* that he called upon Prussia to stop the trials it was conducting against Polish rebels, since—in his opinion—they posed no danger.[21]

Marr, who was not overly modest, aimed high. He (the "German Mazzini") had to make contact with the German Cavour (Bismarck), and this was done through Marr's journalistic activity. The important Jewish publisher from Hamburg, I. S. Meyer (nicknamed Ismeyer), had started a newspaper, *Nessel* (the nettle), as soon as the commotion over Schleswig-Holstein had begun. The newspaper supported the Augustenburg prince, without much success. Ismeyer requested Marr to write an article (*Der Judenspiegel* had apparently been forgotten). Marr called upon the prince to lead a military struggle for German unification. The article stirred up a controversy and was reprinted by the *Norddeutsche Allgemeine Zeitung,* Bismarck's semiofficial newspaper. Ismeyer, who did not receive financial backing from the Augustenburg prince, offered Marr a partnership in the newspaper, even at the cost of a complete change in the newspaper's orientation. Marr had only 1,000 taler, and 2,000 more were needed; he hoped to obtain them from Bismarck, "the only *man* in

Germany."[22] It should be stated to Marr's credit that he was not one of those who jumped on Bismarck's wagon after Prussia's military victories in 1864 and 1866, but before them, when Bismarck was not yet firmly established. The compliment that Marr paid himself, that he had better foresight than many regular politicians, was correct; it had not been at all clear then that Bismarck would be more successful than his rivals in the Prussian capital, who were supported by the king.[23]

The way in which Marr reached Bismarck bore the touch of the conspiratorial style he had adopted in the 1840's, in the underground movement in Switzerland. He wrote Bismarck an unsigned letter containing a request for 2,000 taler, to turn a newspaper into a supporter of the annexation of Schleswig-Holstein to Prussia. Marr requested that the reply be given by the publication of an advertisement in the Hamburg newspaper *Hamburger Nachrichten* under the title of "Florence." The reply appeared in the newspaper under that title two days after the letter had been sent: "Matters such as this can only be arranged through personal contact. It is necessary to talk." Marr then sent an additional anonymous letter: "I will appear before you next Sunday." Marr went to Berlin in January 1864 to meet with "the tiger of the reaction." The former revolutionary, as always in his contacts with the nobility, took pains with his attire and correct manners, and entered the side entrance of Bismarck's house in Wilhelmstrasse 65. Marr writes that Bismarck assumed that he was the writer. He wrote in his memoirs that thus began the meeting between "Mazzini's pupil and friend and the statesman of the future." Marr, the petit bourgeois revolutionary of short stature, felt ill at ease with the huge Junker. He was strengthened and consoled by the fact that the Junker lit his cigar for him three times with his own hands and that he made General Manteuffel wait for twenty minutes, until he had finished talking with Marr. Marr presented the issue to Bismarck, mentioned his record of unpleasant relations with Prussia in the past, and even argued with him about the nature of republicanism, parliamentarianism, and democracy. The meeting ended, but he did not receive the money from Bismarck, which he obviously could not have received by other than devious means.

Marr was forced to raise the 2,000 taler by other means; it is possible that he received some of the money indirectly as a result of his talk with Bismarck. At any rate, starting in February 1864, Marr was the editor of the newspaper *Nessel,* which advocated the idea of annexation to Prussia—not just the annexation of Schleswig-Holstein, but of Hamburg as well![24] He would follow this line not only during the year he edited the newspaper until the beginning of 1865, which was the year of the war between Denmark and the German Bund, but until 1868, when he left the city.

Marr's ties with those close to Bismarck became more ramified. He began to correspond with the Prussian politician Rudolf Schramm a few days before the appearance of the article supporting Prussia as the "sword

of Germany." Schramm, who defined himself as Bismarck's confidant
from their days as university students, tried to influence Marr to write in
favor of the annexation of Hamburg to Prussia, despite the fact that Marr
still attempted to defend the position that Hamburg had to be as independent of Prussia as it was of Denmark.[25] A short time later, after the conclusion of the war with Denmark, Marr corresponded with the editor of
the *Norddeutsche Allgemeine Zeitung,* A. Bras. Marr apparently still
attempted in this correspondence to defend the American or Swiss version
of republicanism, while cooperating with Prussia, possibly with the intention of influencing Prussia's actions.

These contacts explain the position of the *Nessel* newspaper from
the beginning of the Danish-German war. The key word is the "politics of
action" (*Aktions-Politik*), represented by Bismarck. In accordance with
this line, Marr attacked the "chatterers" from the National Union, the
federal solutions, and the proposal to establish a German Parliament while
perpetuating the existence of the thirty-four German states.[26] "In our
desire to support action, we surrendered our weapons to Bismarck, our
most dangerous adversary, but the most highly regarded; we were not so
closeminded as to turn arithmetic into a party issue. We prefer the progressive unification of our homeland to its perpetual division." Marr found
it easy to attack the democrats, his former partners, when the Danish war
was successfully concluded. The personal motive surfaced once again:
Marr stated that the fact that Germany needed a "strict taskmaster"
(*Strenger Lehrmeister*) was a consequence of the ineffectual policy of
"Virchow in Berlin, Wex, Godeffroy, and Wolffson in Hamburg."[27]
Wolffson, the Jewish liberal leader, and Wex, who had expelled Marr
from the "Democratic Association," therefore became the targets of his
attacks. In addition to this, his personal anger was so great that he once
again revealed his thoughts by calling the camp of his opponents on the
question of German unification "the camp of modern Israel [the National
Union, the Progressive Party, etc.], which believes even today that it will
topple the walls of Jericho with its screams."[28]

Marr's activity aroused great anger at him in Hamburg, even when
it was directed only against an independent Schleswig-Holstein, and not
against an independent Hamburg (i.e., until the end of the Danish war in
1864). He was termed "Hamburg's enemy" more than once. Already at
the beginning of the Danish-German war in February, a rumor of cooperation between Bismarck and Marr was leaked through a source in
Schleswig-Holstein to one of the leading newspapers of the state of Han-
over, the *Hannoveraner Courier*.[29] The newspaper even published a report
that Marr had been bribed, to the tune of 2,000 taler, to defend Prussian
expansionist policy. Marr did not respond until August, when he wrote
a letter to Kiel, from where the report originated,[30] in which he totally
denied the accusation. According to the evidence we possess, Marr was
right: first, he did not receive the money, and second, he did not change

his mind and his position to receive financial support; rather, he requested this support *after* having crystallized his pro-Bismarck opinion.

This was not sufficient, of course, to stop the maligners, and Marr lost the last remnant of the popularity which he had enjoyed in his city. The more Marr was attacked in Hamburg, the more his pro-Prussian orientation inclined him to leave the Schleswig-Holstein issue, especially since it was only half-resolved, and to deal with the issue of Hamburg's independence or annexation to Prussia. He did not edit the newspaper *Nessel* from the beginning of 1865 on,[31] when the paper returned for a short time (until it was suppressed by the authorities) to Ismeyer's hands. Marr searched for another newspaper, and published the *Beobachter an der Elbe* (a weekly for Schleswig-Holstein and Hamburg) by himself for two years,[32] following developments in Germany until after the Austro-Prussian war (1866). We do not know whether the money for these enterprises came from his inheritance from his wife and his American dealings or from the Prussian treasury. An essay published in 1866, "Hamburg's Independence and Sovereignty Have Become Anachronistic," testifies, however, to the continuation of his firm ties with Prussia, since it was dedicated to the Prussian Foreign Office[33] while the war between Austria and Prussia was still being waged. In this article, which was replete with harsh criticism of Hamburg's government and society, Marr called upon Prussia not to adopt (*Anschluss*) the small states, including Hamburg, as satellites, but to annex them. "The choice is to be Prussian Helots or Prussian citizens." He feared that joining Prussia would lead to the economic exploitation of Hamburg's residents, while annexation would enable the taxes of twenty-two million Prussians also to be used to cover Hamburg's expenses.[34] He said that if Hamburg had been in the south, he would have proposed annexing it to Austria, if only to end the system of small states.[35] There was a double advantage to annexation to Prussia, in addition to the need for a new Germany: it would be beneficial for Hamburg's honor, economy, and for its future as a city of commerce, and would bring it a more progressive educational and legal system. It is of interest, in light of the Austro-Prussian conflict, that Marr waived, on the one hand, the idea of *one* German state (republic) and took an interest "for practical reasons" only in northern Germany. On the other hand, he explicitly criticized Bismarck for leading Prussia to war instead of solving the German problem through a diplomatically reached partition, without expelling Austria from Germany.[36] This comment, and a pamphlet which Marr wrote for this purpose,[37] are proof that he was not a loyal servant automatically agreeing with Prussia, even if he did maintain contact with Prussia. Also, this position reveals that the German Reich, in the form it assumed from 1871, was not the fulfillment of Marr's hopes concerning the German question.

The essay on "Hamburg's Independence" was the climax of Marr's anti-Hamburg attack. He brought upon himself the ire of the loyal Hamburg residents who were involved in the debate over cooperation with the Prussian customs union.[38] After he discredited himself with the democratic union in 1862, and after entangling himself with Lassalle's supporters in 1863, the following three years helped him to fall from favor with all the rest of the respectable Hamburg residents. Marr became persona non grata in his own city, and he became more embittered than he had ever been before.

Marr did not leave journalism. In 1866 he began to edit a Sunday newspaper, *Der Kosmopolit*. This was Marr's swan song as a publisher and editor; during the following ten years, he would wander from newspaper to newspaper, and from place to place, as a feuilletonist. He went in 1867 to Italy and Switzerland, later publishing a book about this in Hamburg, the *Council of Trent,* which was a general attack on the church and a book written "in Voltaire's footsteps." The book described the church's extremely worldly interests, and would not have added anything to Marr's atheistic repertoire, if it had not been for his incidental attacks on the press. According to Marr, the press was nothing but a product of speculation, guided by business interests and by hand-to-mouth spiritual realism, a product of the literary industry.[39] All the descriptions which he would apply to the Jewish press more than ten years later are already to be found here. This is not surprising; he knew, as a disciple of Feuerbach, that Judaism was noted for realism. The anti-Jewish feeling, which had already found expression in his writings in 1862, and which would be the prime motivation for his anti-Semitic outburst in 1878, was already sharply formulated here. The term "Jew," however, still does not appear in every sentence. A term nevertheless appears once which gives Marr away, when he sums up the entire phenomenon as "compulsory *Orientalization.*" His conclusion here is similar to the conclusion which made his 1878 anti-Semitic book a success: resignation, a surrender to the spirit of the times which cannot be stopped.[40] This is no longer the radical, energetic Marr of the 1840's and 1850's. Marr after 1866, no longer a politician and no longer an independent newspaper editor, was a beaten man. This was the cause of his resignation and surrender. Since the blows which would land upon him in the coming decade both as a journalist and as a man would only aggravate the situation, the accumulated bitterness and frank resignation which would also characterize his book *The Victory of Judaism over Germanism* are not surprising.

Marr was only fifty years old, but all manner of strange illnesses descended upon him and embittered his life. He began at the end of 1867 to write for the liberal newspaper *Post,* the newspaper of the free conservatives published by the apostate Strousberg, and from 1863 for the Hamburg newspaper *Montagsnachrichten,* edited by the talented satirist Zerbst and published by the Jew Jonas Cohn. I intentionally mention the Jewishness of his publishers from the time of the *Nessel,* since he would never have arrived at the anti-Semitism of the end of the 1870's without them. Special mention should be made within this context of Bethel Henry Strousberg, for whom publishing a newspaper was of secondary importance. Strousberg, who was known as the European "railroad king," was considered an outstanding example of modern Jewish success until he was imprisoned in Russia. Marr would later be attacked for being inconsistent, a racist anti-Semite who agreed to work for a rich apostate Jew. Marr replied to this charge in 1879.[41] He claimed he worked for the newspaper for five months without being paid, and did not know that Strousberg owned it. (This claim clearly testifies to what straits Marr was in as a journalist at that time.) He made especial use of the newspaper to attack Hamburg, and wrote several articles about the scandalous exploitation of the "industry" of immigrants from Hamburg. In time Strousberg offered Marr the post of acting editor of the newspaper, or of part of the newspaper; Marr turned him down since he wanted to live in Switzerland instead of Berlin. Marr also writes in his memoirs that he knew nothing of his employer's improper activities, and that he had quite a good impression of his employer, despite the latter's being "the archetype of Jewish nervousness."[42] It is even possible that Strousberg, who himself defined the Jews as a race,[43] unwittingly provided the confirmation Marr needed in this direction.

Marr was eventually put on trial as an "enemy of Hamburg," after one of his vigorous attacks in the press on the Hamburg government, and was sentenced to nine months of imprisonment. His sentence was lessened to ten weeks after his appeal in March 1869. The ailing Marr did not relate to this period of imprisonment with as much equanimity as he had in his youth. The implementation of the sentence was postponed several times for medical reasons, until he received a pardon at the outbreak of the Franco-Prussian War in 1870. As a result of the sentence, he resolved to leave Hamburg for good, but he honored this resolve only intermittently. He lived in Bex (near St. Maurice) in Switzerland from 1870 to 1872, where he wrote articles that he sent to the *Post* in Berlin. He was back in Hamburg between 1872 and 1874, where he wrote a portion of his memoirs that was published in the leftist journal *Reform,* whose editor-in-chief until 1870 was H. S. Hertz, a Jew from an Orthodox family and principal of the Jewish school, followed by Dr. Pizza, the cantor of the Jewish Reform congregation. He lived in Weimar from 1874 to 1875, writing for both the *Weimarsche Zeitung* and *Gartenlaube* (which will be discussed again later). He later moved to Berlin and Leipzig, writing a little here and there in the women's magazine *Der Bazar,* the literary magazines *Die Gegenwart, Politik,* and other journals. Marr was on the way down.

The use of the word "Oriental" in the book on *The Council of Trent* had not been accidental. Marr had developed his own racial theory during the 1860's, without any connection to the Jewish question. As we have seen, his stay in America aroused his awareness of the racial issue, which was also the source of his judgment of the American Civil War. Marr analyzed not only the black race or the Jewish race (both of which he wanted to overcome by intermarriage) but also the European race, which had already aroused his interest while a youth in Switzerland. He was given another opportunity to deal with the issue when he addressed the problem of the Schleswig-Holstein war. The establishment of a tripartite alliance (Russia-France-Prussia) was discussed in October 1864. Marr viewed the proposal as the basis of a new European order, and not just as a diplomatic exercise. "Even Prussia's rivals acknowledge that it is a Power which is meant to head the Germanic sphere. . . . The rule of Europe must be divided into three realms: the Germanic, the Slavic, and the Roman," since the Slavs, Romans, and Germans are "the only cultured peoples on earth," with the rule of Asia also to be divided among them. If Russia were to renounce its expansion to the west, and France to the Rhine border, and Prussia were to be content with northern Germany, an equilibrium would be created on a racial basis that would maintain world order. Each of the three powers would be given a free hand in its apportioned realm: France, in Italy and Spain; Russia, in Turkey; and Germany, in the Low Countries. England and Austria would shrink until they disintegrated.[44] He termed the new order a giant cultural-historic step forward.

The theme of the three European races against Asianism also appears at other times. The trinity of European races, as the basis for a comprehensive European order, he described in an anonymous pamphlet, *The New Trinity,* which was published in 1867.[45] He wrote an unpublished article immediately afterwards, apparently at the end of 1867, for the convocation of the "Congres International de la Paix" by La Ligue Internationale de la Paix in Geneva. The league, which had been founded in France by Charles Lemonier, had as its goal not only world peace but also the replacement of monarchies by democracies, the separation of church and state, the creation of a United States of Europe, and so forth.[46] Its first congress was held in Geneva on September 9, 1867, with subsequent yearly congresses held at the same location. A league member asked Marr to join; as was Marr's custom, his answer was surprising and paradoxical. Marr's proposal for European peace was based on the principle which had already been mentioned in 1864 and 1867: the partition of Europe into three racial spheres of influence, the Latin (no longer Roman), the Slavic, and the Germanic. The basic assumption was that "the faulty use of the term nationalism is the cause of most wars." The peace for which the league aspired would come automatically, as soon as there could be agreement on the meaning of the concept "nationality," and an agreement that this concept would form the basis for the political order. Marr had such a definition: the small nationalities are only excuses for war, ridiculous creations. The only nationality is the great nationality,

"La veritable nationalité c'est la race,"[47] the three races which are the three nationalities "absorb within themselves the little tribes, like the sea the rivers." These races-nationalities are defined, according to Marr, by "language and customs," with the three European blocs being created by a process of "gravitation." Encouraging the process of gravitation does not constitute a threat to peace, but in contrast, is the only basis for peace. Maintaining the peace requires that each racial state refrain from intervening in the process of gravitation to another race (i.e., France cannot intervene in wars such as those of Prussia over Schleswig-Holstein or the states to the south of the Main). Marr's Darwinian philosophy was already explicitly expressed: "Anyone who cannot hold his own—has to go." *This* idea of the league for maintaining peace obviously had very practical significance at the time when Prussia was about to conclude the process of German gravitation. Beyond this, however, it contained an innovation of revolutionary significance, not only as it pertained to the European order (he proposed dismembering Austria, according to its races, and dividing it among the three European racial states), but also in its definition of the concept of "nationality," its definition of "national," and in the use of the term "race" in international relations. This "national triad," in his words, is the "new gospel," even though to some degree the "new" gospel consists of entrusting the mission to the old order, the monarchy, not to the republic. This "newness" does not contradict Marr's past system; as a radical, both the politics of cabinets and the established rights based on subtle dynastic arrangements were strange to him. His proposed racial and "national trinity," even if it were to be directed by kings, is essentially in accordance with the radicalism following the "ancien régime." After attaining the European triad, it would then be possible to reconsider the question of exchanging the monarchy with a republic.

This radical arrangement is of interest not only because it presents the paradox of revolutionary radicalism, or because it laid the ideological foundation for the policy that guided Europe during the 1930's, but also—and mainly—since it also included the Jewish question. We have already seen how this system pits the European races against Orientalism or Asianism. The term "Asianism" surfaces here too, not incidentally in connection with the Eastern problem but specifically linked to the Jews. Marr's convolutions are strange, but not surprising: How does one wage war against war? With the help of money. The trouble is that those with money are interested in war and not in peace; they are the real inciters to barbarism. The socialist in Marr appears here in all his splendor, and here he also lets the cat out of the bag:

> Knock on the doors of the Jews, who are the high priests of the Jehovahism of money, and who give of it to their king, and see how they will answer you. The Golden Calf became a fattened ox who makes

use of his horns, and woe to Moses if he tried to remove it from the pedestal! This is the Asianism which is commanded today, merely in a new form, to cut to pieces the unbelievers, i.e., the vanquished and the poor devils. Asianism must be removed before bringing peace to the world [*il faut desasiatiser le monde avant de le pacifier*].[48]

The war therefore devolved onto Asia, a war against Asia which was a war against those with capital, a war against the Jews. This was written about twenty years after Marr the radical had published a carica- ture in his newspaper depicting the kings of Europe standing around Rothschild, holding their hands out for money,[49] and about ten years before he would publish *The Victory of Judaism over Germanism*. The word "Asianism" would then be replaced by "Semitism," and the horrible product would stand completed.

The Franco-Prussian War, which erupted after this, unexpectedly furnished him with additional ammunition for an attack on the Jews. The role of the "bad guy" was filled by Gambetta, whom Marr thought to be Jewish. In Marr's opinion, Gambetta made false use of republican- ism and unnecessarily lengthened the war. The French paid the price in blood, while Gambetta and Crémieux put its monetary price into their pockets.[50] Gambetta became the target of Marr's pacifist, humanist ire, and the alleged cause of the disruption of the international system which Marr had proposed. Marr's anger at the "Jewish" Gambetta had not calmed down by the time he wrote *The Victory of Judaism over Ger- manism*,[51] nor for many years later, when he wrote his memoirs.

After the capitalistic wars had aided Marr in placing the Jews within his racial configuration, the creation of Germany and the 1873 crisis of the German stock exchange bolstered his conviction that this alien race did indeed rule the world and Germany. A trivial scene in his city, Ham- burg, to which he had returned after an absence of four years, was the pretext for a general attack. It was customary to celebrate for several days before Christmas on the location where the city cathedral had once stood (Domfest). And now, to the shock of the atheist Marr, Jews were taking over the celebration area and turning it into a noisy marketplace: "One would think that they are in Jerusalem. . . . This Orientalism pushes aside every other element."[52] It is an expression of the Jews' racial quality (*Raceneigenthümlichkeit*). "What is called 'the emancipation of the Jews,' or, in practice, the emancipation of Jewish privileges from the general law, has brought us the rule of the 'Golden Calf.' "[53] Marr had so polished his concept ten years after *The Mirror of the Jews* (*Der Judenspiegel*) that *The Victory of Judaism over Germanism*, which would appear in another five years, would add almost nothing. Here he attacks the Jewish press for mixing literary writing with advertisements for the sale of goods: "They use the same pen to write criticism of Feuerbach and propaganda for shoes and sausage." In Marr's eyes, this is how a profession which was "pure literature" turned into a mixture which he could not abide. As in all his writings, the Jewish press was only one side of the coin; the other side was Jewish money: the corruption revealed by the manipulations and collapse of the stock market that took place while Marr was writing the article. Aided by the press and the stock market, Jewry ruled the world, spiritually as well as commercially. Judaism means "war on all ideals; the transformation of everything to merchandise."[54] The church cannot help, "hyperrealism, reaching its peak in Judaism, encompasses the entire world. One who is not a speculator is directly or indirectly dependent upon speculation."[55] In five years' time, these themes would characterize *The Victory of Judaism over Germanism*.

The resignation and despair which had characterized Marr since 1867, and which would deepen in *The Victory of Judaism over Germanism*, already appear here.[56] "I'm not joking. I speak in complete seriousness, from the viewpoint of cultural history. This is the last attempt, and I hope that Israel will award me a medal of honor for recognizing its power to rule the world."[57] The question which must be asked is, why did Marr content himself with articles and bits of articles in dark corners of the press instead of publishing *The Victory of Judaism over Germanism* when these scattered statements were written in 1873?

7

The Victory of Judaism over Germanism

Almost all the historians who have discussed Marr until now have mentioned 1873, and not 1879, as the year in which *The Victory of Judaism over Germanism* appeared. The juxtaposition with the stock exchange crash (*Gründerschwindel*) furnishes a good reason for the selection of this date. The *Jüdisches Lexikon* from 1927, the *Encyclopaedia Judaica* from 1928, the anti-Semitic encyclopedia *Sigila Veri* from 1931, Massing in his 1949 book on anti-Semitism, Alex Bein in his 1958 article on anti-Semitism, Pulzer in his 1964 book, and even a dissertation from 1975 on anti-Semitism in Hamburg all mention the year 1873 as the year in which the book was written.[1] The fact that Dubnow commented in the 1929 volume of his book *Weltgeschichte des jüdischen Volkes* that Marr's book was written before the year in which it appeared, although this comment was not included in his book on modern Jewish history which appeared in 1923,[2] is evidence that this mistake was made some time towards the end of the 1920's. It should be noted that the first systematic historian of anti-Semitism, Wawrzinek, in the book he wrote in Berlin in 1927, attributed Marr's book to the year 1879.[3]

The year 1873 was nevertheless an important year in Marr's life, not because of the stock market crisis or because of the writing of a book which did not yet exist, but because he finally divorced his first wife, who was forty-two years old, after twenty years of marriage, to marry another woman. On February 26, 1874, he married the thirty-eight-year-old Helene Behrend, his junior by seventeen years and a pure-blooded Jewess whose mother's maiden name had been Israel. Marr dealt with this episode in two places: in the *Gartenlaube* journal, for which he wrote during the years 1874–1875, and in his memoirs, written fifteen years later. Marr described what happened to him in a heart-rending manner in *Gartenlaube:* after finally divorcing his rich wife, he married a woman "who was not rich, not young, and not pretty." Their relationship began as a correspondence during his first marriage and later developed into a love that Marr had not previously known. He repeatedly emphasizes that his soul, which had known no peace since his first marriage, had at long last found peace and tranquility.

The happy couple decided to leave the noisy city of Hamburg for Weimar, where Marr had been offered the position of literary and theater critic at the official Weimar newspaper. In Weimar Marr found the spiritual nourishment he sought—the full range of Wagner's music. Marr constantly expressed his admiration for the great Herzog, Karl Alexander of Weimar, for his encouragement of the arts, and especially for already being at the beginning of the 1850's the "protector of the musical direction of Wagner," considerably earlier than Ludwig II of Bavaria, and without the latter's mania for exhibitionism. Marr stated that Weimar was the "Nazareth and Bethlehem of Richard Wagner's musical method."[4] Weimar also aroused Marr's memories of his father's stay in the city during the years 1852–1853 as the head of the royal theater and his friendship with Franz Liszt, who had headed the opera during those years. He had less pleasant memories of the manner in which his father had been forced to leave Weimar, as a result of an insult ("Kiss my . . .") directed at the Jewish casting director of the theater, Jacobi.[5] Marr's stepmother lived in Weimar, and he stayed in her house while he was furnishing his apartment. And then the blow landed: his wife, who was living with her brother-in-law in Mecklenburg, gave birth to a premature baby on September 22, 1874. The baby died, and she herself died three days after the birth, in the arms of her husband.[6]

This heart-rending story incidentally reveals that thanks to his first wife, Marr had lived in financial comfort but in spiritual distress during his first marriage. Marr lost an allowance of 1,000 talers when he divorced. From then on, he would live in increasing financial straits, which would be accompanied by rising and descending levels of spiritual distress. Marr became even more embittered after 1875 than he had been in the past. This bitterness is expressed in *The Victory of Judaism over Germanism*. Another element (of which Marr was not conscious) was that Marr had published his eulogy for his wife in the very journal that two weeks later began to publish Glagau's articles on the "stock market swindle," and especially articles about Marr's previous employer, Strousberg the "railroad king." Marr, who undoubtedly read every word in the journal, was influenced to some degree by these articles, thus sharpening his awareness of modern economics and his hatred of the Jews participating in it.

His wife's extraction is not mentioned at all in the article which appeared in *Gartenlaube*. He filled in this lack in his memoirs: "My wife was a pure Jewess [*Volljüdin*]; since pure blood is always preferable to mixed blood, my life with her was happy." He was not bothered by her bringing her entire *mishpoche* (the Hebrew word for "family") with her.

This presumably should have moderated his hatred of the Jews, if it had not been for the sequel of this episode: the eulogy "Too Happy" in *Gartenlaube* led to a stream of letters to Marr, one of which captivated him. This letter was from a woman, a widow according to the letter, who enumerated all her troubles to comfort Marr. Marr fell in love with her and responded with a letter and his picture. They were engaged on Christmas, and married on April 15, 1875, in Leipzig. His third wife was a twenty-eight-year-old divorcée, a known writer, Jenni née Kornick; her letter to Marr had been a pack of fantasies. From the beginning, Marr's life with his new wife was sheer hell. He separated from her less than a year after they were married, and later returned to her. They were finally divorced in 1877, two years after marrying, a divorce that was very costly for Marr, especially since a son, Heinrich, had been born, and Marr had to support him. Marr cursed himself for this mistake, calling himself an "ass" and "crazy."[7] He drew from this marriage the insurmountable central point of his racism: that pure racial character-istics (his second wife) were preferable to mixed race (his first and third wives). Describing the episode in his memoirs, he wrote that "I at least came to know the Semitic race in a thorough manner, in its most intimate details, and I *warn* against the mingling of Aryan and Semitic blood." If mixed marriages had been the solution to the racial problem in 1862, in *Der Judenspiegel,* or regarding the Negro question, they now became a factor aggravating the same problem. At the end of 1877, the way to the racism and profound despair of *The Victory of Judaism over Germanism* lay open before Marr.

His next marriage, his fourth, would come in 1878, and would be marked by his worsening financial condition. This wife was indeed a "pure" Aryan, but came from the workers' district of Hamburg. During the course of the next twenty-five years, she would bear her husband, twenty-six years her senior, and already poor, aging, and becoming progressively sicker, on her frail shoulders.

Marr's personal problems, both material and spiritual, would worsen along with his marital situation, which had been deteriorating since his first marriage. He stayed in Weimar until August 1875. The reason for his wanting to leave the city where he had experienced such tragedy is perfectly clear. The cause of his leaving, however, is characteristic of his career. A certain Dr. Wolf came from Berlin and told him of the strike at the *Berliner Tageblatt* newspaper. The staff of the young newspaper had revolted against the publisher, Rudolf Mosse. Several members of the editorial staff wanted to publish an improved *Berliner Tageblatt,* and invited Marr to join them. The salary offered by the "rebel" investors, 1,200 talers a year, greatly appealed to Marr. He arrived in Berlin in September, and discovered within a number of weeks that the project had no chance of succeeding. Wolf was left without money, and Marr without work. He went to Leipzig and helped the satirical magazine *Puck,* but this magazine also expired. Marr continued to wander, to Bayreuth, Vienna, and Italy, exhausting his money and his soul.[8]

The years of disappointment in his personal life were not disappointing years for the intellectual advancement of the aging radical. Paradoxically, it is very likely that it was specifically his third wife, the half-Jewess, who helped him to once again take to the path of anti-Semitism. If later developments illuminate initial stages, then the woman who was willing to be a writer for an anti-Semitic journal in the 1880's[9] could already have been infected with anti-Semitism, or well-developed Jewish self-hate, during the 1870's. We cannot know how decisive this episode was, but there is no doubt that Marr's reading, contacts, and experiences during the 1870's developed his pessimistic world view, his awareness of the social problem, and his awareness of the centrality of the Jewish problem within this context. The great luminaries, in whose shadow Marr's soul and thoughts wandered during those years, were Marx, Lassalle, Richard Wagner, and Johannes Scherr.

Marr revealed in the essay which he wrote for the "Congres International de la Paix" in Geneva that the revolutionary fires within him had not been extinguished. "We must accept with all seriousness the sad truth that only a social revolution can guide humanitarian ideas. Look at the bourgeoisie, money-grubbing and egotistical, which is only an imitation of the faults of the tyrants, but without their energy—this is the real source of all the wars." The conclusion was compatible with the spirit of Marx or Lassalle; the problem is formulated in a similar manner. Marr, who consciously lived through the Industrial Revolution, learned to recognize the serious threat posed by the social problem on society as a whole. It is therefore not surprising that we find a newspaper article which he wrote in 1872 on "The Economic and Political Criticism" (*Das Kapital*) of Marx, which appeared in a second edition in Hamburg; it is also not surprising that this article is not a complete negation of Marx's theories (Marr had met Marx in 1869): "The value of Marx's book is that it reveals the faults of social localism [i.e., attempting to solve problems without realizing their full scope], and that it defines the concept 'capital' in a philosophic manner." Marr appreciates the willingness for revolution and the claim that there is a natural law leading to revolutionary change, but nevertheless objects to the logic of a revolutionary such as Marx, since he does not believe that the process of dialectic self-destruction is automatic. Marr is not willing to accept a revolution which is only a puppet show. To reconcile his views with those of Marx, he even claims that Marx is not a communist, since he (Marr) is convinced that the force moving the world is individualism. He therefore thinks that the Lassallians err when they "hitch" Marx to their wagon.[10] Marr accordingly tends to draft Marx for the radicalism of 1848—twenty-five years later. Also, he attempts to draw closer to Marx while trying to attack the social democrats, the Lassallians, who broke with Marr's brand of radicalism. Marr was willing to forgive Lassalle personally, as we have seen, but not the Lassallians. He charged them with the same accusation he had made in 1863, and which Marx had constantly repeated from his point of view: etatism.[11]

Marr's jealousy and hatred of Lassallian social democracy received justification in 1875 (the year of the Gotha program), in light of another element of Marr's old radicalism: atheism. Once again he succeeded in connecting two antipodes. He connected a sharp antireligious attack with an antisocialist attack in his book *Religious Sorties of a Philosophical Tourist*. Marr's supralocal and global thinking which was taking shape paved the way for this. He dealt more and more with "world" phenomena, and this led to his agreeing with Marx on the issue of "social localism"; and hence to his developing the concept of power, which he had learned to appreciate during the 1860's, into the concept of world rule. Everything converges here: Christianity was an attempt to seize world rule, despotic and antisocialist. Its rule was immoral, and its growth was based on the social insecurity and the ignorance of the population. Lassallian social democracy was a new Christianity. It too started small, but advanced faster than had early Christianity. It too aspired to world rule, it too was built on social insecurity and ignorance, and it would mobilize the state, even more than Christianity, to its ranks![12] Marr feared it, but prophesied that it was destined to rule.

So far, there was nothing in this definition of social democracy as a religion which would lead to the painful subject of Judaism. But the cat was soon out of the bag: Feuerbach and Bauer, who had guided the atheist Marr in the past, continue to guide him here:[13] Christianity had been swallowed up by Judaism. When Christianity tried to take control of the world, "Humanity was Judaised by Christianity . . . Judaism rules the world!"[14] An additional element has made its appearance in Marr's anti-Jewish conglomerate: *world rule*. At this juncture, Judaism's supreme rule is connected with the power of religion, economic power, and even with the power of the socialist revolution! When this conclusion is accompanied by a Darwinistic comment on "the freeing of man from the apes" (*Entaffungsprocess*), and by a comment that there is only one difference—race—separating Judaism from Christianity, the picture is complete. All that Marr has to do is to publish a short, direct essay (instead of involved "philosophical ponderings") to state what is on his mind concerning the Jewish question. And still, he did not conceive of such an idea before 1877, and not only because he had not yet divorced. He would explain in *The Victory of Judaism over Germanism* that no "Judaized" newspaper would let him publish anything in this spirit.

This is where Wagner enters the picture. Marr had already published an article in Hamburg in 1873 praising the revolutionary musician.[15] In 1874, as noted earlier, the chance to live in a Wagnerian millieu was an important factor motivating Marr's going to Weimar. Two years later, the year of the controversy surrounding the Bayreuth festival, Marr was one of the more intensive participants in the debate, as an enthusiastic supporter of Wagner and his ideas. He wrote "Letters from Bayreuth"[16] in the Vienna *Illustriertes Musik- und Theater Journal,* expressing his opinion of the festival and the *Nibelungen Ring* which was presented at the festival. He later published two additional articles, entitled "Additional Notes from Bayreuth," in which he described his part in the stormy debate surrounding Wagner. All of his writing was a paean to Wagner and his creations, which were infused with the true German spirit.[17] Marr did not succeed in becoming close to Wagner, but his relations with Wagner's closest friend, the conductor Hans von Bülow, were excellent.[18]

The historian of German cultural history,[19] Johannes Scherr, also put Marr in a pessimistic "twilight of the gods" (*Götterdämmerung*) mood. Scherr had published his book, *The History of German Culture and Ethics,* a clear expression of pessimism, in 1876. According to Scherr, the Industrial Age, which had created the proletariat, had lowered not only the material level of the majority (the proletariat) but also the ethical level. Since reforms in a true German spirit (in Scherr's opinion, such were the attempts of Schulze-Delitsch) had failed, the only foreseeable correction of the situation would come through terrible revolutions, with awful consequences:[20] "the 'twilight of the gods' battle between Capital and Labor." Scherr's ideas do not always conform with Marr's, but the closeness in important matters is striking. Scherr fears Protestant and Catholic religious fanaticism; he opposes German federalism, as created after 1871; he talks of the struggle between Romanism and Germanism; he detests communism; he fears the modern "bestial materialism."[21] All of these are elements with which Marr agreed, and he viewed their appearance in writing, by a distinguished historian, as confirmation of his opinions and actions. An additional resemblance between Marr and Scherr is slightly paradoxical: their evaluation of Heine's and Börne's dealing with the social problem in Germany. The closeness between Marr and Scherr is what explains why the former assigned to the latter, in *The Victory of Judaism over Germanism,*[22] the role of working his thesis into a well-based scientific essay, and why *The Victory of Judaism over Germanism* was more of an expression of cultural rather than socioeconomic Jew-hatred.

Marr in 1877 could be compared to a person drowning in a sea of despair and pessimism: divorced, frustrated, impoverished. He nevertheless attempted, like Baron Münchhausen, to pull himself by his forelocks out of the morass into which he was sinking. He married, for the fourth time, and moved to Berlin to find work as a journalist. But Marr, the successful journalist of the 1840's, was not sought after in the Berlin of the late 1870's. This Berlin was even different from the Berlin he had known during the days of the establishment of the Reich. It was, in his words, "half Jewish, and half Social-Democrat." Also, as a result of his

unsuccessful move in 1875 with the *Berliner Tageblatt,* he could not get
a foothold in the papers of the newspaper magnate Mosse.

As Marr was floundering in the depths of despair, he was approached
by one of his friends, a botanist by the name of Polokowsky, who proposed that Marr join the anti-Jewish party of Stoecker. Marr refused,
since he saw the movement as not having come of age. He told Polokowsky—so he writes in his memoirs—that "if I ever enter anti-Semitism, I
will do it in my own way." He began to write his memoirs then, and at
last decided to present his calling card, *The Victory of Judaism over
Germanism,* which he wrote during February–March 1878 before the
attempt on the life of the kaiser.[23] This story of the direct background for
the writing of *The Victory of Judaism over Germanism* appears twice,
with textual variations: in his memoirs and in "The Testament of an Anti-
Semite." The story arouses our wonder,[24] since Stoecker only gave his
Christian Social party its anti-Semitic designation in September 1879,
not at the beginning of 1878. Marr could not, therefore, have related to
Stoecker's political anti-Jewish position when he stated that "I will do
it in my own way." It is clear, on the other hand, that Marr's memory
did not so fail him that he completely confused matters. Supporting evidence can be found for this in the title of the essay, "From a Nonreligious
Viewpoint." Marr would not have bothered mentioning this in the title
if he had not viewed the essay as a controversial *response* to the position
of the Christian Jew-haters, Catholics or Lutherans. It therefore seems
that Marr's description is true after all. He knew the anti-Jewish positions
of Stoecker and his disciples, and was motivated by one of these disciples
to take a stand. He did not, however, conceive then that he would enter
a debate between political parties. This was still not the case at the beginning of 1878; it was only in the aging mind of Marr that the boundaries
became blurred between the theoretical discussion of the Jewish question
before the end of 1878 and the political discussion which began at that
time, the discussion that we shall elaborate on here. At any rate, this
description can explain why he mentioned Stoecker once again, in his
old age, as the trailblazer of anti-Semitism, in contrast to the schematic
presentation, current in historical literature, according to which Marr
and Stoecker represent two ends of the anti-Jewish spectrum, one a racial
anti-Semite, and the other a Christian Jew-hater. There is no doubt that
designating Stoecker's activity in that passage of Marr's memoirs as "the
beginning of the anti-Semitic movement" is anachronistic, since the term
"anti-Semitism" did not yet exist in 1878. This terminology does, however, testify that in retrospect the disagreement between Christian Jew-
hatred and secular anti-Semitism is not to be found, in Marr's eyes, in
the term "anti-Semitism," in spite of the racial connotation it possesses.
We will discover the reason for this further on, when we discuss the
establishment of the *Anti-Semitic League.*

The question, how Marr arrived at anti-Semitism, or at an anti-

Jewish "forward position," is answered both explicitly and by inference. This reply conforms to the paradigm by which means sociologists and psychologists describe the anti-Semite. Marr states in his memoirs that "the essay was written on the basis of things which I saw in my surroundings in Berlin."[25] He explicitly admits that the Berlin to which he came was not the same Berlin of the past. The change in the city—a change which he felt was for the worse—was too rapid. The motif of a change for the worse is also repeated in his description of Hamburg, to which he returned after leaving Berlin in the middle of 1878. Marr is not aware of the fact that the description of the change in and decline of his surroundings is only a projection of his degeneration and his subconscious relation to this degeneration. What does he find in Berlin that is not to his liking? Jews and Social Democrats! These are expressions of change and threat; he can blame them for his lack of success and helplessness. Since they were his enemies, we can understand why his botanist friend thought that Stoecker's philosophy would suit Marr. Marr's insecurity that sprang from the change was reinforced by the sorry episode of his unfortunate marriage to the "half-Jewess" and the undermining of his financial situation. This episode, reminiscent of the situation in which he had found himself in 1862, but in a much more severe version, produced a similar result. Each time he wrote an anti-Jewish essay. This time, it was *The Victory of Judaism over Germanism;* in 1862, it had been *Der Judenspiegel.* This time, the essay was pessimistic. In 1862, Marr had still been in good circumstances, and it had seemed to him that he would be successful, just as the possibility of halting the negative consequences of industrialization, then in its infancy in Germany, appeared to be feasible. Now in 1878, Marr was a beaten man, in a world which had revealed to him, on a massive scale, what had been a local phenomenon in 1862—his personal failure as well as that of the ideological political trend which he professed. If he had had any hope, he would have become a supporter of Stoecker, just as he had previously been a supporter of the monarchy. Since he had lost all hope, he wrote a book in the spirit of anti-Christian radicalism, with an admission of failure. The book was meant to be the will of one about to die; he himself testified that he thought about committing suicide then, and looked into the possibility of cyanide. The pessimism of *The Victory of Judaism over Germanism* was certainly neither false nor inconsistent.

This pessimism was justified, if only for the reason that no one would publish the essay. There was no publisher willing or daring to do so, until a letter suddenly arrived, Marr recalls in his memoirs, from Munich. The letter was written by Rudolf Kostenobel, who had distributed Strousberg's newspapers at the end of the 1860's, when Marr had worked for the *Post* in Berlin. The two had not met since 1875 (the time of Marr's unsuccessful attempt to start working for the *Berliner Tageblatt*). In the meantime, Kostenobel had moved to Berlin and become a publisher, and he was looking for interesting manuscripts. Marr's response to the proposal, which was a godsend to him, was, "If you dare—publish it!" Marr sent him the manuscript of *The Victory of Judaism over Germanism,* which had been lying in his drawer for half a year. Kostenobel was willing to meet Marr's monetary demands and published the book.[26] This is Marr's later version.

The correspondence between Marr and Kostenobel sheds light on this short description in Marr's memoirs. Kostenobel had by chance received Marr's Hamburg address from his friends on one of the Berlin newspapers, and he told Marr what had happened to him. He had been sent by Rudolf Mosse to Munich in 1876 to be in charge of advertisements and the *Süddeutsche Presse.* He wrote to Marr that despite his success "[Rudolf] Mosse sent a young 23-year-old Mosse around my neck." A quarrel broke out between the two, and Kostenobel was fired. Kostenobel ventured the opinion in his letter to Marr that, "You can rely on a Semite only if he's within arm's reach."[27] He added, apropos the Berlin Congress, which was being held then, "Let us hope that the Congress will reestablish the Promised Land, so that all the rabble will go there, and cheat one another, instead of us." Marr could not have asked for anything better. He and his friend the publisher spoke the same language in their attitude to the Jews, in the personal context in which they found themselves. They both had a common stimulus for their outburst—Rudolf Mosse, the Jewish publisher who revealed to both of them the power of emancipated Jewry during the period of rising German liberalism (i.e., in the mid-1870's).

On July 2, 1878, Marr rushed to send his essay to Kostenobel in Munich, even though the latter still had not yet opened a new business. Marr received a reply only in January 1879! The period of six months during which the essay had lain in the drawer was the time between the sending of the essay to Munich and its being published, not from the writing of the essay until its publication. Marr's mood could therefore not have improved during this half-year. It transpired that only then did Kostenobel move to Bern and open the publishing house in which Marr's essay would be published. He asked Marr to shorten the essay and not to write in hieroglyphics. Marr agreed. The final terms were agreed upon on February 1, and the first announcement was sent to the Berlin *Börsenblatt.*[28] *The Victory of Judaism over Germanism* was finally published during the first days of March 1879, a year after it had been written.

The brutality of the despair expressed in *The Victory of Judaism over Germanism* turned the book into a best-seller. Readers found in the book what Marr had not written: the incentive for a war against the Jews. Marr's despair was honest. The 60-year-old—who had gone from bad to worse, from wife to wife, from newspaper to newspaper, disappointed and frustrated when he compared himself to Dohm and

Kalisch from the *Kladderadatsch* or to his colleague-competitor, Stetten-heim the satirist—painted the entire world in colors which matched his personal career. His readers were unaware of this, and reacted differ-ently from what Marr had anticipated. Paradoxically, his readers dragged Marr himself out of his despair, to hope and rejuvenation as a political propagandist for a short time, a very short time. This led to his intensive activity in his new journal, *Deutsche Wacht,* and in the "Anti-Semitic Pamphlets" (*Antisemitische Hefte*) during the years 1879–1880. Marr was soon to regret this optimistic awakening and dizzying success.

I will not expand upon the content of the notorious essay here. It will suffice to describe it as an attempt at a socio-cultural history of the development of Jewish hegemony in the world in general, and in Ger-many in particular, without blaming this development on the Jewish religion. The book ends in a pathetic cry: "Finis Germaniae!" I hope that the reader will keep in mind the events surrounding its composition. It should also be emphasized that Marr's antireligious stance was both consistent and honest. We therefore see, on the one hand, the continua-tion of the radical arguments of Feuerbach, Bauer, and Marr from the 1840's, and, on the other, the explicit admission that the traditional hatred of the Jews, with blood libels and other slanders, is not deserving of special attention within this context.

There is another issue in the essay that needs to be clarified. The only ray of light in *The Victory of Judaism over Germanism* is Russia, the country in which Jewry had not been emancipated. There is a personal explanation behind this statement, since Jew-haters could not expect salvation to come from someone like Alexander II, the Russian tzar at the time. Marr's closest friend, his neighbor and insurance agent, Scherni-kau, had gone to St. Petersburg as the local manager of Lloyd's. He reported extensively in his letters to Marr of events there,[29] and even made additional connections for him. Marr thus met Ernst Schirmer, a teacher who was the Russian vice-consul in Leipzig starting in 1877 and a ferocious Jew-hater. As part of his duties, Schirmer hosted General Trepov, the governor of St. Petersburg, in the autumn of 1878, when the latter came to Leipzig to recover from the pistol shot fired at him by the famed Wera Sassulitsch. Schirmer talked to Trepov about Marr's plans to drive the Jews out of journalism and the economy.[30] The as-sassination attempt on Trepov reinforced for Marr what he had thought after Nobilling's attempt on the life of the German kaiser at the begin-ning of June in the same year: rumor had it that Nobilling was Jewish.[31] Trepov met Marr close to the time he had given *The Victory of Judaism over Germanism* for publication, and promised Marr that he would at-tempt to talk with the tzar, whose adjutant he was, in this spirit. The talks and the promise filled Marr with hope, but this hope also melted away, until it vanished after the publication of the essay.[32] Yet, Marr succeeded with this essay in doing what he had thought to be impossible: he had driven the Jews off balance, out of their practice of silence, which had always been deadly for him.

Already in March 1879, two weeks after the publication of *The Victory of Judaism over Germanism,* an article, "Against W. Marr," appeared in the distinguished Jewish newspaper, *Allgemeine Zeitung des Judenthums.*[33] Marr had not received such an honor previously. The author of the article knew that Marr was a radical who had previously published *Der Judenspiegel* (information which was contained in *The Victory of Judaism over Germanism,* and which was not obtained from any other source), and denounced the entire essay as ridiculous. This criticism opened the floodgates to further responses, which were quick in coming. Marr was jubilant—at long last he was not ignored! All the responses were of course critical of the essay, but from two different directions: Jewish criticism of Marr's anti-Jewish way of thinking, and criticism by non-Jews of Marr's non-Christian approach.

The Jewish response related less to the racial issue and more to the perpetually pertinent topic of the Jew and the economy. Perinhart, a Reform Jew, saw it necessary to attack the booklet mainly over the claim that the Jews "shirk work" (*arbeitsscheu*). He took pains to correct Jewish history as it had been presented by Marr, to show that the Jews were artisans, and that Judaism should not be confused with capitalism.[34] If the Jews were only capitalists, how was it possible for Marr to interpret socialism, whose founding father was Lassalle, the Jew.

Ludwig Stern, the principal of the Jewish school in Würzburg and an observant Jew, went in the same direction, without striking deep historical roots. Not only were the Jews not "shirkers" from work, but commerce, which was their millieu, is not parasitical: it creates values, since it saves time! Quite a modern argument. Stern indirectly revealed, however, that he had not gotten to the bottom of the issue raised by Marr. Stern stated that only "the money of a few rich Jews fuels modern hatred of the Jews," and proposed that the Jews mend their ways in economic activity, thereby depriving their enemies of justification for their accusations. He accepted the accusation of fraud in the stock market, appealed to Jews to refrain from usury since they were blackening the name of Israel, and even called on Jewish women not to covet luxuries, lest they arouse jealousy.[35] This response, which testifies more than anything to a lack of social security among German Jewry—in complete contrast to Marr's estimation—was chosen to be the propaganda line of the association of Jewish communities, the *Deutsch-Israelitischer Gemeindebund,* which was centered in Leipzig.[36]

The *Gemeindebund,* which had been founded in 1869, and which was considered by Marr to be a prime example of Jewish international power, waged its own campaign against Marr. The association's first response was silence, followed by making use of the anti-Jewish breakthrough to strengthen its own standing among the Jewish communities.

In July 1879, it decided to purchase the anti-Marr pamphlet by Perin-hart, and in October, when Marr was about to found an anti-Jewish newspaper and organization, to take legal measures against the attack on the Jewish religion, but without success.[37]

Besides the need for legal action and the economic argument, Stern's pamphlet, and even more so another essay by Friedrich Israel, made use of a tactic considered to be more effective: a personal attack, an attempt to slander and undermine confidence in the author himself, while casting glances in the direction of liberal principles. Stern claimed that Marr was a radical who had betrayed his party and turned into an ally of the party of the church and the feudalists; he was accused of justifying slavery in America in the past, and there was a "suspicion" that he was Jewish.[38] Friedrich Israel, who had published his attack on Marr in July 1879 in Berlin, hiding behind the name "Sailer," relied on the rumors about Marr which had been mentioned in the *Börsen-Courier,* according to which Marr had engaged in the slave trade in the 1850's, and directed his arrows towards Marr's ancestry, "who had never denied that he was three generations removed from Jews." This attack reveals that its author had delved into Marr's past, albeit not very thoroughly. It was not written with a great deal of taste, either; correcting Marr's mistakes in grammar only reinforced for the non-Jewish reader the claim of Jewish learned conceitedness. The comment that Marr's recommendation to send the Jews to Palestine was based on his experience in exporting humans during the 1850's was not in very good taste, either.[39]

There was an even more arrogant, but not personal, response by a Jew, which Marr made use of in his newspaper *Deutsche Wacht.* A Jew from Dessau, I. M. Cohn, wrote Marr a letter intended for publication in the following language: "You yourself stated in *The Victory of Judaism over Germanism,* Mr. Marr, that the radical revolutionary party, to which you had belonged in the past, could have become very dangerous if it had had enough money at its disposal. And so, Mr. Marr, we have the money. . . . If you press us too much, then . . . anyone can imagine for himself the terrible consequences which are liable to, which must, come."[40] Marr published this in his newspaper, since it strengthened the charges he made against the Jews. This is not a forgery; the letter is to be found in Marr's archives. Marr changed nothing in the letter. On the contrary, he had omitted other sharp sentences: "We have not spent a penny until now to influence politics or the social situation in the country. Nevertheless, I warn you not to go too far in your attacks on the Jews. It is possible that you, who view anti-Jewish agitation as a refreshing novelty or a joyful sport, will greatly regret having acted so stupidly."[41]

The sarcasm and arrogance in these responses came from the confidence in the power of liberalism held by many Jews in the two decades since the time of the reaction. Wit was the weapon which successfully fired its salvos in the newspapers in the service of liberalism. This confidence was no longer justified. Firing salvos from behind the wall of liberalism in 1879 was like taking cover behind a paper wall, and exaggerated self-confidence, while not giving evidence of a developed sense of reality, does explain the response. How can we understand the friendly exchange of letters between Stettenheim, the Jewish satirist, and Marr, the Jew-hater, despite the latter's actions? The explanation is simple. Jew-hatred was a ridiculous absurdity for the Jew Stettenheim, and its being nurtured by his former teacher and colleague seemed to him to be more ridiculous than worrying.[42] The Jews who responded had not read the scenario correctly. They apparently did not properly understand, from 1879 on, the significance of the change in the German customs policy in that year, nor the significance of the establishment's organizing against true liberalism and social-democracy, while effecting a reconciliation with the Catholic Church.

Another pamphleteer opposed the personal attack on Marr, justifiably claiming that Marr, and to an even greater degree, his attacker, were not known for their important works. The main feature of this pamphlet was that it diverted the argument back from the confrontation between Judaism and Germanism to that between Judaism and Christianity. And so, in a paradoxical manner, Marr's attack, like the counterattack against him, became blurred, and Marr's defenders became his liquidators.[43] The controversy returned to its old course, or to the course given it by Stoecker. Another pamphleteer claimed, just like the previous one, that *The Victory of Judaism over Germanism* essentially deals with the conflict between Judaism and Christianity. This pamphleteer went so far as to totally reject the explanation of Judaism as a race. In contrast to Marr, he was an optimist, and justified the hatred of Judaism by Christianity, which had been persecuted by Judaism since Nero's time.[44] A third pamphleteer completed what had been missing: not only did he disagree with Marr's pessimism, he located the source of the illness—liberalism![45]

In the final analysis, Marr's essay aided his opponents. They could use this new form of racism, using the term "Semitism" (still *not* "anti-Semitism"), in order to further Christian and antiliberal views, going beyond the frameworks within which these concepts had been enclosed in the past. Pathetic but significant evidence of this is given by the response of the pastor Paulus Kassel, an apostate Jew. This person, who had devoted his life after his conversion to a war on Judaism as a religion, found himself in a dilemma: his fellow priests supported a party that persecuted Jews, believed in the concepts of race, and thereby undermined Christianity itself. Stoecker himself talked of the struggle between Semites and Aryans. Kassel realized that Marr's school of anti-Judaism was a new paganism, was anti-Christian, and could lead to the victory of a *Nibelungen* Germanism over evangelical Judaism, thereby bringing his activity and his decisive personal step to naught. Kassel therefore tried to turn Marr into Balaam, but was unsuccessful in turning the clock backwards.[46] Marr did not want to be Balaam, and he especially did not want to be pushed aside. He therefore tried to adopt a combination of antiliberalism, racism, and even Christianity. But even this combination, which was alien to Marr, did not help him.

Marr's response was speedy. Four months after the publication of *The Victory of Judaism over Germanism,* during the seventh press run, Kostenobel published Marr's *From the Jewish Battlefield,* in five editions.[47] Less than three months later, a new pamphlet appeared in Berlin, "Don't Elect a Jew," subtitled "The Way for the Victory of Germanism over Judaism." This last pamphlet, a propaganda piece for the elections to the Prussian Landtag, revealed Marr as an opportunist. Not only did he replace pessimism with false optimism but he suddenly made use of religion to this end. "One who cannot remain Christian and German, will remain Jewish," and as such would be a citizen, but without the right to participate in the government. Germany and Prussia were Christian countries![48] In a flyer attached to his newspaper *Deutsche Wacht,* Marr even wrote a sentence that one finds difficult to believe issued from his pen: the goal was "to free Christianity from the yoke of Judaism." Care must be taken "for the defense of Christianity; otherwise, there will be mass emigration and true hatred of the Jews."[49] Marr would even relate later on to the kaiser's call of November 17, 1881, for "practical Christianity" by Germany's citizens.[50] This was an extreme departure from his philosophy until then, and from the motives for his new anti-Jewish activity; the only possible explanation for this is his desire to ride the new wave of hatred of the Jews, which was financed and supported by religious and conservative elements.

Marr was not modest. Not only did he gladly accept the titles of "father of the anti-Jewish movement" or "the new Luther,"[51] he assigned himself command, as "the general of a division," of the anti-Jewish battle, alongside a great statesman who would want this.[52] As a "general," he demanded a "general mobilization," and therefore turned even to those not following his atheistic line. Many of the numerous letters he had received since the appearance of his essay in 1879 counseled moderation concerning Christianity; indeed, the main financing for Marr's new newspaper came from these circles.[53] He did not make light of all these factors—especially not of money, which had become an obsession for him. There is no doubt that Marr's attitude on this issue was again neurotic and not consistent or rational. Anyway, the disagreement he had with Stoecker continued, both in the *Deutsche Wacht,*[54] in which he attacked religious hatred of the Jews or the rejection of the "better classes" by the use of the term "workers" in the name of the party, and in correspondence with the court preacher.

The surfeit of essays by Marr during 1879–1880 is of interest more for the autobiographical elements they reveal than for their message, which did not contain much that was new. It is not necessary to re-emphasize that Marr's bitter personal experience was the main motive behind the anti-Jewish attack in this format. The weight of the Jews in journalism was blown out of all proportion, due to Marr's bitter lot in the realm of journalism, mainly in the years preceding this attack. He praised journalists like him who had dared to attack the Jews, and thereby (in his opinion) endangered their prospects for working in their profession. He denounced those who hid behind pseudonyms, especially his colleague and rival in 1879–1880, Nordmann (Naudh), who had published his first anti-Jewish book in 1860, two years before Marr.[55] He devoted an entire essay to the subject of the Jewish press,[56] in which he expressed his bitterness at the new type of journalism, which no longer needed the services of the old-fashioned feuilletonist: the journalism of Rudolf Mosse, financed mainly by advertisements, and owing most of its circulation to scandals. Marr was willing to be called a reactionary, if the intent was to aim this term at his war with this type of journalism. Indeed, his claims against the press characterize reactionary and conservative elements still current today. The autobiographical allusions concerning journalism which appeared in 1879–1880 already prophesied, however, the breach between him and his anti-Semitic colleagues. He explicitly attacked Nordmann and Hentze, both Jew-hating journalists, who tried to force upon him a journalistic policy that was not to his liking. It would become clear in his memoirs and in his correspondence during the coming years that his frustration as a journalist would not only bring on his anti-Semitic outburst but also—within a short time—cause him to disown it. It should be emphasized that it had already become clear to him, in July–August 1879, that the publisher who had saved him from oblivion, Kostenobel, had betrayed him, and was not willing to offer Marr a partnership in his business.[57] The next publisher, Froben, who had caused the quarrel between Marr and Kostenobel, also betrayed Marr a short time later.[58] When Marr set about editing his newspaper, *Deutsche Wacht,* and organizing the Anti-Semitic League in the autumn of 1879, he had already freed himself of the euphoria that had enveloped him in the spring of that year.

The autobiographical element was also explicitly tinged with the racial theory that Marr presented in these essays. He admitted that the theory of "racial mingling" which he had proposed in *Der Judenspiegel* in 1862 had been fundamentally wrong, since the racial characteristic (*Eigenart*) of the male Jew and the female German do not permit this. A male German and a female Jew may do all right, and were quite a common occurrence, but this would not provide any solution (i.e., Marr himself underwent the experiment, but even if it had been successful, it would not have solved the opposite problem, that of male Jews entering into mixed marriages).[59] Marr completely ignored the fact that his experience was not representative; mixed marriages of male Jews with female Germans were much more common. His bitter experience impelled him both to censure and praise the Jewish woman: she is more arrogant than her German counterpart, and plays the main role in improving the Jewish race.[60] Marr brings examples for Darwinistic principles (he labels them as such) not only from his "Jewish experience" but also from his American past. A description of the mulatto in America leads him to the conclusion that the Jew is a white Negro, marriage to whom spoils the race.[61]

Another autobiographical detail which keeps surfacing in these essays is the experience of the 1848 revolutionary, including his activity on behalf of equal rights for Jews. The frustrated revolutionary peeks out from behind every sentence, and as such looks forward to the next revolution, as we will see further on. "I was a 'rebel' when I fought on behalf of Jewish emancipation . . . and I've remained one today, when I fight against it."[62] "You [the Jews] have to thank German radicalism for emancipation—this radicalism had already turned against you in 1862. This radicalism itself changed the direction of the prominent members of all the parties today."[63] The plural language used here is first and foremost *pluralis majestatis*. The experience which he mentions is clearly his personal experience: 1848 as the year of Jewish emancipation; 1862 as the year of the rift. It was not enough for him to repeat the familiar charge of betrayal of the radicalism of 1848; Riesser's name crops up several times as the archetype of the traitor and slippery Reform Jew, even though most of his readers could not have had any idea about whom Marr was talking.[64]

Anyone who did not know Marr from before 1879 would also have had difficulty understanding the fervor with which he attacked the liberal customs policy which was on the agenda then. In his essay *The Jewish War*,[65] Marr fired off salvos against Nordmann and Hentze, who had tried to force him to write articles against Bismarck's customs policy. The reader can wonder whether it was only his loyalty to Bismarck which caused this attack (a sufficiently good reason in itself, when considering Marr's position). A more intrinsic reason became clear, however, in a later essay, "Open Your Eyes, German Newspaper Readers." Even by 1871, Hamburg had not joined the German Customs Union, and until 1881 there were debates in the city over the issue of its joining, with the new German customs policy (protectionism) only deterring those Hamburgians who were hesitating. The Hamburg politicians opposing the customs union were led by Isaac Wolffson (now a liberal member of the Reichstag), Marr's mortal enemy since the days of 1848. The newspapers that supported his position were the same newspapers which had attacked Marr for his anti-isolationist, pro-Prussian stance during the

Schleswig-Holstein war in the 1860's. There could be no better reason for Marr, who had vigorously opposed protective tariffs in the 1840's, now to fight vigorously on their behalf.[66]

Of interest, and perhaps of more importance, is the viewpoint of the former revolutionary on the future revolution. Marr the revolutionary struggled here with Marr the conservative, being influenced by the analysis of Johannes Scherr. He saw two alternatives: reform from above or revolution from below.[67] This was certainly not an original presentation of the problem; it was Bismarck's philosophy during those years, between laws restricting the socialist revolution and laws for improving the social conditions of the worker. Marr also supported a reform from above, but his and Scherr's pessimism did not permit much hope: power was not in the hands of the state, but rather in the hands of Rothschild, Bleichröder, Mendelssohn, & Co. Even the German socialists, in his opinion, would have preferred an anti-Manchesterian reform, and not a violent revolution along clearly ideological lines, if the socialists had not been misused by the Jews.[68] The guiding hand of the Jews, which the paranoic Marr saw everywhere, was what convinced him to the deepest recesses of his soul that the revolution would surely come, a terrible social revolution, in contrast to which the revolutions of the past would be "like tea boiled for the third time."[69] He thought that the bearers of the revolution would be the members of the fifth estate (*Stand*), the unsuccessful, the tramps, and the criminals, who saw themselves as victims of society, and who would be the true leaders of the next revolution! (This assumption appears prophetic to anyone in the post-1933 era.) But what would be the results of the revolution? Marr painted two different scenarios, between which he could not choose. Would the revolutionary fervor, which at any rate would be directed against the Jews, end in the victory of the Jews, as Marr thought when he wrote *The Victory of Judaism over Germanism*,[70] or in "the victory of the Jesuits over the Jews?"[71] In either case, Marr attempted to extricate himself, theoretically, from this difficult situation with the help of a deus ex machina.[72] Within a few years, however, Marr would lose faith in miracles, and sink once again into melancholy and perpetual fear of the great nihilistic revolution which would destroy all. We shall discuss this fear further on.

Marr the pessimist, who foresaw the victory of Judaism or feared a nihilistic revolution, could not conceive of a "solution to the Jewish question." Marr the optimist, who in 1879–1880 halfheartedly believed in the victory of Germanism, nevertheless had to ask what method was to be employed when the old solution of assimilation and intermarriage had been pushed aside by the belief in racism? The answer is indeed to be found in Marr's writings, in the spirit of Zionism: Jews to Palestine. In 1862, Marr had cast doubt in *Der Judenspiegel* on the possibility of a "second Moses" arising to lead the members of his people to Palestine, in order to establish the "model state."[73] In *The Victory of Judaism over*

Germanism, he bewailed the Jews having left Palestine, but could not conceive of a Jewish retreat from the arena of their victory in Europe to Palestine. Yet from the moment that he began to search for the way to the victory of Germanism over Judaism, he grasped onto the Palestine solution. Paradoxically, it can be said that his "Zionism" was extremely practical: he proposed sending *all* the Jews to Palestine. He wanted to solve two problems in this manner: the problem of Germany turning into a "Persia," headed by a "Mordechai" as chancellor,[74] and the "Eastern problem," which arose in full force since the Russian-Turkish war and the Berlin Congress.[75] By all the Jews, he meant the seven million Jews in the world, including the Jews of America, Asia, and Africa.[76] He uses the term "model state" (*Musterstaat*) over and over again to define the Jewish state in Palestine. He ·found this term in a speech by the like-thinking Istoczy in the Hungarian parliament on June 25, 1878, a speech which Marr cited in its entirety in his essay *From the Jewish Battlefield.* (Istoczy had meant by this a state without an army.) In the opinion of Marr and Istoczy, Palestine had to be the ideal location, since the Jews were racially close to the Moslems.[77] Who knows—perhaps this speech not only directly influenced Marr but also touched a chord deep within Herzl, who was in Budapest writing his matriculation examinations when Istoczy delivered the speech.

Marr closely followed the attempts made during those years, Zionism's first years, to bring Jews to Palestine. He knew that Montefiore was attempting to settle poor Jews in Palestine; he knew that modern Jews wanted to send there Orthodox Jews, who aroused the populace's disgust at home (i.e., in Europe).[78] As far as Marr was concerned, sending the "non-disguised Jews" to Palestine, was only a Jewish stratagem to rule Europe more conveniently. Marr followed Oliphant's plans for Jewish settlement on the east bank of the Jordan as a base for a Jewish settlement in all of Palestine, under British patronage. Marr did not, of course, believe wholeheartedly in the implementation of the plan. Christian settlers first had to settle the land and make it bloom, so that the "Jewish swarms of locusts" would desire to settle in Palestine, or alternatively, Palestine should turn into a Jewish penal colony for Jewish criminals from the entire world.[79] The high point of this mixture of the maximalist Palestine solution with skepticism concerning its implementation is to be found in Marr's reaction to the enterprise of Baron Hirsch: "I will guarantee that our anti-Semitic movement will agree to obtain Palestine a second time for the Jews."[80] Relating to Baron Hirsch's plan to resettle a portion of Polish Jewry for 12,000,000 francs, Marr proposed, "Twelve million francs? For this [sum] we will buy all of Palestine, on shares! We, the anti-Semites!!" Marr's proposal to purchase Palestine for the Jews should not be taken more seriously than his skepticism on this subject. This skepticism became an explicit statement: "Semitism insurmountably recoils from the return to Canaan."

Since he beleved this, he could not have rejoiced at the appearance of Zionism, which actually aspired to fulfill his plan. At the age of 78, a sick and weary Marr took heed of an important event for the Jews, the Zionist Congress, or the "Jewish National Congress," as he defined it. He chose to cite the speech of Dr. Lippe, and to make fun of it:

> The Sultan will announce that he will . . . grant the province of Palestine to the Jews. Before this, he would have to eliminate or expel the Moslem population there, just as the Jews had done in the past to the inhabitants of Canaan, or to give the brave Jews the right to tranfer their businesses there, which—just as in the past, with the Egyptian fleshpot— would be sent back to Europe at the first oportunity.
>   This entire matter is a foul Jewish swindle, in order to divert the attention of the European peoples from the Jewish problem.[81]

It is of interest that Marr—preceding the Zionists and their supporters—took heed of the Arab problem, as a factor which would make the Zionist program unrealistic. It is clear, however, that above all Marr did not believe that the Jews desired, or were capable of, the Palestinian solution which he himself had proposed.

Therefore, Marr helplessly sought another solution: "A 'bulwark' must be erected against the Semitic flood, since the educated person must certainly reject barbaric measures."[82] The formula for the erection of this bulwark included a ban on business dealings with Jews, the severance of social relations with Jews, withdrawing support from the Jewish press and Jewish candidates, and the separation of Jewish from non-Jewish education; in short—"the isolation of Jewry within the state and society."[83] Perhaps in this manner "the Jews would disappear from the Fatherland, never to return."[84] This solution, one of powerlessness, is characteristic of Marr. An analysis of the situation, as constructed by Marr, reveals that a radical solution would not work. In his talks with the Russian general Trepov in 1878, Marr had already raised the idea of putting obstacles in the path of the Jews. Then as now, this would have been only a partial solution, since the adoption of this policy in Russia would have been detrimental to this policy in Germany, which began specifically with the halting of Jewish immigration from Russia. The only radical solution would be by "barbaric measures." The tone of the statements of the bourgeois Marr evokes a feeling of sorrow that his education prevented him from wholeheartedly proposing such a solution. Fifty years later, the Nazis would understand how to rid themselves of nineteenth-century education and morality, to arrive at the only logical solution to what they and their predecessors defined as a problem.

The way to a solution would still be long, paved with daily anti-Semitic activity. *"Anti-Semitic!"* This is the place to discuss the emergence of the term, which would be accepted so wholeheartedly. In 1879, in his second anti-Jewish essay, Marr called himself a "fighter against

Jewish emancipation." In 1880 he still called himself "the father of the anti-Jewish movement," and only a decade later "the patriarch of anti-Semitism."[85] The traditional terms "hatred of the Jews" and "persecution of the Jews" would evolve into "anti-Semitism" *within this decade.* The development can be credited to a great extent to Wilhelm Marr, "credit" which was acknowledged by Marr and his Jew-hating colleagues and disciples. How did this come about?

It is customary to credit Marr with coining the term "anti-Semitism." There are those who state this unequivocally, like the Berlin *Encyclopaedia Judaica,* while others are more reserved, mentioning others who incidentally used this term before 1879.[86] Since it is accepted to ascribe the first use of the term to Marr, the German historian Rürup searched in 1975 through Marr's writings, in an attempt to discover whether there was an explanation for the coming into use of this term. Rürup did not find such an explanation. Furthermore, the term itself was not to be found in Marr's writings until October 1879. Rürup did not investigate the reason for this. To round out the picture, it should be added that Marr, in his 1879 writings, consciously used the terms "Judaism" and "Germanism" as *main* terms, and "Semitism" and "Aryanism" as *secondary* terms. Marr absorbed these secondary terms from the scientific jargon which had developed during the 1870's, and used them, when necessary, as replacements for the terms "Orientalism" and "Germanism," which he had already used to emphasize racial significance. If Marr was troubled at all by any term, it was not by "Germanism," but by "Judaism," which bore such a clear religious connotation. Since Marr's avowed stance in 1879, consistent with his theories, was "antireligious," he needed a term which would clearly indicate that the Jews were a racial unit. Marr apparently felt in his 1879 anti-Jewish writings that the content of the essays and the use of the term "Semitism" on occasion ("World Rule—for Semitism") would impart a new, nonreligious, connotation to the term "anti-Jewish," and that he would therefore *not* need another term in place of it. He continued to talk in this manner in August and September 1879 about the "anti-Jewish newspaper" he would publish, and about the "anti-Jewish organization"[87] he would create. And indeed, the newspaper which began publication in November 1879 was called *Deutsche Wacht,* The Monthly of the *Anti-Jewish* Association (emphasis added). During the five months it was published, not a single headline appeared in the newspaper containing the combination "anti-Semite"; the contrast between "Jew" and "German" was common. Even the contrast between "Israel" and "the *goyim*" (non-Jewish nations) appears more frequently than the contrast between "Semitism" and "Aryanism." Indeed, the term "anti-Semitic," as a substitute for "anti-Jewish," might have appeared to be unsuitable to Marr during the period when he had to decide about the nature of the association and newspaper which he would establish (i.e., July–September 1879), due to its novelty and lack of clarity. These were the months during which Prussia prepared for the elections to the Landtag (to be held on October 7), for which Marr had written his essay "Do Not Vote for the Jew," with its "deviation" towards the traditional religious orientation. As we learn from Marr's copious correspondence during these months and from his memoirs, he found himself then under a complicated set of pressures, which disinclined him towards the innovation of anti-Semitism, both on purely semantic grounds and contextually. Marr was too dependent upon partners who promised him financial assistance in return for determining policy, to act freely.[88] Notwithstanding this, how can we explain the fact that in October, when Marr at last founded his anti-Jewish association, it was called the "Anti-Semitic League," and *this* is where the new term gained currency? How can the contradiction between the "Anti-Semitic League" and the "anti-Jewish monthly" be resolved? How can we explain the fact that Marr, not one for modesty, did not take credit, even in his memoirs, for coining the term?

The "League" came into existence on September 26, 1879, on the Day of Atonement. The *Allgemeine Zeitung des Judenthums* rightly suspected that this date was chosen for the meeting by its organizers for fear of massive Jewish opposition.[89] All of Marr's writings testify to the fact that he honestly feared the Jews, believing that they possessed much power; this was a clear expression of what has been labeled "paranoic honesty."[90] He kept repeating the claim that his career as a journalist had been obstructed in the 1870's by the Jews; he believed that his fellow anti-Semites, who were hiding behind pseudonyms, were doing so to escape the heavy hand of the Jews. Conducting the founding meeting of the Anti-Semitic League when the Jews were occupied with the prayers of the Day of Atonement fast was well suited to the paranoid character of the Jew-fighters. This paranoia may also explain why the term "anti-Semitic" was needed in place of "anti-Jewish." The former term, specifically because of its novelty and its being somewhat vague, was a good cover both against attacks by sensitive Jews and concrete legal suits, claims which the association of Jewish communities in Leipzig did indeed try to raise against Marr in Berlin starting in October. (This is, of course, no more than a reasonable assumption.) Another assumption, which has a solid basis in the written material before us, is that Marr did not coin the term alone, but did this in conjunction with another founder of the League, whom Marr calls "tapeworm," or perhaps Hector de Grousillier. De Grousillier was Marr's partner in organizing the League in October, and to Marr's displeasure he even delivered the first two speeches at its meetings.[91]

The League came into being completely by chance in the following manner. Not many people had paid any attention to the fact that Marr had planned and published his newspaper *Deutsche Wacht* with the subtitle *Monthly of the Anti-Jewish Association*. Such an association had never been formed. Marr had even admitted that he did not believe that he was capable of forming such an association. In a letter to his publisher, Kostenobel, in July 1879, he had bitterly complained that if he were to found an "Anti-Jewish Association," he would be its president and only member.[92] Marr was dragged *by chance* to the League, which was called "Anti-Semitic," and his newspaper was never the League's official newspaper. On September 20, de Grousillier had sent Marr an invitation to take part in a meeting of a "small association" named the "Lessing Association."[93] He told Marr about a newspaper which the Association planned to publish in November (this was the newspaper *Truth [Warheit]*, which did, in fact, appear then), knowing full well that Marr was about to publish his own newspaper. De Grousillier humbly informed Marr that he would "put his resources at his [Marr's] disposal." Knowing that Marr was basically an atheist, he wrote a sentence that is repeated in many letters which Marr received: "We will march separately, but strike together." Marr appeared six days later at the abovementioned meeting of the Anti-Semitic League, which had in practice been united with the "Lessing Association." This furnished the subject of de Grousillier's maiden speech in October 1879: "Nathan the Wise and the Anti-Semitic League." The legerdemain involved in the change in nomenclature joined the legerdemain involved in resolving the clearly Christian stance of the Lessing Association with the non-Christian term "anti-Semitic." This act of legerdemain revealed not only how differently the two partners, Marr and de Grousillier, interpreted the term "anti-Semitism," but also—and even more importantly—that the term "anti-Semitism," which is considered by historians as an innovation in the transition from the religious basis of hatred of the Jews to the racial basis, was *not* so initially. De Grousillier stated in this speech that "we have chosen the terminology of 'Anti-Semitic League,' and not 'Anti-Jewish League,' in order to show that we recognize the difference between Jewish Germans and that bunch; we also designate those [non-Jewish] Germans who deny their Christianity as Semites. [!]" Let it be absolutely clear: when de Grousillier spoke of "that bunch," he meant the "[Jewish] *kahal* [community] as a religious band of robbers," not the Jews in general.[94] The term "anti-Semitic" was interpreted by Marr's partner, one of the League's founders, in exactly the *opposite* manner from what Marr presumably intended and from the accepted interpretation of this semantic innovation: a *religious,* and *not* a racial, interpretation. De Grousillier did this to reconcile anti-Semitism with his goal, "With God's help, for the Christian faith, for the Kaiser, the princes, and [our] dear Fatherland."[95] Such an interpretation of the term held no advantages for Marr, no matter which direction he chose. If Marr wanted to cooperate with Jew-haters in the spirit of Christianity, he had no need of the new term; if he wanted to separate from them, the official interpretation given by de Grousillier to the new term could only be detrimental. There is no doubt that as much as Marr tended to cooperate with Christian-inspired Jew-haters for financial and tactical reasons, and for reasons connected with his increasingly conservative tendencies, this interpretation *contradicted* his line of thought. This contradiction prevailed in the League. The League's bylaws indeed speak of a war against the oppression of Germanism by Judaism and putting the Semites in their proper place, which, by itself, was a noncommittal slogan. Beyond this, however, the League's propaganda was clearly Christian: its symbol was a (German) oak leaf and a cross.[96] The newspaper published by de Grousillier called *Truth* used the following language, as cited in a cartoon with this title: "When the State and the Church quarrel with each other, the Jew rejoices; but when they join together, each [Jew] will hide."[97] Right *from the beginning,* Marr had lost control of the Anti-Semitic League. The philosophy of de Grousillier, the Christian anti-Semite, had won out over that of Marr, the atheistic anti-Semite—this is what Marr would state in his "Testament" twelve years later.[98]

Marr, however, was the one who *proposed* the term "anti-Semitic," for reasons connected with the date of the League's establishment: precisely *one week* after Stoecker's first anti-Jewish speech ("Our Demands from Modern Judaism") in his Christian Social party. Marr and his fellow anti-Christians did not want to be identified when the League would be established with a Christian-social movement which suddenly became avowedly anti-Jewish. The change in Stoecker's policy of September 19, 1879, when Marr and his colleagues were still planning the establishment of an anti-*Jewish* party, ended their monopoly on that term. As we recall, Marr had been motivated to write *The Victory of Judaism over Germanism* by his refusal to join or to appear to be a part of Stoecker's movement, even before it had chosen anti-Jewishness as the focal point of its activity. His dissociation from Stoecker was even more emphatic in the case of the league. Unfortunately for Marr, the Trojan horse had already entered the gates: de Grousillier and his colleagues, guided by the spirit of Christianity, had completely distorted the innovation in the term. De Grousillier's explanation for the term "anti-Semitic" just cited sounds like hair-splitting, rationalization by a person who had the term "anti-Semitic" forced on him against his will. Marr, with his notorious bad luck, was once again pushed aside.

We can gauge the extent to which Marr's fears of having his movement identified with that of Stoecker were justified, and the extent to which the League was identified specifically with de Grousillier's orientation, from the following passage from the Hebrew newspaper *Ha-Magid,* which was published in Lyck in eastern Prussia, far from Berlin:

> A new society has been recently founded in our country. It has been called the "Anti Semiten Liga" by its founders, meaning, "a society against the Semites" (against the Jews). Its aim is to raise a lot of money and to do everything in its power to ill-treat and harm Jewry. . . . The number of its members increases daily, in all districts of the kingdom.

Who heads it, and who is the guiding spirit in [determining] its nature? Stoecker.[99]

No mention was made of Marr. Even his propaganda stunt of using a new name, the "Anti-Semitic League," was not enough to distinguish him from his rival Jew-haters. Certainly not when his partner was de Grousillier, who held views opposed to his.[100] The writer in the newspaper did not know just how right he was—Stoecker was indeed invited by the League (not by Marr) to give a lecture. Stoecker apparently even agreed to join the League. Afterwards, in a speech in the Prussian Landtag, Stoecker denied all connection with the League, and even denied knowing the people from *Deutsche Wacht*. He undoubtedly lied: Stoecker himself reveals this in a letter which will be cited later.

There was also a prosaic reason for not mentioning Marr's name: he had not been chosen as chairman of the Anti-Semitic League! Marr attributed this to his own hesitations and to the history of the "Lessing Association"; the press thought otherwise. The *Berliner Tageblatt* stated that Marr had disqualified himself from being elected as chairman, because he was "politically unreliable" (*politisch anrüchig*).[101] The newspaper did not go into detail, but Marr's opponents attributed this description to his past betrayal of the radicals and "Young Germany in Switzerland." (This does not appear to me to be a sufficient reason to damage his reputation here.) Marr himself was furious, and set out to discover the identity of the anonymous writer who had published the article. Neither the editor of the newspaper, Perl, nor its owner, Rudolf Mosse, responded to his entreaties and threats (even including a challenge to a duel) in this matter.[102]

The bylaws of the Anti-Semitic League were published ten days after the elections of the Prussian Landtag, on October 16, 1879. The *Ha-Magid* reporter was deceived by Marr, who told of thousands of members joining the League.[103] Its actual success was much smaller: there was much strife within the League, and its demise was speedy. The League acquired a bad name right from the start. Stoecker addressed a letter to Marr[104] in these words: "You perhaps are connected with the management of the Anti-Semitic League. If this is indeed so, I beg of you to return to me the letter which I had written in answer to the invitation to deliver a lecture. After the unpleasant incident which has occurred, I believe it would be preferable if there were no document written by myself in the hands of the management of the League." The nature of the "incident" and the content of the letter are not known; it is of interest, however, that Stoecker viewed Marr (who had sent him the pamphlet "Do Not Vote for a Jew") as holding similar views to his within the League—specifically Marr, the former atheist.

On November 21, a Berlin newspaper published the names of all those registered as League members,[105] thereby deterring many others from joining.[106] Marr himself apparently realized the extent of the failure that week, and began to contribute his efforts to the anti-Jewish "Deutscher Reformverein," which had been founded in Dresden, on November 28, 1879, by Alexander Pinkert (under the alias of Waldegg). Marr had been in contact with Pinkert since November 15, but had made his help conditional upon the acceptance of the racial principles of anti-Semitism (i.e., rejecting apostates).[107] It is therefore not surprising that Marr's newspaper, *Deutsche Wacht,* which had begun publication at the same time in November, did not bear the subtitle which may have been assigned it, *Monthly of the Anti-Semitic League.*[108] The Anti-Semitic League was, in practice, suspended about a month after it was established, and was revived only a year later.[109] Marr's newspaper, *Deutsche Wacht,* did not have a better fate, and ceased publication in March 1880, due both to financial problems and an ideological dispute between Marr and the publisher, Hentze. An attempt was made to continue *Deutsche Wacht* in a smaller format, in pamphlet form entitled *Der Judenspiegel,* with press excerpts and pertinent reports on the subject of anti-Semitism. This enterprise also did not last for more than two months. Marr's anti-Jewish effort once again centered around bitter writing. In the meantime, however, the term "anti-Semitism" had received a favorable response, disconnecting itself from the casuistic interpretation given to it by de Grousillier. The term "anti-Semitism" became popular specifically among writers and scholars, not only because of its scientific pretensions but also because it cast a cloak of uncertainty over the intent of hatred of the Jews (which people were still careful not to mention explicitly). The fact that the prominent historian Treitschke used this term in his anti-Jewish article in November 1879 undoubtedly legitimized it, among both learned and unlearned Germans. The term still served during the years 1879–1880 the purpose which the term "anti-Zionism" serves today—evading the accusation of engaging in something improper. It should be remembered that the period under discussion is 1879–1880, the years when German liberalism with its well-polished rapier in the press, law, and parliament was still feared by some of its opponents. Marr himself, at any rate, felt free to use the term, in whose shadow he had acted in October 1879. In February 1880, he began to publish the *Antisemitische Flugblätter,* which were sold for the low price of 10 Pfennige (a copy of *Deutsche Wacht* had sold for 1.20 marks). The first "anti-Semitic leaflet" was actually a reprint of an article from *Deutsche Wacht* on the subject "Israel in Every Spot," an article in which the term "anti-Semitism" does not appear, and which deals entirely with the "Isaac" who pushes himself everywhere.

The next project would be the "Anti-Semitic Pamphlets" (*Antisemitische Hefte*), the title of Marr's pamphlets during 1880. After a breach with his publisher, Hentze, and with his partners, de Grousillier and Nordmann,[110] Marr searched for a new publisher, whom he found in Chemnitz. This was Schmeitzner, a racial anti-Semite in his own right, who had already published Wagner's *Bayreuter Blätter* in 1878. *The Jewish War,* the first "Anti-Semitic Pamphlet," publicly revealed the details of Marr's dispute with his fellow Jew-haters until then; in actuality, this was Marr's method of settling accounts with them. Now that he had freed himself of his dependence upon his financial patrons (who had deceived him) and his Christian-oriented colleagues, Marr could once again present unadulterated anti-Semitism: an anti-Jewish, nonreligious, movement, which had fundamental differences of opinion with Stoecker.[111] Although he did mention "the Christian state" from time to time, race and the social problem set the tone, also in the following two issues of the "Anti-Semitic Pamphlets" which he would publish in 1880. This was the case in the venomous attack in *Golden Rats and the Red Mice* ("Anti-Semitic Pamphlet" No. 2) and in *Open Your Eyes, German Newspaper Readers* ("Anti-Semitic Pamphlet" No. 3), which dealt with the issue which had personally bothered Marr more than anything: the press.[112]

While Marr was busy with this flurry of anti-Semitic writings, the anti-Semitic movement had already passed him by. Public activity was concentrated on the anti-Semitic petition which was presented to Bismarck, party activity had split into a number of groups with various names, and Marr found himself—once again—powerless. This time, however, he was too old to start new projects. The reputation he had won from *The Victory of Judaism over Germanism* still held a circle of admirers who were extremely verbose in their letters, but not for long. More than 50 percent (one hundred people) of those who had begun to write to Marr concerning *The Victory of Judaism over Germanism* wrote only one letter, or stopped writing within a year. Between 3 and 8 percent of those corresponding with Marr stopped writing during each of the next five years, and only about 20 percent continued to write to Marr after 1886, or saw any purpose in writing to him during this period. Marr's health had also totally deteriorated. From here on Marr's activity would only take the form of spasmodic twitches, but not death throes. The "patriarch of anti-Semitism" would live for two more decades, not letting his pen rest, even though he himself had been pushed aside into oblivion.

8

The "Business-of-Anti-Semitism" Syndrome

The same phenomenon is found repeatedly in most of the correspondence which Marr conducted from 1880 on: the writers turn to Marr appreciatively as the "father of anti-Semitism," but they are soon disappointed. There were those, of course, who never thought Marr a luminary, even though they were Jew-haters themselves. Richard Wagner, who Marr held in such esteem, responded laconically and noncommittally to Marr's letter in 1879:[1] "Your essay gave us much pleasure"; "We found in it new aspects" of the struggle against the Jews; this is a difficult question, like the question of the Jesuits, "which our demagoguery dealt with, without thought." The next pamphlet which Marr sent to Wagner earned him only a short reply by Cosima Wagner. In Wagner's opinion, Marr was "superficial."[2]

Pinkert, the founder of the "Deutscher Reformverein," wrote to Marr in November 1879 with a great deal of admiration and a certain amount of trepidation. This submissiveness vanished within two months, however, to be replaced by insolence. The reason for this is clear: Marr had been in increasingly dire financial straits from 1877 on. He enjoyed some relief after the publication of *The Victory of Judaism over Germanism,* and he was even able to go to the south for a long vacation. Afterwards, however, when he began to publish *Deutsche Wacht,* he quarreled with both the publisher of *The Victory of Judaism over Germanism* (Kostenobel) and the publisher who replaced him, Froben. He also quarreled with Hentze, the newspaper's publisher, and got into even more trouble with the patrons who had promised him financial support, but had not fulfilled their undertaking. Marr almost became a welfare case; the fact that he was willing to cooperate with de Grousillier, Stoecker, and Pinkert, without considering the ideological differences separating them, only proves this. The condition which he imposed on Pinkert for his attending the meeting of the *Reformverein* in Dresden was the payment of a travel allowance! Marr later tried his best to have his articles published for payment in Pinkert's newspaper. Pinkert, who came to know Marr, answered him rudely: "Contribute to the popularity of our newspaper in Berlin, and you will attain the position of which you are worthy in our newspaper, and which I would give you, if I could; I am not a wealthy man."[3] He was even ruder half a year later: "You thought you would obtain 500 additional subscriptions for *Reform;* we have not received a single additional subscription to the present day." Marr was then living in his city, Hamburg, which had not shown an outstanding degree of enthusiasm for anti-Semitism. The key sentence in the letter was casually tossed out: "I will be able to give you a decent wage later on." As became clear later on, this "later on" never materialized. Pinkert did not even invite Marr to the first Anti-Semitic Congress, which was held in Dresden in September 1882; nor was Marr invited to the second Congress. Schmeitzner, the editor of the journal of the recently founded Anti-Jewish Alliance, did not even require Marr's journalistic services.[4]

Despairing of Pinkert, Marr turned once again to Stoecker, after having attacked him in his newspaper at the end of 1879.[5] The latter responded by expressing his wonder at Marr's profound pessimism; he apparently did not know to what degree this pessimism was a function of Marr's personal fate, more than it was a function of the general fate of the anti-Semitic movement. Stoecker listed the successes: the failure of the Jew Strassmann in the 1880 elections in Berlin: the Tisza-Esler trial in 1882, the Jewish press becoming less strident, and so on. He felt that Marr's lack of faith sprang from his being anti-Christian. Christian Jew-haters had greater faith regarding the prospects of the war against the Jews. The problem which bothered Marr—livelihood—can only be glimpsed between the lines: Stoecker wrote to Marr that "a Berlin newspaper will publish your articles. You must write to me in greater detail concerning your request." Stoecker was reminded of Marr once again in 1884; when the latter offered him his help for the elections, Stoecker asked, "Were you a socialist once? In this case, your assistance would be of special benefit," since Stoecker was then fighting for the votes of the socialists.[6]

Marr also offered his assistance to Stoecker's rival party in the same year, 1884. In July he wrote a letter to August Bebel, the socialist leader, in which he apparently proposed cooperation between the Social Democrats and the anti-Semites. Here also, Marr turned to the wrong person. Bebel replied to Marr in a cool and reserved manner.[7] He was not certain that Marr had voted for him in the last elections in Hamburg. The fact that Marr had chosen him as "the lesser of two evils" did not make him especially happy, and he was not willing to abandon his principles for the votes of Marr and his kind. Bebel was sufficiently polite to end his letter by stating that he would not evade Marr, if the latter were to

seek him out. Marr apparently did not know Bebel sufficiently well, while
Bebel, on his part, did not know that there was a precedent for Marr's
1884 vote: A by-election had been held in Hamburg in 1880, with the
Social Democrats achieving an impressive degree of success. Marr already
had an explanation then.[8] The Social Democrat candidate Hartmann had
not been elected by the Social Democrats; he had been elected by the
Jew-haters. Hartmann's two opponents were the progressive Anton Rée
(a member of the Reichstag until then), and the national liberal Riege,
an apostate. According to Marr, the Reform Jews voted for the former,
while the Orthodox Jews voted for the latter, with the Jew-haters voting
for Hartmann. This explanation, with which Marr settled accounts with
his democratic colleague-rival Rée,[9] is not an explanation of the 1880
electoral results in Hamburg, but rather an explanation of his later turning to Bebel and supporting him in the 1884 elections.

Marr's decline is graphically reflected in his correspondence with
other leading anti-Semites as well. Liebermann von Sonnenberg discovered Marr in December 1879, after the establishment of the Anti-
Semitic League, and presented Marr with a submissive request to cooperate with him. The new admirer apparently did not know, or did not
understand, the Marr of *The Victory of Judaism over Germanism* period,
but only the Marr who cooperated with Stoecker and de Grousillier. If
this were not so, how could he possibly have contemplated writing, "My
slogan also is 'With God's help, for our German Christian Kaiser and
the new Reich.' " Liebermann, a rising star in the anti-Semitic constella-
tion, quickly came to know Marr. In 1884, when the latter, out of the
bitterness of his despair, tried his luck with all of the anti-Semites who
had risen in the world, Liebermann replied only after several letters, and
even then with sharp criticism: "Don't send me the delivery costs." Marr
had thought that Liebermann's desire to economize was the only reason
for not sending him articles.[10] He would not have received any answer
at all, if Liebermann had not needed certain information from him.

Only colleagues who had suffered similar failures were sympathetic
to Marr. In 1881, Henrici, the Berlin anti-Semite, responded to Marr's
desperate appeals with the necessary terseness ("I am busy at present"),
reluctantly agreed to publish an article by Marr, and finally revealed that
he answered Marr only because Marr might be useful to him (in organizing a mass anti-Semitic gathering in Hamburg). In 1884, when Henrici
had also been cast to the sidelines, he admitted to Marr that "I changed
my mind in a fundamental manner. . . . I no longer believe in the
'square' German; . . . I am an anti-Semite who has become a pessimist. Yours."[11]

Paradoxically, Marr enjoyed a revival a few years later, since the
influence of the first generation of anti-Semites (except for Stoecker) had
waned. To the next generation, Marr was not an aged, cynical, unstable
acquaintance but a heroic figure, the "patriarch of anti-Semitism." This

next generation did not arise thirty years later, but rather after the seven lean years of the initial anti-Semitic activity. Indeed, the anti-Semitic movement had become, after six or seven years, an obscure matter, a family quarrel, and a public failure. The new anti-Semites had to begin anew. And so Marr once again floated to the top. As in the past, his rise lasted only a very short time.

An exchange of letters between the new star, the Sachson engineer Theodor Fritsch, and the aging one, Marr, sheds light on this matter. The background is described by young Fritsch in a very picturesque manner:

> Externally, anti-Semitism (or at least anti-Semites) is going increasingly bankrupt. Stoecker is wiped out; the *Volkszeitung* has been closed, and along with it Liebermann has vanished from the scene for the present; [the entire movement] wants to emigrate. Otto Hentze has offered to sell me his anti-Semitic publishing house. Schmeitzner has gone into the lighting business, after the discovery of the spiritual light of the century had brought him no luck; Pinkert apparently cannot hold on, Glagau's *Kulturkämpfer* appears irregularly; Henrici is silent. Förster only comes here as a guest. . . . The old man Marr talks of death. It's possible that one day I may remain the only anti-Semite.[12]

Not only was this description accurate but it undoubtedly caused the aging Marr pleasure. All of his partners, colleagues, and rivals who had treated him, the enfeebled anti-Semite, with contempt three or four years previously, had suffered a fate no better than his. Marr was even more pleased by the fact that Fritsch, representing the young generation of anti-Semites, had pushed aside all the other anti-Semitic activists to offer him the "leadership of the rejuvenated anti-Semitic movement,"[13] despite the usual slanders about him being "quarrelsome" (*Murrkopf*). Fritsch agreed with Marr, and labeled the guiding principles of his opponents' actions as the "principle of begging." He averred, "Yes, there are many 'stupid guys' who serve in leading roles [*macher*] in anti-Semitism. It seems at times that people receive their salaries from the Alliance Israélite Universelle."[14] "It is now stated in public that these people—who in the eyes of the masses of naive and ignorant anti-Semites still have some glory surrounding them—are all *swindlers* . . . I have despised the foolish and complicated essential nature of de Grousillier, Pinkert, and Schmeitzner for some time."[15]

As usual, Marr did not understand the message. He thought that the time had come for the "slaughter of [these] begging street musicians,"[16] that his hour of revenge had come. "Revenge" meant for Marr, as usual, a new newspaper. He accordingly turned to Fritsch with a proposal to aid him in starting a conservative anti-Semitic newspaper in which he would wipe out all the competing anti-Semitic factions. This was not Fritsch's intention: he wanted to close the ranks, even going beyond the slogan previously cited ("to march separately but to strike together"). He understood perfectly well that the mutual attacks by anti-Semites against one another were the Achilles' heel of the anti-Semitic movement. He understood that a hair-splitting, learned debate and novel articles were of no value to a movement such as his, in comparison with constantly repeated slogans which descended like the blows of a sledgehammer on an unaware and uneducated public. Fritsch felt no commitment to, or respect for, the revolutionary outlook of 1848 and the accounts between the old radicals (Marr, Wagner, Glagau, or Scherr). Since Fritsch was the one who had purchased the newspapers and legacies of previous anti-Semites, he could also know to what degree they had been successful. Fritsch himself told Marr that he had found forty-five hundred copies of Marr's "Anti-Semitic Pamphlets" in Schmeitzner's estate.[17] If we take into account the fact that these "Pamphlets" were only published in one edition, we can conclude today, as Fritsch undoubtedly concluded then, that Marr's popularity had already waned in 1880. Fritsch committed an act of charity when he reissued them in 1885.

In place of the newspaper proposed by Marr, Fritsch founded, as he had planned, the *Antisemitische Correspondenz;* Marr was not even appointed editor of this newspaper. Fritsch, the mechanical engineer, declared, "My principle is to rub the contrasting elements against each other, until the sharp corners will have been smoothed off. . . . The opposites Stoecker and Dühring will both reside in the *Antisemitische Correspondenz* amicably—or not amicably—together, and the elderly Marr will also take care that the flame does not grow cold. But not one-sidedness! This has been the source of the illness of the anti-Semitic prattler up to the present. Each anti-Semite created his own special nuance. In my eyes, they are all right—whether free-thinking or religious."[18] Fritsch carried out what he said. It became clear to Marr within a year of Fritsch's contacting him that his star had indeed descended and that his teachings and past were no longer linked to the new society and its anti-Semitism. His task on the newspaper was reduced to merely reading the articles before they were published and writing responses to readers.

Fritsch spread before Marr a theory unequalled in its primitiveness and crudeness, cheap Darwinism. According to his theory, the Jews were vermin (*Ungeziefer*) in the form of man, which God had created in order to test man. These vermin had to be eliminated. The fact that the Jews were stronger than the "good" Germans was explained by comparing the two to wheat and weeds, with the bad always being stronger. Fritsch placed much importance on proving that Lessing was a Jew, with *Nathan the Wise* accordingly not worthy of study. Marr had to swallow such ideas in order to stay on Fritsch's newspaper, upon which his livelihood depended.

Marr was willing to forgo his honor, up to a certain unbearable point—his ex-wife (his third), the author. This woman, who had embittered his life, put his manhood to the test in a degrading fashion, and dragged him down to poverty, became at the age of thirty-nine the lover of another anti-Semite, Oswald Zimmermann, Pinkert's partner. Zimmermann had already aroused Marr's ire, since he, and not Marr, had been chosen as editor of Fritsch's newspaper. To add insult to injury, Oswald Zimmermann offered his lover a position on the newspaper. Marr, in a state of excitement, wrote two urgent letters to Fritsch in October 1885 to prevent the double scandal.

It was Fritsch's primitiveness, conservatism, and narrow-mindedness, of all things, which saved Marr from this disgrace. Fritsch described at length to Marr what motivated him in this episode: the woman's Jewish extraction and her "wanton behavior." Zimmermann tried to explain to Fritsch that his lover was noble-spirited, and that all the slanders came from her disappointed lovers. Fritsch replied that "I, for my part, cannot understand how a noble-spirited woman can dress in a more scandalous fashion than prostitutes do."[19] Even if she had behaved like a nun, Fritsch's stand was clear from the start: "I reject the idea that a female would be a party to such a matter [the anti-Semitic newspaper]. No, faithful Marr, our enterprise is not dependent upon women's underwear."[20] And so the former Jenny Marr was removed from anti-Semitic activity, and her lover with her. The petit-bourgeois Fritsch could not stand a "scandal" in his anti-Semitic community, and made Zimmermann choose between the newspaper and his lover. Zimmermann chose his lover (who had custody of Marr's eight-year-old son), and his name as editor was deleted from the masthead at the last moment. Zimmermann did not forgive Marr and soon joined Böckel, becoming one of those responsible for splitting the united anti-Semitic movement between Fritsch and Böckel. Marr gained nothing by this episode. Despite his ideological closeness to Zimmermann (secular anti-Semitism), he remained hostile to him for personal reasons. This was only a passing episode, but very instructive concerning the nature of the anti-Semitic movement. The attitude towards women and the conventions concerning relations between sexes reveal the combination of the authoritarian personality (Adorno) and reactionary petit-bourgeois morality which form and explain anti-Semitism and its actions.

Marr's attitude towards women, as opposed to Fritsch's, was more complex. Marr regarded the woman as an important element in the anti-Semitic struggle, an element of weakness. He would express this belief in an article from 1891, which apparently reflected the results of his last marriage to an Aryan woman. He accused women of causing the failure of the anti-Semitic effort "Don't Buy from Jews." The women broke the boycott by buying from (presumably cheap) Jewish stores and by filling the theaters which had been taken over by the Jews. The problem seemed to him to be so serious that he wanted to apply Fichte's proposal of "replacing the heads of the Jews" (in order to cancel their Jewishness) to "the philo-Semitic portion of the members of the fairer sex." Marr was radical even on anti-Semitic matters concerning women.[21]

The strange battle over Jenny Marr was the last one Marr was to win during his partnership with Fritsch. The gap between Marr's intellectual obstinacy and his financial condition blocked his path. He had cold water dumped on him every time he censured his disciple for tactical or theoretical mistakes. The rift began to widen in March 1886, a few months after Fritsch published *The Anti-Semitic Catechism*. Marr was once again enveloped by the darkest pessimism. In his letters he attributed this pessimism to the fate of the entire anti-Semitic movement. It is difficult not to discern, however, the personal factors behind this pessimism; even the unfeeling Fritsch understood that Marr had sunken into real poverty. Fritsch was not, however, a sensitive psychologist, and when Marr continued to claim that anti-Semitism was doomed to failure, Fritsch responded, not only by stating that anti-Semitism was alive and well but also by presenting Marr with a clear choice: either to agree with Fritsch, or to leave.

> Anti-Semitism . . . is the step before the ideal maturity of humanity. . . . If you are willing to write in this spirit, I will glady accept your articles, and make sure that you receive your wages for them. Pessimism has no justification in great spiritual movements; it is a sign of weakness and lack of ability. I thought that your pessimism was a mask (as you once admitted to me). It had its purpose, in inflaming the passions, and in impelling extremely powerful defense, but this was its only purpose. Its time has passed now. . . . You are sick, and I therefore make allowances for you. Become well in body and spirit, and then come to us. Only *healthy* people are of value on the battlefield. . . . I ask you once more, tell me openly what your condition is, and then we shall see what can be done.
>
> In addition, you yourself are to blame for your difficult condition. Not everyone is capable of swallowing your rudeness. A veteran soldier like you should have learned during his lifetime to be a bit of a diplomat. If you quarrel with everyone, what friends will come to your aid in time of trouble? You have already said to me things which someone else would not forgive.[22]

This response stunned Marr, and he responded with an attempt to explain the historical background for his pessimism and the need to wage war on the anti-Semitism which had come into being since 1879. Fritsch had no patience for Marr's wrestling with the anti-Semites of the beginning of the 1880's:

> I don't know, old comrade, why you struggle so hard on behalf of dead anti-Semitism. Let the dead enjoy the peace they deserve. The "current anti-Semitism" does not *have* to disappear. It has *already* disappeared.

We represent the anti-Semitism of the *future*. The King is dead—long live the King. I am surprised at you impractical 48'ers, for still dragging a tape measure with you. I really find it ridiculous that you are fighting the dead. You are a true war hero. My greetings to you; it would be advisable that you improve.[23]

Marr was insulted, and the two did not correspond for half a year. Fritsch was busy in establishing the German Anti-Semitic Association (*DAV*). Their correspondence was renewed only at the end of 1886, for a number of possible reasons: the rise of the rival anti-Semite Böckel, financial reasons, or Marr having become the feuilletonist of the anti-Semitic newspaper *Österreichischer Volksfreund*.

Marr attempted at this time to take advantage of the new crisis within the anti-Semitic movement. The DAV had pushed Stoecker out when it was founded in June 1886, according to the anti-Christian line with which Marr agreed. Marr apparently expected that the renewal of the debate over Christian and atheistic anti-Semitism would make him the center of the theoretical discussion. He threw down the gauntlet in a letter to Stoecker. The latter was prepared to take up the challenge, and was convinced, of course, of the rightness of his position. Not only this, but Stoecker felt that the renewed debate would revive his movement at this time, and was only sorry that the debate would harm the anti-Semitic movement as a whole.[24] This was a comment which Marr had already heard from Fritsch, but it was not enough to convince him. He regarded the struggle over the path of the anti-Semitic movement as a matter of life and death, with its participants being of prime interest for him. He wanted to teach a lesson, not necessarily to Stoecker, but to Fritsch, Böckel (Fritsch's rival), and to Zimmermann (Böckel's partner—and the lover of Marr's ex-wife).

Marr's efforts did not bear fruit, and he turned more and more to sweeping accusations of the anti-Semites and their leadership. As he would testify later, he was influenced then by the publication of his idol, Johaness Scherr's last book, *The Nihilists,* to push aside the Jewish problem as a special problem, in favor of the great social problem and the chaos which was about to envelop the entire world.[25]

The charge which Marr now repeatedly brought was that anti-Semitism had become a business. This charge was rejected by Fritsch, who explained to Marr how he had managed to keep the *Antisemitische Correspondenz* alive: with private investment to cover debts, contributions, and income from sales. All this for a newspaper whose circulation did not reach two thousand copies! The breach between Fritsch and Marr was complete. Marr mourned the death of his idol Johaness Scherr; Fritsch did not think that the loss was so terrible. Marr criticized an article in Fritsch's newspaper; Fritsch accused Marr of not making his criticism clear after proofreading the article. Fritsch would be a bit more generous only when he would republish *The Anti-Semitic Catechism* in

1887, and would need the services of the "expert." The beaten expert gave his assistance. When he did not receive any recompense, Marr once again began complaining about "commercialized anti-Semitism." Marr could take no more, and he began to write his work, *Im Philosemitismus,* which was supposed to be published only posthumously. This essay is the first manifestation of the "patriarch of anti-Semitism" returning to the straight and narrow. He gives a factual description of his life together with Jews. His purpose is not to defame the Jews but to lay a basis for comparing the Jewish business world with the anti-Semitic one (*Geschäfts-antisemitismus,* as he called it). The results of the comparison were supposed to present the latter in a negative light. This essay, which is of great interest for us, waited almost a century before it was published for the first time; it appears in the Appendix.[26]

Pathetically, Marr also opened his heart to Fritsch himself, along with a request for aid—the beggar reproaching his patron. Fritsch responded with the coarsest frankness: "I would help you if I could. The anti-Semitic movement has a dozen invalids like you, and each one expects that *I* will help him. . . . You talk ceaselessly about the 'fraud' of 'those who make a business out of anti-Semitism.' Who is befrauding? In what manner? Who calls himself the President of the Anti-Semitic Association? Old comrade! You fantasize at times. . . . 'A muzzle for the snout of one who cannot bite' is an appropriate inscription, and it would be advisable for you to hang it on your door."[27]

Marr, the dog who barked without biting, came back to serve Fritsch a year later, with his tail between his legs. Fritsch continued to make use of him, mainly to correct and improve *The Anti-Semitic Catechism* at the end of 1888. Marr was behind the new edition of the book and its pocket edition.[28] Fritsch suddenly became more generous towards Marr, for as long as the latter could be of use to him. Fritsch thanked him for the abovementioned article "Baron Hirsch," and sent him a blood sausage as a Christmas present. Marr would mention this present as a humiliation in his essay *The Testament of an Anti-Semite,* which appears in the Appendix. Marr had for all intents and purposes ended his role in Fritsch's service at the beginning of 1889. The occasional letters during the years 1890 to 1892 cannot be considered as correspondence.[29]

Fritsch would contribute from now on to the expunging of Marr's role from the history of anti-Semitism. Marr's birthday was indeed still mentioned on November 16, 1889, in the *Antisemitischer Volkskalender* published by Fritsch, but Marr himself was described only as "an anti-Semitic writer." Minor individuals received a more detailed, and more flattering, description. The portion of the chart dealing with the "Harbingers of Anti-Semitism" mentioned Glagau, B. Förster, Liebermann, Fritsch, Stoecker, Schönerer, and Radenshausen in 1888 and 1889. Marr was conspicuous by his absence.[30]

Marr found a spark of hope in his own city of Hamburg. No matter how sick he was or how difficult it was for him to move, he could at least still take part in anti-Semitic activity in his home town. On July 7, 1888, seventeen members founded the "Deutscher Verein" in Hamburg, a society whose declared aim was the "fostering of the Germanic spirit," and which in fact was simply an anti-Semitic party.[31] Marr was invited to be among the founders, but he did not win any post or standing within the society. When the society sent its delegate to the Anti-Semitic Congress in Bochum in November 1889, Marr could no longer be a member of the society with equanimity. This congress had adopted the program of Fritsch, Liebermann, and Paul Förster, which he abhorred.[32] The society's slogan in the 1889 elections, "Christianity, Kaiserism, Fatherland," was also not in line with Marr's views. Marr remained a member of the society in name only until his resignation in 1891.

The question of the workers and the Social Democrats contributed decisively to the worsening of relations between Marr and Fritsch, and between Marr and the other anti-Semites. The question of the workers and Social Democracy was the center of attention from the end of 1888, a short time after Wilhelm II took power. The new ruler's stance, and the policy which led in 1890 to the nonrenewal of the socialist laws (a ban on the socialist party's activities) created for the anti-Semites, as it did for many conservatives, a difficult dilemma—how to continue with a conservative policy and compete with Social Democracy. Marr, aware of the seriousness of the situation, began to direct most of his anti-Semitic arrows against Social Democracy. He published an article, "The German and French Social Democrats," at the end of 1888 in the *Österreichischer Volksfreund,* and, immediately afterwards, in the *Antisemitische Correspondenz.* He praised the French Social Democrats for focusing their struggle with the "gold International" against the Jews and even for having prepared a plan to attack rich Jews in case war broke out. In contrast, he angrily attacked the German Social Democrats: "We've been able, for some time, to identify the German Social Democrat as the slave of the Jews."[33] Such statements were in line with Fritsch's philosophy; this was not the source of their disagreement. Three months later, he sent Fritsch an additional article on the same subject, "Why Are Anti-Semites Generally Conservatives?,"[34] which was published in *Antisemitische Correspondenz.* In this article, Marr engulfed the Social Democrat issue in a wider problem, the economic history of mankind. In his attempt to reverse everything, to turn what was accepted as "progressive" into "misleading," and "reactionary" into right, he concentrated on the economic question as the major question faced by anti-Semitism. He had already said in 1879 that the Jewish question was not a religious question, but rather a social one. Now he developed this idea into a general criticism of the existing economic system. "Anti-Semitism requires breaking away from the deceptive economic philosophies which exist thanks to the Jews." This break meant reaction; Marr proudly admitted this, once more,[35] as one who had held liberal economic views in his youth when he had fought against the Prussian customs union and protective tariffs. He included a call to the Social Democrats in the same spirit: "You will not attain anything, as long as you let the nation of Jewish speculators drag you by the nose. In this manner you lose the sympathy of social revolutionaries, who view you as the bodyguards of the Jewish stock exchange and bank." There is no doubt that the term "social revolutionaries" is a case of *pluralis majestatis,* with the intent being to Marr himself. He continued, "Since I do not have to make allowances [i.e., that he did not belong to any of the petty, quarreling anti-Semitic parties], I can state openly: the future belongs to socialism. The question is whether this will be Aryan socialism or Jewish socialism." We can appreciate what is apparently a diagnosis of the direction in which the social problem was developing, along with an interesting and dangerous preamble to a theory of special German socialism, which would be developed by Spengler, Moeller van den Bruck, and the National Socialists, after Marr's death. He expressed this even more strongly in another article, declaring, "I view today's Social Democrat workers as traitors and Judases to the great idea of our time—the idea of the socialist struggle of work against the great floating capital."[36]

Fritsch did not make use of the anti–Social Democrat weapon which Marr had developed for him only by printing Marr's articles in his newspaper. He also deceived and abused Marr by publishing a pamphlet entitled "Open [Your] Eyes," which consisted mainly of the article which Marr had written on the German and French Social Democrats, but *without* crediting Marr as the author.[37] The impression thus fostered was that the idea was Fritsch's. Fritsch mentioned Marr at the end of the pamphlet and cited a short passage from another of Marr's articles. However, Marr's pessimism is more conspicuous in this passage than his analysis of the situation. The most striking sentence in the passage is, "I call upon the Social Democrats at the end of my life." Marr appears here as a washed-out animal. Adding insult to injury, Fritsch called Marr, in this same pamphlet, "a veteran 1848 revolutionary" and "an old hothead [*alter Brause-Kopf*]."[38] No wonder Marr began now to write his memoirs, which were a settling of accounts with the anti-Semitic movement.

In the meantime, Marr tried to render battle, as best he could, in the *Österreichischer Volksfreund.* He presented over and over his theory of "correct," anti-Semitic socialism, and attacked established anti-Semitism for its failings in the struggle. Marr, in whose veins the blood of 1848 boiled, demanded "a moral revolution [*sittlich revolutioniren*]," a revolution in "great waves," and infiltration of the Social Democrat ranks in the large cities. After a prolonged silence, Fritsch responded at the end of 1890 in a letter which clearly shows the difference between Marr (concerned with the general social problem) and Fritsch (who saw the entire problem only from the perspective of the anti-Semitic movement).

Fritsch wrote that he did not desire a revolution, negated the "great wave," and insisted upon "small" daily work. In addition, Fritsch rejected Marr's more modern approach concerning the need to conduct the moral revolution in the large cities. Fritsch, whose reactionary opinions have already been presented, reinforced them here: "The fact that we concentrate our activities in towns and villages is of tremendous importance! The large cities are a heap of corruption! Health is to be found in the village. The reform will set out from there."[39] It is ironical that the "garden city" (*Gartenstadt*) movement, of which Fritsch was a mainstay, influenced the tendency among Jews and land reformers, as well as among Zionists, to escape from the city.[40] Marr did not see this type of romanticism as a solution to the great problem he had identified, and accordingly he continued to develop his philosophy of the approaching social revolution. In "Anti-Semitism—Momentum and Failures," an article which appeared in installments in 1891, he presented anti-Semitism as a socialist movement and as a revolutionary movement. Anti-Semites were the "unconscious pioneers of the social revolution. . . . I hate Social Democracy as I hate Beelzebub. But the truth must be said: Beelzebub is more effective than we, the Christians and Aryans. . . . When we, the anti-Semites, take five steps forward, Judaism and Judaised Social Democracy take a hundred thousand steps. . . . We have become powerless, even in the little things which would protect us from Judaization and from social revolutionary ferment. Why should you be surprised if old, battle-wise men become pessimists?"[41] Once again Marr refers to himself in the plural, and he alone will draw the logical conclusion: if the social revolution is inevitable, how can anti-Semitism be of any value in solving the problem? And indeed, he arrived at this conclusion in his unpublished writings from that same year, 1891.

Marr began to write his memoirs in 1889 at the age of 70. These memoirs comprised six volumes, covering his life from birth until 1891. When he finished his work, he began to write *The Testament of an Anti-Semite,* which he completed at the end of 1891. Marr rid himself in this *Testament* of the anti-Semitic movement, even though he did not expunge the anti-Semitic prejudices which had become part of his personality. The *Testament* was not published, even after Marr's death, and is published here for the first time (see Appendix). The readers of *Österreichischer Volksfreund* had already learned of Marr's critical tendency without seeing his memoirs; with the publication of his article in the newspaper on April 26, 1891, they became acquainted with two terms aimed directly at organized anti-Semitism: what he called "those making a business of anti-Semitism" [*Geschäftsantisemiten*] and "anti-Semitic begging policy" [*Klingelbeutelpolitik*].[42] The Jews naturally made immediate use of the term "business of anti-Semitism" in their defense against anti-Semitism.[43] If Marr had also published the *Testament,* he would have furnished the Jews with a lethal weapon against their opponents. It is ironical that

Marr, who felt that he was about to die, would live for another thirteen years. After he died, however, no one was interested in the legacy of the forgotten dead man. Certainly no admirer could be found who would be willing to pay 1,000 marks for the strange manuscript, as Marr had demanded.

Despite the declaration that the essay was to be published only posthumously, Marr attempted to sell it during his lifetime. Paradoxically, it was Julius Stettenheim, the talented satirist who was Marr's disciple in 1850 and his critic in 1862, who was supposed to act to have the essay published. After moving to Berlin, Stettenheim continued to correspond with Marr until 1895. He related to Marr with sarcastic forgiveness in his letters, despite the latter's anti-Semitism. Stettenheim did not take anti-Semitism seriously, not even at the end of the century. It was therefore almost natural that Marr, the repentant anti-Semite, would turn to him, the Jew, for aid in the publication of his book. Marr was so suspicious, however, that he did not send the manuscript to Stettenheim, but only told him about the essay. And so, despite Stettenheim's efforts, the work was not published.[44]

There is no doubt that Marr's personal fate, his decline and the humiliation he suffered, are what directed him against his former colleagues, the anti-Semites. After analyzing his statements and articles during this period, I cannot, however, accept the "obvious" assumption that all his new ideological arguments were only the rationalization for this personal response. These arguments have their roots in the old Marr and are therefore very sincere. Why did Marr abandon anti-Semitism?

> The social question is more important today than "Thron und Altar" [monarchy and church], Semitism and anti-Semitism, and partisan, progressive, national-liberal, or social-democratic quarrels. . . . This is the reason for my drawing away from modern anti-Semitism, [even though] I am one of its pioneers and most veteran fighters. . . . Practically, the Jews have lost their importance for me, in the face of the fast-approaching social upheaval.

He viewed accounts with the Jews as settled. "The Jews related to me, on the personal level, ungratefully. As a result, I didn't pat them on the head, either! Personally, our accounts are therefore even."[45]

Marr had come full circle and had balanced accounts; there was therefore no need for him to change his basic assumptions about the Jews. The "repentant" Marr still believed that the Jews ruled the world—but now he complimented them on this account instead of fighting them. He still saw them as seasoned merchants—but he was convinced now that the anti-Semites were worse than them in this area as well. He still toyed with the idea of Jewish migration—but had ceased to believe that this would solve anything. "The present mass migration of Jews from Russia," which was quite noticeable in Hamburg in 1891, "will only lead to their flooding the world with their special characteristics. . . . No nation wants them, but everyone wishes they were among his enemies. It is therefore inconceivable that *international diplomacy* will find a separate area for their settlement."[46] This is testimony to Marr's having closely followed the efforts of the predecessors of Zionism. Two of those pre-Zionist essays had been published that year in Hamburg: Gustav Cohen had published *The Jewish Question and the Future,* and Max Bodenheimer *Where Will the Russian Jews Go?* Marr was undoubtedly responding to these essays.[47] Here again we find traces of the pessimism of 1879: "I no longer feel hatred for the Jews. . . . Yes! I bow my head before the mysterious phenomenon, before the *Sphinx* of history, before Judaism, which has known how to impress its special mark on humanity during the course of four thousand years."[48] Marr revealed here in the *Testament* that he understood his times. He explicitly wrote that it was industrialization and modernization which had created the social problem, and not the Jews, and that the confrontation was with these factors and not with the Jews. He openly requested the Jews' pardon for having erred in isolating the problem.

When Marr understood the essence of the period in his old age, he saw Social Democracy, to whose sources he had been close in his youth, in a different light. Marr returned in 1891 not only to the pessimism which had enveloped him in 1878 but also to the socialist radicalism which had guided him in the 1840's. His criticism of the path he and the anti-Semites followed (collaboration with the conservative monarchy, and even with the church, instead of joint action with the workers, within Social Democracy) is expressed throughout the *Testament.*

It makes no difference, at the end of this depressing settling of accounts, who was the partner on the way to the abyss; yet, Marr finds it preferable to admit that one of the two paths leading to the abyss is less logical: the conservative path, which he had followed since the 1860's.

Despite the resolute conclusions he reached in 1891, Marr hesitated for more than a year before he published openly (i.e., in the press) his disavowal of, and separation from, anti-Semitism for the reasons which have been listed.[49] Yet, when the dramatic disavowal of the anti-Semitic movement by the "patriarch of anti-Semitism" was published, it did not receive a response. Except for Hamburg, I could not find any mention of this in the Jewish press that year. The degree to which Marr had sunk into oblivion can be learned from an incidental remark made by his friend and opponent Stettenheim in the *Allgemeine Zeitung des Judenthums* in 1893, five months after Marr's announcement. Stettenheim told, in remembrances of his childhood, of his work for the newspaper *Mephistopheles,* which was edited by Marr. Since Stettenheim was certain that Marr was not a known personality, he wrote that "Marr was an anti-Semite at the time, and later returned to liberal principles." This was the allusion in the

Jewish press to Marr's "repentance." Stettenheim's source of information was the correspondence he continued to conduct with Marr, and not the press.[50]

The Berlin *Encyclopaedia Judaica,* which was published more than thirty years after Marr's "repentance," stated that "Marr disgustedly abandoned anti-Semitism."[51] The encyclopedia's source of information was a book written in 1892 by another of Fritsch's disappointed disciples, Hermann Lucko.[52] Lucko, who had been asked by Fritsch to edit one of his newspapers (the *Leipziger Tagesanzeiger*), and who had been fired by Fritsch a year later, felt that he shared a common fate with Marr, his senior. Lucko accordingly began his book with the motto by Marr, "I am sorry for that portion of our German youth and the middle- and lower-class bourgeoisie which has fallen, due to the 'petty leaders' of the party, from the Semitic frying pan into the fire of the business-of-anti-Semitism." He cites a letter which Marr had written in July 1891 during the period when he wrote *The Testament of an Anti-Semite.* It was stated in that letter that "modern anti-Semitism . . . has become irrelevant for me. . . . It has swollen like the frog in the fable, and will eventually burst like it."[53] Lucko naturally quoted this sentence in his letter to Fritsch during the same month, adding another quotation from a letter by Marr to another anti-Semite:[54] "After thirty years of war against the Jews, I have grown to despise the cheating business-of-anti-Semitism. I will never part from this belief." This citation was apparently the reason for the end of the relations between Fritsch and Marr, and its publication in Lucko's booklet is the best-known evidence of Marr's departure from the anti-Semitic movement. The German *Encyclopaedia Judaica* cited it, as well as the researcher of the Jewish question von Freienwald, who was mentioned at the beginning of this book.

What had begun with *The Victory of Judaism over Germanism* with thunder and lightning ended in 1891–1893 with a whimper.

Marr did not stop writing, even though nobody bothered to publish what he wrote. He worried about his future image, and turned his writing into vocational therapy. He continued writing diaries in bed until the age of 81 in 1901. In 1896 he summed up his life in the article "Ecce ego," which remained in his legacy:

> My hair and beard have turned white. The list of my physical illnesses . . . includes gout, sciatica, rheumatism in my hands, and problems with my eyes, liver, heart, and kidneys, resulting in almost total infirmity. Last but not least, if I'm not misinterpreting the signs—mental decay and blindness are fast approaching. And so I'm expiring in solitude, abandoned by my "best friends" and the best of my enemies. The former, since I can no longer amuse them, and the latter, since I can no longer annoy them. . . . All this comes after 76–77 years of active, turbulent, life, about which the "everyday people," who live both materially and spiritually from hand to mouth, know nothing.[55]

The philosophy which accompanied Marr in "the five years' study of world history" (1891–1896) was the profound pessimism of Schopenhauer. This philosophy apparently compensated him for his general helplessness in the twilight of his days:

> I must thank the "German Buddha" for the self-awareness, for the awareness that I cannot be so presumptuous as to [think of myself] as solving all the world's problems. When I realized that everything is madness in the "world as *image*," I also had to realize that it was presumption to implement social and political methods in the "world as will."

He admitted that he was most depressed by the knowledge that "among the everyday people, an everyday person is of value only as long as he is healthy and can take part in the costume ball of life." He concludes with a statement to his friends and enemies: "You will not be able to say that I owe you money, nor will you be able to say that I ever borrowed from you—and this is the main point in the everyday life of everyday people."

These are sad conclusions for an idealist and reformer. They arouse compassion, even if the memory of his hatred for the Jews cannot be expunged. The next eight years, during which he would be completely bedridden in the workers' quarter of Barmbek in Hamburg, forced him to swallow what remained of his pride. Not only did his wife have to borrow money for him, he had to ask for aid from the Hamburg Journalists' and Writers' Association.[56] Marr died on July 17, 1904, at the age of 85. Fortunately for him, the Hamburg State Archives responded to an advertisement his wife placed in the newspaper about her husband's enormous legacy, allowing those who came after him a glimpse into the recesses of an anti-Semite's soul, and into the social environment in which he evolved.

The Decline of the Term "Anti-Semitism"

It is not absolutely certain that Marr coined the term "anti-Semitism," but it is very likely. As we have seen, the meaning of the term when it was first used (i.e., when the "Anti-Semitic League" was established), and presented publicly by de Grousillier, was completely different from what we would have anticipated and from the racist meaning which it acquired later. The "Anti-Semitic League" was only an abortive attempt to compete with Stoecker's Christian Social brand of Jew-hatred. We have already seen that the Jewish newspaper *Ha-Magid* thought that the League had been founded by the minister Stoecker. We find in an 1879 essay, written in response to de Grousillier's inauguration speech which contained the definition of the term "anti-Semitism," that the writer attacked the League primarily as a *Christian* society.[1] We should not look far: Marr himself said retrospectively, "modern anti-Semitism has existed since 1878, when the court preacher Stoecker first raised the Jewish question from his 'Christian Social' point of view."[2]

The term "anti-Semitism" was unsuitable from the beginning for the real essence of Jew-hatred, which remained anchored, more or less, in the Christian tradition, even when it moved, via the natural sciences, into racism. It is doubtful whether the term, which was first publicized in an institutional context (the Anti-Semitic League), would have appeared at all if the "Anti-Chancellor League," which fought Bismarck's policy, had not been in existence since 1875. The founders of the new organization adopted the elements of "anti" and "league," and searched for the proper term: Marr exchanged the term "Jew" for "Semite," which he already favored. It is possible that the shortened form "Sem" is used with such frequency and ease by Marr (and in his writings) due to its literary advantage, and because it reminded Marr of Sem Biedermann, his Jewish employer from the Vienna period. The sentence "Sem took over" or "Sem wanted," short, without the definite article, strikes the mark more than "the Jew took over" or "the Jew wanted."

We have already stated that "anti-Semitism," a striking expression phonetically, apparently won wide circulation due to its lack of clarity, on the one hand, and its scientific pretensions, on the other, without a great deal of attention being paid to its contents. It seems to me that it was Treitschke's incidental use of the term in November 1879 which gave it much momentum, since his writings were read by tone-setting Jews and Gentiles alike.[3] Yet, the few who considered the contents of the term, were quick to protest against the use of the concept.

The *Great Brockhaus* lexicon, dating from 1882, defines "anti-Semite" without superfluous embellishment: "Hater of Jews. Opponent of Judaism. Fights against the qualities, appearance, and intentions of Semitism." The original Semitic aspect is pushed aside here. And who if not Fritsch himself aimed to undermine the term which his master used: when Fritsch organized his followers, during the years 1885–1886, whenever the issue of whether to establish an anti-Jewish party was on the agenda, the question of whether to use the term "Anti-Semitic" also arose. Fritsch's newspaper, called *Anti-Semitic Correspondence,* debated whether to call the organization "anti-Jewish" or "anti-Semitic," aware that the term "Jew" included only those affiliated with the Jewish religion, and not all of the Jewish people.[4] The organization was finally called "DAV," the "German Anti-Semitic Association," but the term was explained entirely in the spirit of the old *Risches* (Jew-hatred). In an abridgement of Fritsch's *Anti-Semitic Catechism* dating from 1889, when the term "anti-Semitism" celebrated a decade since its appearance,[5] we find: "What is anti-Semitism? Anti means against, Semitism means the essence of the Jewish race. Anti-Semitism is therefore the struggle against Semitism. Since almost the entire Semitic race in Europe is Jewish, we therefore understand [the term] 'Semites' in its narrow sense—Jews. In our case, 'anti-Semite' is a Jew-hater, one opposed to the Jews." This is the formulation which also appeared in the *Anti-Semitic Catechism* in the 1890's.

This formulation provoked the sharp criticism of the famous opponent of the anti-Semites, Graf Coudenhove-Kalergi. "The anti-Semites . . . assure us that anti-Semitism has no connection with religion. If this is so, it is surprising that they call themselves after a personality in whom they cannot at all believe without the supernatural aid of religious writings."[6] This is the question which Marr, the atheist, should have considered, if he had thought scientifically and methodically. This is the question which is directly aimed at the Achilles' heel of the consciousness of hatred of the Jews, which is allegedly racial, modern, scientific, and secular.

It is of interest to follow the attitude of the camp of Jew-haters—in the *Anti-Semitic Catechism* (or as it was called afterwards, the *Handbook on the Jewish Question* [*Handbuch der Judenfrage*]) and in later anti-

Semitic literature—towards Marr and his handiwork, the term "anti-Semitism."

Paul Förster, one of the founding fathers of anti-Semitism, said in 1907 that "it should be noted, by the way, that the expression 'anti-Semitism' appears to me to be unfortunate (*unglücklich*), but it must be accepted as it is. Its meaning is identical to what you [the Jewish editor Julius Moses] call 'the solution to the Jewish problem.' "[7]

The blurring of the special connotation of the term "anti-Semite" continued as Marr was sinking into oblivion. We know that Marr had already been pushed to the sidelines in 1889 in the *Anti-Semitic Diary*. In 1910, the editor of the *Anti-Semitic Catechism*, Fritsch, did not bother to cite him more than once, and did not even mention the dates of his birth and death next to his name. By the beginning of the 1930's, the *Handbook* even included criticism of Marr. It was not enough that he had been demoted to the seventh place on the list of founders of the anti-Semitic movement—he was attacked for coining the concept. The concept is unfortunate (once again *unglücklich*) "since there are other peoples with a Semitic language[!], who are opposed to the Jews." It was preferable, in the opinion of the *Handbook*'s editor, to use the term "adversary of the Jews" (*Judengegner*).

This same edition, more comprehensive than its predecessors, also included an attempt to find a substitute for the term "anti-Semitism," since the problem was not primarily racial but spiritual[!]; it would be preferable to use the term "anti-Rabbinical (*Anti-Rabbinisimus*).[8] This term was removed from the edition which appeared in 1933, the year of Hitler's rise to power, to be replaced by the reappearing claim of the unsuitability of the term coined by Marr. It was therefore proposed once again to use the term "adversary of the Jews." This was the guiding line of the *Handbook*, which appeared in twelve editions from the death of its first editor, Fritsch, in 1933 until the Second World War.[9] It may be stated that the *Handbook* still reveals some degree of moderation towards the term, stating only that it is "unfortunate" or "incorrect." Hans Günther, the German (and Nazi) expert on racism, wrote in his standard book on race that the term "anti-Semitism" was "badly chosen," and should be replaced by "anti-Jewishness" (*Judengegnerschaft*). Graf Reventlow, the veteran imperialist and Jew-hater, went further: he called Marr "the father of the unsuitable and harmful word 'anti-Semitism.' "[10]

The concern not to harm the non-Jewish "peoples speaking Semitic languages," which was present among the Jew-haters even before the Nazis took power, became a political and practical guideline after 1933. Already in 1935, before the enactment of the Nuremberg laws (which use the contrast between Jew and German, and not between Semite and Aryan), Goebbels' office had given an order to the press not to use the term "anti-Semitism," since the war of the German people was directed only against the Jews.[11] The explicit statement that the intent was to exclude the Arabs only appears in the *Handbook* during the war itself, when hatred of the Jews was a component of international policy, and not just an internal German affair. It is symptomatic that the defamation of Marr came at the same time as the extreme conclusion concerning the harm caused by the use of the term "anti-Semitism." The *Handbook* stated in 1944 that "the concept anti-Semitism, which was coined by the descendant of the Jews Wilhelm Marr in 1879, is unsuitable, if only for the reason that there are other peoples with Semitic languages, such as the Arabs, who stand in complete opposition to the Jews." This sentence is a repetition of what had appeared in earlier editions, with the addition of two words: "descendant of the Jews," the description of Marr, and "the Arabs," a people which proves the unsuitability of the term "anti-Semitism." It was very convenient to blacken the name of the man recognized as the father of the term "anti-Semitism," in order to overcome the problem which the term had created for National Socialist policy. To close the circle, the term "anti-Semitism" was removed from the last editions of the *Handbook*. Even the quotation from Herzl's *The Jewish State,* which had appeared in the previous editions under the subtitle "Anti-Semitism," would appear from now on under the title "Anti-Judaism," the term which—according to the recommendation of the book's editors—had to replace the term "anti-Semitism."[12]

National-Socialism paradoxically dealt the coup-de-grace to Wilhelm Marr's name and work. Marr drifted into oblivion, leaving behind only an occasional and inaccurate footnote in books dealing with anti-Semitism. We may indeed wonder at the irony of fate for taking Marr at his word and "letting the dead bury the dead." Then why defy fate and make Marr the hero of a biography? The answer lies not only with Marr's extraordinary career, so illuminating for the understanding of the anti-Semitic personality and the emergence of modern anti-Semitism on the background of the nineteenth century; nor with the fact that Marr was the man who introduced the term anti-Semitism into politics; not even the fact that the same Marr turned his back on anti-Semitism and became the sharpest critic of that movement. It is the astonishing insight of the man Marr regarding the main trends in modern European history that render his biography particularly interesting. Marr, who rightly defined himself "the man of the nineteenth century," deserves the attention of the world of the twentieth century: he was aware of the forthcoming and inevitable social upheaval, of the threat of communism and of the probability of a takeover by the "fifth estate." This is why he came to consider anti-Semitism as an unrealistic and erroneous way to solve the problems of a society caught between modernization and reaction.

Appendix

The "Bremen Letter"

In June 1862, Marr addressed a letter to Hobelmann, a friend from Bremen, who was a supporter of the emancipation of the Jews and sought Marr's backing for a law granting equal rights to the Jews of Bremen. Marr's letter was the opposite of what Hobelmann intended. Yet Hobelmann published it in the supplement to the *Courier an der Weser* No. 161, June 13, 1862, Bremen:

Hamburg, 4th June, 1862

Dear Sir,

I hasten to answer your letter and regret to tell you that I cannot be your ally in the matter mentioned therein. Without intending to influence your view in any way, I still consider it my duty to reward your trust in me by explaining the motivation of my opinion, and you may use these lines in any way permissible among honest men, i.e., publish and oppose them, as you may wish.

In the first place, there is no question of emancipation in the case of the Jews. This is a matter that concerns only them (the Jews) and not us. In every body politic the minority has to obey the rules of the majority, and I consider it foolish if the latter wants to grant the former exceptional legal privileges. If the Jews want to live in our state and enjoy equal rights with us, they have to live as we do, to be as we are. Above all, not to form a religious or political state within the state.

But I can tell you in advance that the Jews will refuse to live in Bremen as a non-Jewish community, i.e., to leave their temple [synagogue] to the discretion of the individual. They will demand of the state protection and privileges of the sort that every Jew will be compelled to become a member of the Jewish state within the state, and with their official temple they have founded an official sub-state which must become detrimental to their civil liberties, not by reason of religion—this is of secondary importance—but as a necessary consequence of their innate tribal peculiarity (*Stammeseigenthümlichkeiten*). That mixture of all sorts of human races, as confirmed unanimously by science as well as by the Jews' own tradition (Isaiah, Jeremiah, Ezekiel), is incompatible with the Germanic elements in the pure, better sense. And our instinctive antipathy to the Jews is based on history and experience. That race which under Joseph's ministry introduced slavery, which under Mordechai's ministry committed mass slaughter of men, which even to this day celebrates the memory of these horrors in the political *Purim* festival, is not entitled—don't get me wrong!—as Jews to equal civil rights. Just as we had been incapable, and therefore ineligible, for freedom, until we had emancipated ourselves from our prejudices and slavish particularities, thus also the Jews.

If I wanted to live according to my principles in any particular state, the externality of a religion, believe me, would not deter me, and as I leave the nexus of one state, I never would have the cheek to demand of the majority of that state to legislate special regulations in my favour.

But the problem lies deeper. According to my opinion, Judaism, which is the same today as it has always been, since it is a tribal particularity, is incompatible with the life of our state. By its very nature it must always strive to form a state within a state. You cannot exterminate the instinctive popular aversion against Judaism through so-called emancipation, and it takes its revenge by becoming a satellite of reaction, of which we have distinctive proof here in Hamburg. The oriental element is politically and socially incompatible with ours, just as black and white will never produce a colour other than gray. At one time I, too, dreamed about this question, but later on I found only renegades in politics, and in social life only . . . and the few exceptions among the Jews had simply ceased to be Jews.

In one word: don't look at this question from the religious side; examine it from the aspect of cultural history, and you will discover a tribe of mongrels whose vital principle, from the time of the patriarchs who traded away their wives, to this day is—selling to the highest bidder. The honourable exceptions (who any way have better blood in their veins) should not induce a state to allow its own element to be affected for the sake of an ideological conception. You would not permit 10,000 monks to settle in Bremen. Not for religious reasons, oh no! But because monasticism endangers the common weal. Judaism, however, is nothing else than a social congregation, the congregation of a tribe whose whole essence is beyond our morals and who, once they have struck root, will strive to take hold of everything for themselves. Religiously they are commanded to do so, socially this is their nature, politically this is a consequence of both.

You are asking: where is freedom of religion? And I answer: if material interests are dearer to the Jew than his religion, let him give it up; if his religion is dearer to him, how can he demand of us to adapt our state to it?

If you can prevail upon emancipation to stipulate formally that no Jew may be compelled to contribute to the upkeep of his temple, but that he must also contribute his share to the levies borne by all other citizens—just you try it. But as soon as you accord official recognition to Judaism in your state, you will experience the bitter consequences in less than three years!

I am making no secret of my aversion to the Jewish character; as a rule and almost always I have found among the Jews only masks instead of real human beings. The religion and its precepts are nothing but products of their consciousness, their particularities are manifestations of their organism.

And now to the end, for one could write a book on this subject.

Emancipation can only be the fruit of one's own effort. If the people, the plain, simple people, inexperienced in the arts of dialectics, demands emancipation with equality for the Jews as emphatically as it demands political or social reform, then this has become a necessity. *It depends on the Jews to make themselves so popular that the demand is raised as a necessity in the consciousness of the people:* it is not up to us to enforce emancipation. Emancipated by us, but remaining isolated in the consciousness of the people, the reaction is as inevitable as it is certain. You will create allies for despotism and through the exclusivity inherent in the tribe you will form a limited company which *viribus unitis* will also be detrimental to the economic life of your state. Tribal particularities cannot be legislated away with the stroke of a pen. But there is still something else, and this you cannot dispute. So long as the separation of the church from the state has not been consistently introduced and carried out by us, it would be self-contradictory to talk about the emancipation of the Jews.

But, if a state religion, viz., a Christian state, is not enough for you, then you may, as far as I am concerned, allow a temple and synagogal state by its side. I wish you success.

Don't be angry with me for being so frank. I am doing nothing against the Jews, because people learn most quickly from experience, and here with us nine-tenths of the population—and the most intelligent radicals at their head—are cursing the artificial and spurious emancipation. But I can do even less for a tribe whose best critics are its own prophets! I and several congenial friends no longer attend the local parliament, our 'constitutional caricature,' where Abraham's descendants play the role of faithful satellites of reaction.

When the party which, like ours, itself is being oppressed, wants to spill its cornucopia over others, it is being pulled instead of doing the pulling.

I should like to cry out: if you, Jew, are as disgusted with your temple as I am with my church, then attach yourself to me, not I to you. Do not shy away from a few drops of water, when it is a matter of replacing orthodoxy by free humanism. If you are a hydrophobiac, then you are orthodox, and I have nothing in common with orthodox people.

Adieu!

Yours sincerely,
W. Marr

Within Philo-Semitism*

Introduction

The following writings will be released to the public, if at all, only after my death. It therefore follows that it cannot be claimed that the criticism

---

* StA Hamburg, Nachlass Marr BVa "Im Philosemitismus" 1887. The symbol (. . .) signifies a deletion, and the symbol [. . .] signifies a word which is illegible in the original text.

which I level at modern anti-Semitism is intended to create publicity for myself. Furthermore, I will deal with issues and individuals with all possible discretion; at the same time, I will give expression to stringent self-criticism. I promise all my anti-Semitic "colleagues" to act according to the principle of speaking well of the dead. I will not use words of praise for my acts (as a justification for filling whole pages), which leave the logician within me apathetic, nor will I mention the bitter reactions, which aroused in me attacks by many of my "colleagues." I addressed myself to only one issue: *Won't "Sem" greet this composition gleefully?*—possibly so. But I agree that the joy of the Semite may prod my "colleagues." If not, it would not be a great tragedy if today's anti-Semitism would disappear, to be succeeded by *Realpolitik*.

Accordingly, "let my fate be tied up with this booklet" [Habeat suum fatum, Libellum].

W. Marr
Written on the tenth of August, 1887, Hamburg

My earliest memories on this subject go back to 1824 or 1825. My father, Heinrich Marr, who was a famous dramatic actor, poet, and director, was employed at that time by the Royal Theater in Hannover. I, his only son, a wild and mischievous child, went to elementary school, in which boys and girls, together in the same class, learned the alphabet, the multiplication table, and the "Our Father." Jewish children could not attend such schools then. The Jews had special elementary schools for their children, which were called "Jewish schools." The Jews managed, however [. . .] to "smuggle" some Benjamin or Rebeka into the Christian school.

In our school, which was administered, to the best of my recollection, by an old maid named Mademoiselle Bertram, there was also one of the offsprings of Jacob, a funny *Bocher* [sic; lit., "youth"] with burning black eyes and curly hair. His name was Blank. This child was the target of all the childish attacks by the Christian-Lutheran German racial instincts which were in fashion then. The children chased, pinched, and pushed him at every opportunity; when this was forbidden to them, they sang nice songs to the little Jew, such as,

"The Jews slaughtered a pig"

or

"Moses took the Jews
through the Red Sea
And Pharaoh pursued them
with all those accompanying him."

I never took part in these songs. I rebelled against this taking advantage of the power of the "majority." I still hadn't learned that a *minority* group could be several times worse than a *majority* group. I still didn't know that one of these could also be brutal, treacherous, devious. I even saw in my mind's eye the images of the "noble-spirited Jews" which my father protrayed in the theater. My chief feeling, however, was empathy for the suffering of the defenseless youth, who bore all the insults and harassments with indifference, and whose parents had apparently not given any thought to the bad treatment he was receiving. The little *Bocher* remained in the school.

During one of the recess periods, when we were in the schoolyard, my anger was aroused, and I began, without a declaration of war, to hit the group of those attacking the Jewish child. The results were a great number of injured faces, bruises, and torn clothes. I, of course, was the most "seriously injured," since the Jewish child did not do anything to aid his savior. In the end, I was the "troublemaker" who started the entire affair, and the prize I received from Mlle. Bertram was six blows from a ruler on my hand, and staying an hour after school as punishment. My father, who did not object per se to the chivalry which I exhibited, nevertheless added two slaps for the *form* of my chivalry, and decreed that I fast, since I had spent dinner-time in confinement.

In my childish innocence, I thought that "if so, then I have to continue, even more forcefully." Father only protested about the form. I would no longer chivalrously intervene on behalf of the "stronger sex" among the Jews, but rather on behalf of the "fairest sex." (Do not forget, dear reader, this was the period during which Romanticism flourished in art and literature, and a stupid little child always absorbs something from the conduct of adults.)

I went to a higher elementary school, where they even dared to touch upon the science of spelling. The former school had actually been a "kindergarten" within four walls. There was not a single Jewish boy, but rather 2 Jewish girls, in the new school. These two were teased just like Benjamin Blank, this time by the girls. This time as well, I set out in defense of the girls, and loudly slapped the cheeks of Christian German girls. Matters did not develop into a big fight this time, but the ruler, the hour of punishment, the fast, and my father's slaps repeated themselves once again. The two girls, however, proved to be better than Benjamin Blank, and secretly brought me a cake ("Jews' cookies," as they were called in Hannover). It seemed to me (the imagination of the children of actors is always more developed) that I had fallen in love with these two Rebekas (perhaps, actually, with the sweet cookies).

And so I already appeared during my youth as a "philo-Semite." I obviously didn't give much academic thought to the Jewish question. Like today's adult philo-Semites, I saw only the oppressed and the oppressors;

out of the pursuit of honor and a lack of understanding, I took a stand by the side of the former.

I stopped such childish philo-Semitic "acts of chivalry" later, when I was a student in the Braunschweig gymnasium, and later a student in the boarding school of a business school. I acquired a certain contempt for anti-Semites, however, in the latter.

The principal and owner of this institution was a true Jew-baiter. It was stated explicitly in the institution's program that "Jews are not accepted as students" (1834). Nevertheless, there were two Jewish students in the boarding school, and two attended classes [. . .] The anti-Semitic clause nevertheless remained in the program, since, externally, it was a sort of compliment for an educational institution not to permit the entry of Jews. Our institution was really "not religious," and most of the children had not even been confirmed. The principal of the institution used to say to his closest friends, "Commercial studies have no connection with the catechism."

But before I forget—here as well, I once performed a philo-Semitic act of bravery which ended in blows. One of the two external ones (cousins by the name of O.), Joseph—a very tall fellow with an offensive blondish appearance, who was called "the goat" by all of us—was a Reform Jew. This being the case, he gladly received from his fellow students a ham sandwich or sausage which he chewed with demonstrative pleasure. The second one, Benjamin O., was a small good-natured lad from an orthodox Jewish home. Joseph "the goat" was such a rotten person that once he gave his cousin Benny a piece of ham sandwich without the latter being aware of this. Poor Benny began to cry when he learned what a sin he had unwittingly committed. "The goat" made fun of him and even teased him to his face; but then several of us fell upon the pork-eater—and I was not the last of them—and rained our blows on him.

It was here that I first felt the instinctive disgust for Reform Jews.

Benjamin was not a sympathetic phenomenon either, but he wanted to remain what he was, and he didn't want to give the impression that he was somehow different. Somewhat later, the healthy childish instinct also revealed within me liberal sophistication.

My father was already known as an artist. It was unavoidable that Jews came into contact with him, since they pushed themselves every-place where they could stick out. (The Jews no longer need this today. They *throw us* out if we don't dance to their tune.) But the truth must be stated frankly: I was blinded by the "spiritual riches" of the Jews, by the Jewish joke, and—first and foremost—by the Jewish irony which was directed at themselves. I found among the Jewish eaters of pork those who had attained complete "emancipation." Heine, Börne, and associates had already made their appearance as well. Prophets of freedom! The lack of equal rights for Jews appeared to me to be an injustice.

I was too young and inexperienced to examine the *racial question,* and my father was too naive for this. So naive, that years later, when I was already an anti-Semite [. . .], he asked me the question, half in jest and half-seriously, Weren't all humans descended from the Jews? Adam was, after all, the first human. My father wasn't expert enough on the Bible to think of Sem, Ham, and Japheth.

The essence of his philo-Semitism, and for a long time of mine as well, was *"A people which gives us so many spiritually rich pork-eaters must receive equal political and civil rights from us."* This erroneous and convenient conclusion, which turns exceptions and shallow external charm into the rule, caused us to take the path of philo-Semitism.

It should be noted, however, that I could not withhold my criticism of the inconsistent and lazy "Christian state." Just as the Jews "outwardly" could not be accepted to the schools in Hannover and Braunschweig, the same was the case in Bremen, the city in which I had to spend my time on my commercial studies, and in which, legally, Jews could not even reside. These places hummed with Jewish students, clerks, and retailers; many half-Jews were also to be found among the merchants. The Christian Bremenites believed, or presumed to believe, that the waters could not only cure rheumatism, but also change *Jews* into Germans. Yes! They went even farther! "Mr. Cohen etc., is being baptized, he left Judaism."

Yes. [. . .] We will return later to report on anti-Semitism and philo-Semitism.

An anti-Semitic comedy was being conducted in the city of my forefathers, Hamburg, but not as in Bremen. Hamburg had been a haven for Israel since the persecutions of Jews in Spain and Portugal. Jews could **"reside"** in Hamburg without numerical restrictions. They could not be **"citizens."** They were "protected residents," without political rights. They were forbidden to own homes. They registered their homes in the names of their Christian servants; to be on the safe side, the Jew demanded from his servant a note stating that he was only the nominal owner of the house, in accordance with the regulations, but not in practice. Jewish lawyers were not permitted to appear before any court. The solution was to find a Christian "assistant." In places where there were "juicy" positions, they preferred to *be baptized* to Christianity, and became the presidents of the commercial court. . . .

All this was a long time before 1848. They were all learned people, pleasing in their contacts with their surroundings.

I am perfectly knowledgeable of the Jewish "spiritual riches," the Jewish joke and self-irony, but as an adult, I add that these qualities among the Jews *are not suitable to my society, which aspires to be Christian-German;* I think that religion and nationalism cannot, *to their detriment,* ignore racial differences.

*

I now come to the second chapter of my career as a philo-Semite. I ask the reader not to censure me because philo-Semitism had not left me at this stage. I'm returning to the period during which I ignored many negative Jewish characteristics because I saw the positive few, and during which being a *consistent* philo-Semite found favor in my eyes. Yes, found favor in my eyes. I was blinded then, all the time, by the wisdom and the enticing qualities which the descendent of Sem left—then—for the philo-Semite.

1839–1841: Vienna

In the meantime, my father had become a member of the Imperial Theater, and a famous artist.

I completed my commercial studies in Bremen. I wanted to see the world, of which I knew only Hannover, Braunschweig, Bremen, and Hamburg.

It was very easy for my father to find work for me among his Jewish friends in Vienna in the office of a trade company. It was self-understood that this would be work for Jews, since already then, in 1839, all the banking and commercial transactions were in Jewish hands, even the Hungarian pig trade.

I therefore entered one of the distinguished businesses. There were two owners, brothers, friends of my father: one was Samuel (Sammi) B., an old wizened bachelor, and the other was Pepi (Joseph), who aspired to be a sportsman, with 24 horses in his stable. Every day he scattered straw in the large yard so that the "race horses" could stroll around in comfort. A man with a good soul, and a large amount of Jewish pursuit of honor. For him, world history always began when he, Pepi B., "traveled with the **Prince** Trautmannsdorf to London, to purchase horses." This was his weakness. "Wait, such and such happened when I was in London with **Trautmannsdorf.**" All the memories of my master, Pepi B., were tied up with his trip with this nobleman. When they teased him about this, he would respond cordially, since he was not an ignorant Jew, but rather an educated person, who knew how to dress properly. In short, I came *stante pede* as the only non-Jew in the office of a first-rate Jewish business.

I can only state that I was received by the employer and all my associates—despite my being the only non-Jew—in the best and most collegial manner. (Much better than I was received by my colleagues, the *modern anti-Semites,* to whom my bluntness was repulsive!)

There was also an old Jewish *jack-of-all-trades* named Sch. in the business, with a red, fox-colored wig. My employer's father had brought him into the business in his will, as a sort of supervisor or chief clerk; I soon felt, as a "goi" [sic], and even more so as one who was liked by the employer and the workers, that I displeased him.

This same redwig had a nephew in our branch, a fellow so stupid you could smash walls with his head. The business was in a decline. The branch in Pesch was closed. The redwig and his nephew in Pesch needed a new place, and so, **the redwig fired me, the goi, behind my employer's back,** without giving any reason. It was *my father* who received the dismissal notice. I returned home in a good mood, and found my father depressed.

"Did you do anything which could be held against you?"

"Me? Why would you think that? I'm perfectly in order!"

"Read this!"

Damn. The next day, I stormed into my employer's private office, as was fitting for a "coarse Hamburgian." *What's going on with Mr. B.?* !!!— — —

Neither Sam nor Pepi B. had the slightest knowledge of my dismissal. But the "jack-of-all-trades" appointed by my employer's dead father, the redwig, did what he did as the chief clerk [procurator] of his own accord, and the business had to lump it.

To tell the truth, Pepi B. called in the chief secretary, and I received an exceptional letter of recommendation about my industriousness and ability. And so—the act of a good Jew—he found a place of work for me within two weeks, working for A. von W., Rothschild's nephew.

Dear reader, I am trying to be fair. This time I was a victim of *Orthodox* Judaism, to which the redwig was affiliated. I would later fall victim to Reform Judaism.

I was liked and privileged ten times as much in my present place of employment as in my previous one; once again, I was the only "goi" in the office.

Why was I so liked? Why did I receive presents on my birthday and the New Year? A disciplined north German clerk, loyal to his work, would smile: because, for the sake of convenience, I completed the accounts in the books after work hours. It was the custom in Vienna then to close accounts precisely at 5 o'clock, with everyone leaving afterwards. During the course of several weeks I stayed in the office, at times until 10 at night, in order to make the work easier for myself, i.e., so that I would not have to go over the accounts during the day's tumult. And so I became the favorite child of the master and mistress. The latter would bring me tea, wine, and sweets at the office when I stayed there—and I repeat this—*out of practical considerations of convenience*—5 hours more than my fellow workers during the November and December evenings. When I had to go out on errands, my employer's cab was at my disposal, with a decked-out coachman and a purebred horse. In short—I was in Heaven.

And then the Stock Exchange crisis came (1841). Cutbacks. There was a "colleague" in our office, who was even stupider than the nephew of the redwig at B.'s, and who was the butt of ridicule by the employer and all the workers. Someone who was about to be fired twice a month. The chief clerk, a Jew from Breslau, called him a "genuine rhinoceros."

And what happened? I, who was liked by the employer, his wife, and the workers, including the "genuine rhinoceros," I, the "goi," was fired, together with another non-Jew, a storeroom worker. Of course, I received a letter of recommendation even better than the one I had received from B. I don't want to quote what was written there about the *"qualified and loyal* young man." This evaluation naturally served as a letter of recommendation for all Israel and the surrounding area.

Why shouldn't I call *this* employer by name? Adolf von Wertheimstein took his leave of me personally, with tears in his eyes. He was a complete gentleman, a good person, but—he had no alternative. It was the "goi" who *had* to bear the consequences of the economic crisis.

Good manners prevent me from writing what he and his wife said to me when we drank our last cup of tea.

I went to Switzerland. I received a letter from one of my associates after three months, stating, "The employer misses you. Matters have improved. Come back to Vienna. I am writing on behalf of the boss. Your salary will be doubled." I rejoiced. And then the afternoon sun shone on the Alps. Lake Zurich was a carpet of the colors of the rainbow, and the music of the celestial spheres resounded within me: "My thoughts [. . .] are towards the Alps" (Herwegh).[1] "My dear colleague Julius Fischhof!" I wrote back in a letter, "Greetings to the boss, greetings to his wife, greetings to the old servant. Greetings to everyone, even to the 'genuine rhinoceros' there. I am staying here in Switzerland."

What was the moral of the story? I had been in two Jewish companies. Except for the "redwig" at B.'s, the supervisors and employees were all wonderful people. My Jewish colleagues really were. But *the racial question* was of decisive importance, even for these Jews. The "goi" had to be sacrificed, as much as they liked and pampered him. On the one hand, the German "noble horse," and on the other a Jewish rhinocerous or ass—but the noble horse *had* to make way for the ass and the rhinoceros.

These thoughts did not cross my mind then. I was, and remained, a philo-Semite, since I had not considered, beyond the personal friendliness which cost nothing, the racial sentiments of the Jews *against the "gojim"* [sic; "non-Jews"].

I have become wiser now. I am certain that the two *Biedermanns*— there! I'll call them by name—and Adolf Von Wertheimstein had clearly not wanted to fire me. They showed this in their statements, their documents, and the presents they gave, beyond what was coming to me.

---

[1] George Herwegh, 1817–1875, poet. He fled to Switzerland in 1839, moving to Paris in 1841. He was one of the prominent revolutionaries of 1848. Marr had been influenced by his poetry when he was still in Switzerland.

The race simply *could not* act differently. The biggest Jewish rhinoceros or ass was worth more than the best "Aryan."

When I reflect once again on those hours . . . dear reader, I am filled with bitterness, since I am aware that I fell victim to racial hatred by educated Jews. I don't want to attack Pepi Biedermann or Adolf von Wertheimstein. From the material aspect, the two Jews treated me much more fairly than my "colleagues" who made a business of anti-Semitism. I am merely establishing a fact here: the Jew cannot overcome his race. The Jew will prefer to sacrifice the Aryan, who is of benefit to him, when his *race* is the deciding factor.

Modern business-of-anti-Semitism— — —

But I do not want to put the cart before the horse.

(. . .) If some of the friendly Jewish associates of my youth are still alive, I would ask them to smile together with the old clown. The old clown runs on at the mouth now. This essay is an anti-Semitic will with humor. I'm willing to bet that the modern anti-Semites will be angrier with it than the Jews!

And so, to the matter of J.W. Moss, the chief clerk of H. Biedermann's sons in Vienna! (. . .)

When I was with Biedermann and Sons in Vienna, I learned about the usurious "strangulation" deals with the Hungarian nobility, which were conducted on a large scale, since I was the one who copied the contracts in this area in German, Hungarian, and even in Italian. I must state, however, that the members of the Biedermann family, copying the nobility, did not become rich from the "strangulation deals" with the noble masters. Pepi Biedermann was so possessed by the obsessive pursuit of honor, wanting to be a nobleman himself, that the masters made deals at his expense, and not the opposite.

The "contracts" with the Hungarian nobility—[. . .]! This is the truth. They had to mortgage in advance the pigs, the plum crop, the wool, the wine, etc., at half of their real value. And this was not all! They had to waive the "right of appeal concerning their property" for themselves and their heirs. Dear reader, the "right of appeal concerning their property" (*appellata in Dominium*) meant at that time that it was forbidden for a nobleman to mortgage part of his estate. I don't find anything wrong with this. Why should lazy noblemen in need of money be able to hide behind class rules from the Middle Ages when they need money. The emphasis in these usurious deals was that the Jew received the produce from these lands at a price *30–50% lower* than the market price, and received high interest, between 10 and 15%.

The noblemen Graf Betllin, Ziesig, Pesteticz, Nowogy, Blucosiz, and others came to our office then [. . .]. Impressive-looking fellows, swimming in riches [. . .]. The biggest speculator, Pepi Biedermann, could write off 50% of the debt owed him by the Hungarian noblemen, the same people who today grovel *in the dust* before the Jews. My boss, Pepi Biedermann, was himself a "nobleman"—due to the pursuit of honor. This pursuit of honor can be explained, however, by human nature.

Once I had to appear in the reception room and announce the appearance of Mr. [. . .]. He liked me and my northern German. I was polite but reserved; I already possessed a revolutionary temperament to some degree. I didn't debase myself before the nobility like my Jewish associates; when they spoke French among themselves, I also spoke French. It seemed to me that my French was better and more elegant than theirs.

And so, I also came to know on these occasions the German-Bohemian prince Trautmannsdorf, whose mustache was indeed not as intimidating as that of the Hungarian noblemen, but who was much more polished than they were and had more class pride than they did, for which I had always appreciated the nobility. Nothing is more repellent than a nobleman addressing one with the haughty formulation "my brother" or "my friend." I prefer [. . .] and, thank God, I know *German* noblemen, whom I have known for 25 years, and with whom I correspond, but I always maintained *the rules of etiquette*. I'm sorry for the nobleman who tries to arouse the impression that he's associating with his social inferiors, and I'm contemptuous of the bourgeois who aspires to push himself *higher*.

And so, Count Trautmannsdorf was pleased with me, and he turned to my boss, and said, "Send me the little Hamburger with the contract" (a loan, of course). I appeared in the office [. . .] the following Sunday, at the beginning of July 1840, at 10 a. m.

"But Mr. von Marr! Don't you know? You are supposed to go to Prince von Trautmannsdorf!!"

"Yes, but I want to wash first."

"Please, forget about washing. Go put on a frock coat."

"I won't hear of it! I'm going on business matters to the prince."

"You're ruining the good name of the company," the cashier shouted.

"Nonsense." In short, I went down to the Danube and washed. To the cashier's amazement, I returned to the office, wearing the elegant [. . .], and strolled to the nearby [. . .] street. I gave my coat to the doorman.

"His Excellency is busy."

"Damnation! He's the one who asked me to come."

"His Excellency is in the stable."

"It doesn't matter. Then I'll go. Give him the card. I'm coming from Biedermann's business house."

(Remember, dear reader, that you are a Prussian by birth and a *Hamburger* by birth appears before you.)

The fellow with the brass buttons and the three-cornered hat on his empty head sent the card in, and, within half a minute, a servant led me into the stable. His Excellency "Long" Trautmannsdorf (he was a very tall person) was sitting on a chair of hay in a night coat, and was marking horses.

"One moment please," the prince said. "Can't you see that this filly is exceptional?"

"She indeed is, but the Walachian horse there seems to be just as superior to me."

"Are you an expert on horses, Mr. Von Marr?"

"Your Excellency, why do you need that draft horse [. . .] I prefer the Meklenburg breeding stables. The next generation can be created there. Perhaps [. . .]"

My fluency concerning horses impressed the prince.

"Natzil! Natzil! Bring the guest upstairs. I'm coming immediately, Mr. Von Marr."

Natzil (Ignaz), the stable boy, led me to a living room which was neither too narrow nor long, and which was full of plants, 4 parrots, and 2 monkeys. I amused myself greatly with the latter. His Excellency Prince Trautmannsdorf came a quarter of an hour later, and apologized for the long delay. I was tactful enough *not* to say, "Not at all, it's perfectly all right." The contract and loan were read and signed among the plants, parrots, and monkeys.

"Now we will eat breakfast," the prince said.

I was hungry after swimming in the river. We ate a solid, not extravagant, breakfast. A cold meal. Fine wines. There were also excellent cigars.

Three p. m.

I returned to the office; the cashier was still there.

"God in heaven, where did you stay so long?"

"With Trautmannsdorf! I ate breakfast."

"In *that* suit? Without a *frock coat!!* Unbelievable."

Dear reader, you can rest assured that even without the frock coat I was the perfect "dandy" in Vienna.

The next day, Monday, the entire office was abuzz!

What? Marr visited the Prince's stables? He invited Marr to breakfast? Marr returned to the office only after three hours!! The world is collapsing!!

Yes, dear reader, this is an example of Jewish humility in Vienna in 1840!

An educated nobleman receives an educated German madman, who comes to him on business matters, as an educated *person*.

And Israel is amazed!

As far as I was concerned, I am convinced that the proud nobleman would not have given me even [. . .] if I had appeared in a frock coat and white tie. No. When all's said and done, clothes do not make the man. The external impression does this. I think that I could reveal my gentlemanliness, in accordance with education and life style, in my home. But there was an uncomfortable excitement in the Jewish office over Marr's eating breakfast in the place in which his associates had been dealt with *previously* with businesslike and pertinent brevity, coolly and politely.

It must be stated, in all justness, that my Jewish associates did not bear a grudge against me after the initial wave of amazement had passed. They said, "Yes, *that's* it. Our nobility prefers something *new,* and you, Mr. von Marr, are a novelty for them."

Now let us go from the aristocratic circles to those which give off the smell of garlic.

As with almost all the Jewish businesses, A. Von Wertheimstein also had a "jack-of-all-trades." Like the errand boy in the newspapers, he was a messenger for everything, even for the type of transactions which honest people prefer not to do.

Isak Loesch was the name of the small Jew, Polish of course, dressed in a dirty caftan shiny with grease and made of some unknown material. When he appeared in the office, he announced his presence, even before he himself came through the door, by exuding a cloud of unpleasant Oriental odors. We all closed our noses when he opened his mouth to speak, and the chief clerk passed his snuff among us. Apart from his "inherent characteristics," however, Isak was a very amusing fellow. Since I was still a philo-Semite then, I was ired by my Jewish associates' petty and painful teasing of their poor coreligionist, the soap-hater. I filled my two nostrils with snuff and took a stand for the Pole.

"Mr. von Marr! Your friend Isak Loesch has arrived."

"Give Loesch a kiss."

This was the kind of teasing I received from my Jewish associates.

Isak was grateful. On occasion he would bring his defender an orange, which gave off such a strong odor of garlic as to render it inedible, but I was touched by his good intention.

Isak had the disgraceful habit of embezzling a small sum every month, to the company's detriment. In simple language—he hid small sums of money on their way to the cashier's. Since he was valuable, and useful in every matter, the matter passed without problems. The chief clerk made do with reprimands: "Loesch! I've got *rachmones* [sic; Yiddish "pity"] for you; I already should have put you in *tefisah* [sic; Yiddish "jail"] ten times. The next time that you'll be a *ganef* [sic; Yiddish "thief"], this will really happen, even if Mr. von Marr will be your friend ten times over."

The good-natured chief clerk said to me, "Make your 'friend' Loesch mend his ways."

"My friend" Loesch embezzled 400 gulden the next month. This was too much. The entire office was in uproar, and Isak threw himself *at my feet,* begging that I help him to escape unscathed once again. He promised "in the name of his children" (whom he did *not* have), and in the name of who knows how many other sacred objects, that he would not return to his evil ways. I made a mistake. I treated the entire matter with humor, went to the boss, and said, "Mr. von Wertheimstein, give the little thief another chance, but don't entrust him with even a single gulden! You yourself are guilty for his having stolen." The boss was, as I have said, a goodhearted, gentle fellow. He forgave "my friend Loesch" for this transgression also, and did as I had suggested: Isak was forbidden to touch the cashbox.

And now comes the most interesting part!

I became the best-liked personality among the Polish Jews, from the *schnorrer* [sic; Yiddish "beggar"] to the millionaire dressed in silk and satin.

—The good little blond *orel* (*orel* was the name used then in the language of the Polish Jews for a Christian, in a positive sense, as opposed to *goy*), they called me.

And so the "good little blond *orel*" saved the member of the Jewish religion from his Jewish oppressors!

"Mr. von Marr," it was said in the office, "if you want 10,000 gulden pieces from the Polish Jews, you will receive them."

Dear reader! I was a "featherweight" then. "My friend Isak Loesch" should have been hung ten times, and I was his "defender," since the ridiculous thief amused me.

The moral! A serious moral from this story! *Israel rejoiced,* since *Israel* was not obliged *to hand over Israel to the flame* of the gallows. The little blond *orel,* in a mischievous mood, saved the little Jewish thief, and all the Polish Jews, all the Polish-Jewish stock exchange loved the "little blond *orel*" even more, since he didn't demand anything in return.

Isak Losech was apparently hung later in Krotin for other small thefts . . .

You see, dear reader, I had proved my good attitude towards the Jew from my youth until I was 21 years old, out of pity and a youthful philo-Semitic tendency. I even gave ten gulden *out of my pocket,* which was not overflowing, to this Isak Loesch, so that he would mend his ways. My Jewish associates filled their mouths with laughter at my pursuit of philo-Semitic principles. My Jewish associates erred! It was *humor,* critical irony, which motivated my moderate spirit to stand by the Jewish thief who had cheated his Jewish brethren. I asked myself, "Why should the small fry be hung when the giants go free."

I was the "favorite" of all the Polish Jews in Vienna, who drank my health whenever I paid for the beer they drank in the "3 Ravens" inn, taking advantage of the "little blond *orel"* with their sympathy reeking of garlic. I, Wilhelm Marr, today's Jew-baiter, was a "most desired person" among Viennese Jews in 1841, since I defended the Polish Jewish thief with my youthful philo-Semitic *humor,* without being aware of this. My sense of humor doesn't regret this, even today. (. . .)

In conclusion: I confess to the charge that, due to philo-Semitic humor, I became the defense attorney of my ridiculous Jewish thief, who nestled within the business of his fellow Jews like a louse in wool.

Man is only a "young fool" at the age of 21; I confess to the *charge* that I was a *philo-Semitic* "young fool" until the age of 41![2] And afterwards . . . as well, but in *another* area.

I want my confession to be complete, because it is only after this complete confession that I will have the right to level severe criticism no less at *modern anti-Semitism* than at Judaism. No less? No, much more!

*

I don't know of anything more embarrassing than rich Jews and bedbugs. "Your Jews, Germans of the Reich, have more political rights than ours, in Austria. But ours have much more social power in Vienna, and this is intolerable." The author of these words was a Jewish clerk in the business of Herman von Wertheimstein, my employer's brother [. . .] with Rothschild. The Jewish clerk was named Sendler—he was a perfect devil, both in his external appearance, and in his soul. Furthermore, he was a sort of "black sheep" within Israel itself. Of course, he was immature, as I was. But "beautiful people find one another," and we, the young ones, formed a sort of circle. Our circle comprised 4 Christians, including one French-speaking Belgian and myself, and 5 Jews.

Heine and Börne were our prophets. It is the undeniable truth that these two Jews were pathbreakers to the ideas of freedom during the period in which the foolish and hypocritical reaction ruled. There is a simple explanation for this. Israel was even more oppressed than we, the Germans, were. Israel incited us, in order to attain achievements for itself. This, in the final analysis, is the entire secret of liberal and revolutionary Judaism, in the past and in the present as well, with Judaism aspiring towards unlimited power.

I'll remind myself here, in time, that the intention of this essay of mine is not to serve as a chronologically arranged political autobiography, to which purpose I fill paper during my leisure hours with philo- and anti-Semitic thoughts. It will therefore suffice to state that we would read *Heine and Börne* in secret in our circle, and were excited by them. At times, when the windows and doors were tightly closed, we sang the "Marseillaise." This was the time of the rule of Metternich and Radetzky

[2] I.e., until Marr published *Der Judenspiegel.*

in Austria, and we knew the nature of the residence [the prison] in Spielberg, near Brunn. We also knew that the Italian *Carbonari* were not committing crimes different from those which we, foolish youth, committed twice a week in Vienna.

Our circle also included the son of a rich Jew from Poland named Ziller, from Lemberg. The father was involved in various Polish subversive activities, i.e., a "freedom fighter." His son was a volunteer in a Jewish commercial office and a member of our circle.

"Read," Ziller said to me one day when I visited him in his room.

"These are Hebrew letters, I can't understand them."

"I'll translate them into German for you."

Ziller *senior,* the "freedom fighter," had written three pages of reproach to his son! "You dared to go and be *baptized!*" the letter began. "You dress like the Christians!" (The removal of the caftan and *paias* [sic; "sideburns" worn by observant Jews]—this is what they said then in Yiddish-Polish about Jews who had been baptized.) Thus began a flood of reprimands by Ziller *père* against Ziller *fils.* As far as I can remember, they did not lack a dark Molochistic tone. The young Ziller was broken.

"How is it possible," I called, "that your 'old man,' a liberal Jew, knows how to scold and curse in such a manner. Why, your father was with us when you, his son, went in a 'caftan' to the coffee house. Why, your father was a Polish lover of freedom. But," I added, "what are you doing? Are you packing your bags?"

"Here, on the fourth page, there's a message for me," Ziller wailed to me: *"You must come immediately to Lemberg, or else a curse and destruction will come upon you, and you will not find rest even in the grave."*

Dear reader, I was 21 years old then. The young Ziller had a beautiful sister whom I courted energetically, with honorable intentions, since she was an inspired girl.

I proposed, with youthful mischievous humor, "I'll dictate the reply to your father's letter *to Rosalie."*

"Forget it," the young Ziller said, "you don't know the rules preserving *the link between us Jews.* None of us can break the *iron ring."*

"But Heinrich Heine broke it," I shouted.

"Just wait and see, Heine too will return to being *Jewish."*

I didn't understand the meaning of my friend Ziller's prophecy then.

"Leave me alone! I must!" Ziller cried when I wanted to empty out his half-full suitcase.

He cried. Not the suitcase, but my friend young Ziller. Two days later, he was on his way to Lemberg. I heard no more of him.

I can conclude my Viennese philo-Semitic memoirs here. I feel the need to add, however, so as not be considered a clown chasing after honor, that I spent many very fine hours in Vienna with beautiful Jewesses. Beautiful Jewesses from "good families." This is how it was.

My father Heinrich Marr, an actor in the Hofburg Theater, was liked by the Jews *since*—since he played *Jewish roles* on the stage, not like the virtuosos, Jewish caricatures (*abmauschelte*), and not in the usual theatrical personification of the Jew.

All Israel believed that Marr had been, at the very least, a converted Jew! And the father and son were philo-Semites! The father—due to a misunderstanding, and the son—out of *idealism*.

It was already contemptible *to speak* of "the religion." Anyone who was *a friend of the Jews* was thought to be a Jew or was "annexed" to the descendants of Jews, without having a say in the matter.

And as for myself? I didn't ponder the Jewish question. I found people with "revolutionary" positions close to mine among the Jews. The revolutionary diletantism which guided me then found kindred spirits mainly among the Children of Israel.

From the political, social and [. . .] aspect, in "the art of love," I was then a philo-Semite in Vienna.

Yes, the "fairer sex" among Israel did not become unfaithful to me, even when I became a famous "Jew-baiter." *The Jewish vanity*—of the *women* . . . but I will not put the cart before the horse.

The Testament of an Anti-Semite*

To my sorrow, I must begin this essay, the last one dealing with the Jews, with a *self-accusation*.

I assume that most of my readers are familiar with the pamphlet "The Victory of Judaism over Germanism, from a Nonreligious Viewpoint," which was published by H. Kostenobel in Bern. I began to write this pamphlet in 1878, and it was published in the spring of 1879. Its motto was *"Vae victis!"* and its concluding words were *"Finis Germaniae."* Eleven editions were published, and not "piddling editions," as the Jewish and philo-Semitic press initially tried to establish.

I received countless letters of appreciation and thanks from all sides, from proletarians and princes, Counts and [. . .], and so on. In truth, all my windows should have been broken for the despairing statements about my German people and the censure of Israel which I published openly.

But that's the way people are. When you put a mirror before their

---

* StA Hamburg, Nachlass Marr BVb Testament eines Antisemiten, 1891. Due to the many repetitions and erasures in the manuscript, I have deleted extensive sections of the original text, especially in the latter portion of the *Testament*. The symbol (. . .) signifies a deletion, and the symbol [. . .] signifies a word which is illegible in the original text.

nose, so they can look at their shame and degradation—they jump for joy (see Heine and Börne). If you praise them for qualities which they don't at all possess, which they may have possessed in the past, they rejoice. The important thing is to be properly excited, whether you mock or flatter the people. Viewed objectively, the latter activity appears to me to be more harmful than the former, if it becomes necessary to choose between the two. Judge *Heine and Börne* as you will, you cannot deny that they put Judaism before "patriotism," which was for Heine, specifically, "[. . .]." The two were a *stimulating* phenomenon in their time. It's not necessary to have *lived* then in order to understand that their destructive derision, which should, by right, have aroused every patriotic soul, enjoyed such success with the German nation! Did I say *"nation?"* Why, there isn't any German nation! Bored cosmopolitanism ruled Germany, both internally and externally. This cosmopolitanism found for itself, and had to find for itself, an easily impressed audience. Its mouthpiece: these two authors, from among cosmopolitan Israel.

Today, when I reread Heine's writings, and am reminded of those times, I have to smile to myself. After the miserable romantic madness of Germanism [. . .] of the student members of the German *Burschenschaften* (whose members were virtuosos in later becoming honest citizens, courtiers, and confidential advisors), we all became supporters of the cosmopolitan spirit, so much so that we related to Israel as the representative of cosmopolitanism, and it was considered *fashionable* to be a philo-Semite.

Just as *Börne and Heine* were the recognized political leaders of the Germans during the 1830's and 1840's, Karl *Marx* and Ferdinand *Lassalle* sprang up as socialist semi-gods.

The younger generation of our day, which did not live through those times, and especially the modern anti-Semites, does not *understand* these phenomena at all.

But, did we then have *other progressive leaders* besides *these four Jews?* Did we have the right to make "the Jews" responsible for the national "failures" of those times, now that 40–50 years have passed?

Have we forgotten that the political disappointments following the "wars of liberation" had already created in the 1830's a cult of idol worship for the dangerous despot—*and genius*—Napoleon I? Have we forgotten that a pure German such as Richard Wagner wrote the music for Heine's song, *"Two Grenadiers Marched to France,"* a song which was sung and publicized in all the concerts, (. . .)

Do you who are making a business-of-anti-Semitism from anew want to learn and understand how it was possible that four insolent and brilliant Jews became political and socialist guides—two in the elite of society, by means of *Börne and Heine,* and two in its bottom rung, among the proletarians, by means of *Karl Marx and Lassalle?* If so, try to reenter that period and its mood, the real conditions of that period, which in 1844 had forced even Arnold Ruge, the most faithful and pure German patriot, the republican exile from Brighton, to cry, *"Nulla salus sine gallis"* ["only the French will bring deliverance"]. This was the same Ruge—a person whom I was proud to call a *friend*—who wrote in 1870 from exile to the *Gartenlaube* newspaper, when it *seemed* that the dawn was rising on a better future: "Anyone not supporting Prussia and Germany is a traitor!"

This same Ruge had also taken part in the war of liberation; he had spent much time in the company of the Teutomanic *student associations* with their black-red-gold colors, and had paid for these harmless games with a term in the prison cellars. This would not happen, of course, to the modern Teutomanic business of *anti-Semitism.* These try to draw close to [. . .] liberals, to Kaiser Friedrich III, to the "throne and the altar," despite the fact that those *prefer to ignore them!*— —(. . .) My dear modern anti-Semites: *Börne and Heine,* who have been resting in peace for the past 40–50 years, had a greater influence on the German nation during one decade than you will, with your retrospective romanticism, in the course of fifty years.

The influence of *Börne and Heine* was not moral, according to the conceptions of our time, but it was an outlet for the feelings of many millions who opposed the *status quo* of *those* times with much more clarity and skeptical awareness than modern anti-Semitism thinks fit while licking the boots of the "throne and altar." You no longer have any support *among the people.* The people is afflicted with social democracy. Its [anti-Semitism's] influence is also limited among the "educated" and semieducated bourgeoisie. The latter still speaks, to the present day, *in the language of Heine and Börne,* and is not interested in the lives of the beer-drinking leaders, the gay "Heil" shouters of modern anti-Semitism.

You haven't taken over a single *large city,* so that you could say, we set the mood (. . .)

I am a *nineteenth century man, and I experienced* all the metamorphoses and crises of this century, its mistakes and truths, honestly, and with complete faith! But I am incapable of degenerating to the *decadence* of the worldview of modern anti-Semitism, in whose eyes *Heine* is not a *poet, Börne* is not a master of *style,* and *Spinoza* is not a philosopher.

I have learned to understand people in the context of *their times;* this nevertheless did not *prevent me* from *opposing* the erection of a monument to Heine in Düsseldorf. I *reveal to you today* that I wasn't content *with articles in the press,* but I also acted *privately, in places of authority. . . .*

Does the learned "mob" know Heinrich Heine? When the struggle surrounding the memorial to Heine was at its climax, I read *selections* from Heine to the wrathful anti-Semites, *without citing their source!*

Despicable! It was despicable!

My God in Heaven! Look at your animal kingdom! I thought, how large it is.

And God knows!—I would have been, *to this day, Heine's* bitterest enemy, if he had written *today* what he had *justifiably* written fifty years ago.

But I don't have the *ability* to be a drunken anti-Semitic *vandal,* judging people apart from the context of their times.

You can wriggle like a worm around a needle! The Jews *Börne and Heine, Lassalle and Karl Marx* have remained the fathers of today's political and socialist *revolutionary movement.* They will remain so for a long time to come, since the boot-lickers who make a business out of anti-Semitism, surrounding the "throne and altar," gathered only an insignificant minority around them, and were never a *factor of historical-cultural importance.*

I'll say this without embellishment; the "throne and altar," which are *immersed in materialism,* are making *better deals* with *circumcized* Judaism than with commercialized anti-Semitism which calls "Heil" and downs a mug of beer, with its leaders who lead a debauched life, at the expense of the organization, and who made anti-Semitism a business [*Geschäftsantisemitismus*].

I want to state my piece as an anti-Semite!!

If we cannot shake ourselves free of the yoke of the *leaders* of the business-of-anti-Semitism, then it would be preferable for *the Jew* to rule us, for the Jew, out of his own interest, would not suck *our last drop of blood* from us!

As much as I'm an avowed enemy of social democracy, I can't shut myself off from an awareness of the fact that social *democracy*—despite all its mistakes and errors, yes, and even despite all its *"Judaization"*—belongs, if not to the *future,* then at least to the *present.*

II

This, or something like this, was my mood in 1878–79, when I published the above-mentioned essay, after already having challenged Judaism's increasing power in my *Der Judenspiegel,* 16 years earlier (1862). I had done this *from the ultrarevolutionary outlook which I possessed then,* since I was not concerned with the Jewish question, but only demanded that the Jews discard their religious [confessional] Judaism on the junk pile of world history, and the same for the Christians. I claimed then that the "crossbreeding" of the Semitic race with the Aryan one would take place naturally the moment that the religious barrier was torn asunder. The influence of the somewhat confused *Der Judenspiegel,* which appeared in five editions within a year and a quarter, vanished a long time ago. Israel forgave me for having gone too *far.* The hidden anti-Semites forgave me for *not* having gone far enough.

But *Der Judenspiegel* did have results, not only for me personally. *All* the writers who challenged the absolute Jewish rule *were removed from the daily press in the course of time.*

How great was the foolishness of the Jews!

The personal bitterness in the struggle for existence against Israel was thus created. I don't intend to deny that I also shared in this personal bitterness.

Since 1862–3, however, I distanced myself from dealing with the Jewish question, and did my best in journalistic life.

I lived in Berlin in 1878. My best friends, Jews and Christians alike, put obstacles in my way, so that I would not be able to earn my *daily bread* in the Berlin press, not even as a belletrist. The former did this from pent-up *hatred,* the latter from *fear* of the power of the Jewish press.

I met then in Berlin a young, travel-wise botanist, Dr. G. P., a hair-raising anti-Semite (Shh! Don't let anyone hear!). This person was excited then by Stoecker and his social Christianity. This person was excited at the same time, however, by the ultraconservative newspaper *Germania,* and so I jokingly called him "Mortimer," according to Schiller's *Maria Stuart.*

"Come join Stoecker," he called to me.

"I wouldn't consider," I replied, "cooperating with orthodox, church-Christian anti-Semitism."

"If so, then join the anti-Semitic ultramontagnists."

"From the frying pan into the fire. No thank you."

"If so," P-Y called, "join the *social democrats.* Maybe you'll succeed in attaining there what Stoecker couldn't."

"I'm sorry," I replied, "Nature has not granted me the talent of playing a *comic* role in *serious* matters."

The Victory of Judaism over Germanism came into being in this mood.

I recognized the *historical fact* that, during the course of 2000 years, Israel in Germany had succeeded in encircling the German world time and again, and Protestant or Catholic *Christianity* are powerless against this encirclement. And so is even social democracy. The chemical mystery of Judaism's mission in society, if one can speak in such a manner, became clear to me. It was a crude fabrication by the Semites and philo-Semites, not to evaluate my essay as being of a serious nature. At any rate, I made a great, serious, terrible mistake, when I permitted myself, *after* the writing of my essay *The Victory of Judaism,* to return to activity in the anti-Semitic movement. I paid for this dearly, and profoundly regretted it. For the fraud of business-of-anti-Semitism was later built on the popularity of my name and at my expense.

"Let's forget this." I am *forbidden* to complain about the thievery of the business-of-anti-Semitism, even if it came at my expense, after I was foolish enough to fall into the net of those making a business out of anti-Semitism.

It was my cultural-philosophical duty and commitment *to shut my mouth* after *The Victory of Judaism, and to rest my pen,* instead of being swept up in the struggle which was only "the anti-Semitism of thieves" by *gangs* of anti-Semites.

But even today I still acknowledge the mysterious mission of Judaism in world history. Whether it is pleasant for us or not is not relevant. World history teaches that *it is impossible to kill Israel.* It is most certainly not possible by means of the collection of alms by those making a business out of anti-Semitism and by means of nice manifestos written by Fritsch.

For the anti-Semitic "business" cannot compete with the Jewish one.

I admit that I "sinned" against Jews and Christians. Not for *writing The Victory of Judaism,* but for falling from the *frying pan* into the *fire* of the business-of-anti-Semitism. (I admit to my sin of cooperating, for ten years, with a gang of swindlers, if we are to use the expressions of Johannes Scherr.)[1]

All this did not befall me because of my arrogance, since I refrained from any acclamation when I was in Berlin, making do with the saying, "The pen is mightier than the sword." I did not attend party congresses and conventions, nor did I belong to any anti-Semitic society. These were the soil from which the various public figures sprouted. They can be forgiven with philosophical tranquility for having squeezed my time, money, and energy to the last drop, like a lemon. Most of the guilt lies with me. I *should not* have become personally involved in the movement after *The Victory of Judaism,* especially after I had already seen in the first months into whose hands the movement had fallen! All anti-Semitism was a *sport* for distinguished people, and a *business* for untrained anti-Semites, and this is so to this day.

III

I will mention a number of moments from my personal experience, only in order to satisfy curiosity, only for amusement and the drawing of conclusions among Jews and Christians. I won't refer to big, tremendous swindles. (These will be mentioned in my memoirs.)

To my misfortune, I was always considered to be an affluent person, since I did not borrow money and did not participate in *vulgar celebrations,* but rather *worked* at the seashore for a number of weeks in the summer, in order to get a breath of fresh air. Naturally, I served, until very recently, as a bird to be plucked by those making a business out of anti-Semitism. And they plucked me with a vengeance.

I worked on a steady basis for 6–7 anti-Semitic newspapers during

---

[1] The sentence in parentheses was crossed out in the original manuscript.

the past ten years. A few even offered me author's royalties, but of course did not pay me a red cent. I have in my possession plenty of revolting Byzantine flattering statements, with which I was "bombarded." I replied to this flattery in my usual manner, *rudely,* in such rude words that, if I had had them slung at me, I would have replied with slaps to right and left.

But now, when I have disassociated myself from all of modern anti-Semitism, breaking all ties with it, I can speak *with humor* about personal matters, by presenting the *honest* business-of-anti-Semitism. Jews and Christians will thereby reach the conclusion that all modern anti-Semitism does is either to increase impotency or be a *vulgar commercial fraud.*

But I repeat: the following statements are *ironical, aimed at myself.* It will be very distressing if Jews or Christians will view this as self-sacrifice on my part. I refer to a weekly published outside of Germany, for which I was a steady correspondent for *more* than ten years. Let's say, for only ten years, i.e., 520 issues of this journal. One or two of my articles appeared in each issue; I have *written testimony* from the publisher that my contribution was one of the mainstays of the journal.

Let's make an accounting—*humorously*—in a businesslike manner with *those making a business out of anti-Semitism.* [Sending the copy to Vienna + payment for distribution of 10 copies each time: 260 marks.]

I have the ability to write *easily and quickly* on matters in which I am spiritually involved. But it would be haughty on my part to think that my weekly contribution took *less* than 4 hours each time (I won't mention trifling matters, such as ink, pens, and paper.) The sum total: 4 × 520 issues = 2080 *hours of work.*

Every construction laborer and helper earns 50 pfenig *per hour of work* today. And so my 2080 hours of work on behalf of the modern business of anti-Semitism should amount to a total of 1040 marks (together with the 260 marks—1300 marks), if *the modern business of anti-Semitism* was not anything other than—the modern business-of-anti-Semitism, interested, either innocently or maliciously, in using the skin of *honest people, strip by strip.*

The owner of the newspaper with which we are dealing, which I have brought as an example,[2] was, besides this, the *only* honest entrepreneur with whom I came into contact as a journalist. He was affiliated with the Catholic Christian-social trend, in which I did not have to take an interest in his newspaper. The fact that his newspaper was not flourishing commercially testifies to the narrow base which its orientation enjoyed among the public. My writing was a sort of *spice* to make the dose of Catholic Christian socialism more piquant. The person himself, however, was good-natured and honest.

2 The *Österreichischer Volksfreund* newspaper.

After innocently conversing with him about Frankfurt sausages in a letter in 1882, he sent me, twice, a half-dozen of the famed Viennese sausages. Furthermore, when I fractured my right hip in a fall five years ago, I received as a present, without asking, 50 or 60 bottles of inexpensive Austrian wine, one after the other, in order to *"strengthen* my nerves." Despite it being clear that the Catholic Christian socialism to which the newspaper and its owner were affiliated was a party to an endless number of societies, which spoke forcefully, drank forcefully, and danced forcefully, while *I* wore myself out for the newspaper, I nevertheless viewed the Viennese sausages and inexpensive wine which I received during the course of ten years as a sort of sign of *"good will,"* and I paid for this.

I can't say the same for the *German* "entrepreneurs" of the business-of-anti-Semitism.

As with the newspaper from outside of Germany, and to an even greater extent, I wasted *time, money, and labor* for 5–6 German "entrepreneurs." And if we're wrapping ourselves in a cloak of humor and irony directed at ourselves on matters of wages, then I must confess that two years ago I received a night's lodging with someone who today plays a leading role as an anti-Semite, and that I later received from this colleague two liver sausages and one blood sausage *free,* paying only mailing expenses for them.[3] May ten myriads of demons take me if I received any wages at all during the past ten years from the press of the anti-Semitic *entrepreneurs and merchants.*

You see, reader—Jew or Christian!—I relate to my disasters *with humor and irony directed at myself.* It is possible that commercialized and businesslike anti-Semitism *could not* conduct its affairs honestly, and it is possible that it *did not want* to. The Jews and Christians will judge for themselves, in either case.— — —

The best horse will become embittered if run incessantly for ten years; the best lemon will dry up after ten years of *squeezing.* My advice to the Jews: don't be afraid of *modern commercialized and business anti-Semitism,* which lives a life of revelry with its friends, while permitting *honest anti-Semites* to be worn out and used (. . .)

IV

I had an opportunity this year (1891) to send out "feelers" against the commercialization and business of anti-Semitism "in a diplomatic manner."

The anti-Semitic newspaper from outside Germany published an article, "From the German Reich," which I had written (Hamburg, April 26, 1891):

---

[3] Cf. Fritsch A67, December 22, 1888.

The revised, new edition, the 13th in number, of T. Fritsch's *The Anti-Semitic Catechism* has just appeared (Leipzig, pub. T. Fritsch, 1891). The first edition, containing 212 pages of text, appeared in 1887. The new edition has 362 pages. The price has remained the same: one mark.

It is only on rare occasions that a book appears which deals with the Jewish question in such a clear and concise manner, and in a manner which exposes the "rivals," as this *Catechism*. The name itself is essential for advertising, for both the Jews and the Christians (. . .)

The chapter "Quotations from the Bible" is of especial interest to both the members of the "Special Tribe" and philo-Semites. Take your heads out of the sand, people!

What will our Jewish liberals, for example, say to the following saying of Jesus: "Alas for you, lawyers and Pharisees, hypocrites! You travel over sea and land to win one convert; and when you have won him you make him twice as fit for hell as you are yourselves" (Matthew 23:15).

Doesn't it seem that this was meant for "The Society for the Protection of the Jews?" [sic] And even more clearly: "There are all too many, especially among Jewish converts, who are out of all control; they talk wildly and lead men's minds astray. Such men must be curbed, because they are ruining whole families by teaching things they should not, and all for sordid gain" (Letter of Paul to Titus 1:10–11).

These "archaeological excavations" are an unforgettable service provided by the book. I personally was specially interested in the chapter, "The Present State of the Anti-Semitic Movement," which reports objectively, without sparing self-criticism.

(P. 291): "The battle began when our armies were small. The small group of enthusiastic leaders, who had only meagre material resources at their disposal, could not endanger the united Jewish armies, with wicked arms. The popular masses had not yet fully understood the new ideas, and a small group of those too enthusiastically sharing the same ideas at times harmed more than it helped."

I am more extreme in my criticism of the anti-Semitic movement. At first only four people appeared in the publicist arena under their own name: Otto Glagau, in his essays on the founders' swindle [1871–1873]; Stoecker, as a Christian-socialist; Dühring, as a scholar and philosopher; and, last but not least, W. Marr (*The Victory of Judaism over Germanism,* pub. Kostenobel). Before this, and afterwards, they appeared only anonymously, or under pseudonyms. In Berlin in 1878 it was still only possible to "whisper" about the Jewish issue in public places, or in the company of those of like opinion. Yes, even in 1879 (the essay *The Victory of Judaism etc.* appeared in February and caused a great tumult and a wave of anti-Semitic writings) the pamphleteers remained anonymous or used pseudonyms. Alexander Pinkert was one of the first to

disclose his name (December 1879). That after hiding behind the pseudonym Egon Waldegg when he published two excellent anti-Semitic book-
lets, and founded a newspaper which was not viable, since it is impossible
to wage war without money.[4]

After people realized that Israel did not have the power to finish
Glagau, Dühring, Stoecker, and Marr on the gallows as they had done to
Haman, the desire of the anti-Semites for literary credit increased. Anonymous articles and those under pen names became rarer; at the same time,
however, the business-of-anti-Semitism came into being—I will not judge
this severely, as long as it uses business-like methods in order to wage a
business war," in a business-like manner, against the Jews.

The business of publicist anti-Semitism blossomed then. It was built
partly on hallucinators, and partly on speculators whom I suspect of trying to turn anti-Semitism into a "product" (. . .)

In either case, both the voyeurs and the cheaters of business-of-anti-
Semitism lacked working capital, and therefore became, had to become,
the ones "cutting strips" from the skin of the idealistic anti-Semites.

Let's talk plainly! An "investor" in an anti-Semitic newspaper—
whether a hallucinator or a fraud—has only a single concern: that he can
pay the printer and the paper supplier!

In order to circumvent this obstacle, this dangerous cliff, the anti-
Semitic "investor" must adopt a worse attitude towards his colleagues
than the Jewish clothing manufacturer who, according to the anti-Semites,
"gives starvation wages to the pale German seamstresses."

The *Catechism* was therefore right: "We set out to do battle with too
small forces and with insufficient material means." The printer demanded
his pay, the paper merchant demanded his payment, the "investor" did not
have money for the advertisements which are indispensable today. And so
the work and the expenses fell upon the partners, who worked without a
salary, and were not even reimbursed for shipping costs, but who had
lived until recently with the awareness that they were writing only for a
limited circle. It is impossible to maintain the body and wallet of professional writers in this manner, and indeed, the circle of anti-Semitic professional writers remained very small. A writer who presented himself as
anti-Semitic was immediately left without a livelihood, and the "investors"
who made experiments, without the public being aware of them, without
means, also went bankrupt. "The material means" were the main thing.
If this were the case, it would have been possible to organize anti-Semitism,
from the beginning, on an honest commercial and pertinent basis, instead
of collecting alms and revealing weariness, inaction, and apathy in the
face of the Jews. I repeat, I had nothing against the attempt to put anti-
Semitism on a commercial basis, but I warned many times against delu-

---

[4] Alexander Pinkert, the leader of the Deutsche "Reformpartei" in Dresden and the
organizer of the first anti-Semitic congress in Dresden in 1882.

sions. It was impossible to arouse esteem among the Jews with such a form of anti-Semitism, or to arouse confidence among those close to our point of view. Another element enters the picture: the logical anti-Semitic worker (the writer) must ask himself: *what future is there in a matter* which has provided a profit, until now, only for the printers and paper suppliers. As an idealist, he must learn to make do with little, but not to starve. I can list a whole line of people broken and collapsing after having given the business of anti-Semitism time, money, and labor. This sounds prosaic, but since the prose of the "business" was a necessary "means" in the service of the idealistic end, the means had to have been turned into means, instead of making irresponsible experiments, and instead of using idealistic anti-Semites as "commercial guinea pigs."

I am happy that the *Catechism* had the courage to allude to self-criticism, and I think that anyone who does not have the courage for self-criticism does not have the right to criticize others.

It is impossible to claim against the objectivity of my statements that I speak from personal reasons, since I cannot take a central role in the movement, even if I wanted to, for purely medical reasons. It is the public's concern to provide the means for the movement if this is what it wants. If not—the movement will vanish, despite its transitory and local accomplishments, as had already happened to it many times throughout history. The "citizen Sem" counts on this. This is a people which knows how to count and calculate.

If this pessimistic verdict will aid in improving the movement, I would be very glad to note this at the conclusion of my "Memoirs." In the meantime, I wish that the *Anti-Semitic Catechism* will have a thousand editions.[5]

A "supplement" to the above self-criticism of anti-Semitism is to be found in another place. As in many other locations, a Social Democrat movement for women's emancipation was also organized here in the second largest city in Germany[6] (after the cancellation of the socialist laws). Five-six "women from the people," who did indeed possess the ability to persuade and dialectic, albeit superficial, power, organized women's and girls' associations in all the professional branches: seamstresses, cleaning women, pressers, salesgirls, etc. The flow towards these associations was insignificant from the beginning.

There are 3–4 times as many men as women in these associations. The fiery speeches were made; enthusiastic articles appeared in the social-democratic newspaper *The Echo* so that women would awaken from their apathy, organize, and join the associations: all in vain. Yes, *does an unfortunate creature* such as "the pale German seamstress," who earns 5, 6, 7, or at most 9, marks a week, have 50 pfennigs to pay to the "associa-

---

[5] Marr concluded the article at this point in the original; the rest is a postscript.
[6] Hamburg.

tion's treasury?" And on top of this, the special expenses for strikes, etc.? The "female proletariat" accordingly ignored the initiatives and leadership of women's emancipation. They prefer their *practical "starvation wages"* to the theoretical *promises* of their leaders, both male and female, and their female public figures.

"History repeats itself" in our unfortunate times. Even the "pale German seamstress" cannot be oil for the wheels of the leadership, owing to material reasons! And she doesn't want to, either. In our practical times, everyone honors the rule, "the worker is worth what he is paid." As long as the public does not agree with this—and it doesn't matter to which party you belong—"capital" rules, swallowing up everything good and noble.

The terrible, open secret of our time is the surplus labor force among the proletariat in all areas of life, a labor force which cannot make material sacrifices for ideals and theoretical leaders and public figures.

And just as the "pale German seamstresses" ignore the Social Democratic emancipation of women, there are not more than two dozen of the 20,000 German writers who have the means to commit suicide against Sem, and to give profits to idealistic investors or to speculators, printers, and paper merchants, who live well.

This must be said once and for all! Social Democracy is lost, just like anti-Semitism, if it is unable to operate capital in order to fight capital. Take note of this—it doesn't matter to which party you belong—"the worker is worth what he is paid" if he is supposed to work for you!

The "pale German seamstresses who earn starvation wages" accordingly prefer to work for a Jewish employer and a Christian employer than for penniless Social Democrats and anti-Semites.

This capitalism at least pays its workers, albeit in a degrading manner. That is not the case for the business of Social Democracy or the business of anti-Semitism. . . . Yes. *Begging!* I was sharp and coarse in my words. But ask yourselves if there isn't a grain of truth in the sharp and coarse wrapping? (. . .)

V

The article hit the target! My diplomatic "propaganda" on behalf of the *Anti-Semitic Catechism* was a *two-edged sword* which I wielded.

A letter [. . .] by the leading and *capable* business and commercial anti-Semite, Mr. Fritsch of Leipzig, is lying in front of me. The gentleman complains in this letter that the anti-Semitic writers (. . .) want him, Fritsch, to make a *contribution* without any *reimbursement*. I also found my name among the string of names he listed.

I answered the gentleman, coldly and politely, that I don't know when, where, and how I made materially promising proposals to him, and

I requested him to strike *my name* from the list of his admirers who make a business-of-anti-Semitism.

You Jews! Don't be apprehensive of modern commercialized and business anti-Semitism, of the anti-Semitism of beer halls and tumult! As time passes, more and more *honest* people are drawing away from this anti-Semitism, preferring a *compromising modus vivendi* with the Jews to the tumult of impotent anti-Semitism and its commercialized deceit. Anti-Semitism today is only exhibitionist impotency or commercialized deceit!

VI

I was somewhat inflamed concerning these matters. Let's cool off once again and examine, with humor, the "relevant" jester's leaps of modern anti-Semitism, the only intent of the business of anti-Semitism being to protect the foolish masses [. . .] with the aid of illusions. Fraud! Only fraud!

I'll make my statement moderately: these are unconscious frauds. But *it's fraud,* all the same.

For example: everything which is called the *Bochum program*[7] on "the Jewish question"—which in my opinion is *childish,* to use the mildest manner against modern anti-Semitism, despite it being only speculation by merchants, entrepreneurs, and those "having a good time."

And so the *Bochum program* on the Jewish question.

"Clause 7: the 'German-Social Party' gives top priority to *a solution to the Jewish problem.*"

Good God! Two million cannon rounds had to be fired in order to announce this great work the world over. A small group of people, whose hands are at each others' throats, like the Church fathers in their first conferences, with their prolonged disputes around the question of whether the nose belongs to smell or smell belongs to the nose. I refer to the premier question of the party: "It views the *Jewish question* not only as a question of race or religion, but as a question of an *international, national, socialist, and ethical-religious* nature."

Didn't you get entangled in a plethora of words?

"Even in a German state of a socialist bent, Judaism—whose two-thousand-year history testifies to its *inability* to assimilate into other nations—will remain a thorn in our sides, and will gorge itself and swallow our nation, by means of its perverted ways and influence, and will riddle our laws and order with holes."

The most simple and direct conclusion of this [declaration], which announces to the entire world Judaism's infinite power, is:

"First of all, let us beat to death as many Jews—apostates and non-

---

[7] The 1889 Bochum congress of the anti-Semitic associations.

apostates—as possible." This was the most logical conclusion of the Bochum program, the program which, as I will show further on in my criticism, is only a guide for *the deceit of the business-of-anti-Semitism.*— — —

"The German-Social Party therefore views it as its responsibility to fight by legal means against the influence, harmful to the people and dangerous to the state, of international Judaism in all areas of public, social, and economic life, to open the eyes of the German people concerning the Jewish danger, and to press the government to attain international agreements, especially against the dangerous amassing of Jewish capital.

"In order to shed light on the question, whether the religious principles incumbent upon the Jews constitute a threat to the state, there is an immediate need for a state department of scientific investigation to examine the Talmud and the religious, ceremonial, and ethical rules which have been written in the rabbinic literature."

Yes! Dear children. Hasn't this been done for eons? Wasn't it the first *Prussian king* who ordered the inspection of the thick book of Eisenmenger and its publication, *at the state's expense?*

So don't bother me with these petty [demands].

"The new social order, based on circles of employment and avenues of livelihood, must permit these to drive out ethically harmful elements, and especially to protect itself by means of the right of free acceptance and courts of honor against the infiltration of Jews.

"The German-Social Party has as its goal the cancellation of equal rights, and the placing of the Jews under the aliens' law in Germany. The implementation of this goal will lead to the following results for the Jews:

"—The Jews living in Germany will not be permitted to be judges, teachers, government officials or technical functionaries of the state or local authorities, or attorneys or doctors with official powers.

"—The Jews will not have the right to vote, passively or actively, in state or local elections.

"—Jews appearing as witnesses will take only a precise Jewish oath before a rabbi. Jews cannot be jurors or bear other honorary German positions."

As for the first clause, this is already the *de facto* situation now.

The points raised in the other four clauses were in existence in Germany until the beginning of the second half of the century—at times with extreme severity. Thus, for example, Jews could not *own homes* in Hamburg, so they would register the house under the name of a servant or an apostate Jew.

Jewish lawyers could not appear before the commercial courts. They preferred to convert, and even the President of the commercial court, Dr. Hall[er], the son-in-law of Solomon Heine, was an apostate. This was also the case with many senators. In many places, such as Dresden, Frankfurt, etc., they were at times *officially forbidden* to enter certain public places.

Entrance forbidden "to Jews and dogs."—

And now the program wants to *return* to regulations which proved themselves, during the course of more than a thousand years, as *unsuccessful?* — —

"The state will protect the Jews in the implementation of their religion and customs, to the extent that this will not arouse public complaints or will be in violation of the laws of the land, such as, e.g., the torturing of animals during slaughter.

"The Jews will be permitted to engage in the vocations of labor, handicrafts, factory labor, and agricultural and commercial work, excluding peddling."

The first clause is more plausible. As for the second clause—*peddling* has ceased for some time in the large cities to be mainly the lot of the Jews. The [. . .] social misfortune patently drove masses of people who lived from hand to mouth to "peddling."

As for the other points, I will put myself in the most *radical* anti-Semitic point of view. From this point of view, the Jew should be totally forbidden to employ a person of Aryan descent in physical labor (for the Aryans employed in *spiritual* labor in journalism . . . he has no need). I think that half of the non-Jewish Aryans employed in physical labor will rebel if the Jewish "entrepreneur" and "employer" were to vanish from the scene. According to my experience concerning [. . .] viewpoints, I have my doubts whether the Aryan entrepreneur and employer would be more congenial and humane towards the worker after having rid himself of the *competition* of the Semite entrepreneur and employer.

The French cried "Hurrah for the Charter" after the 1830 revolution.

They cried "Long live the Republic" in 1848.

Yes, indeed! The "Charter" and the Republic were abstract achievements on paper; in reality, however, the working people were increasingly enslaved by the *capitalistic economics* of Jews and Christians.

This is, inter alia, the reason why *the Social Democrats do not want to recognize us. They are afraid of falling from the Semitic frying pan into the anti-Semitic fire.*

"As much as we must consider these fundamental means, we must nevertheless welcome, on a temporary basis, the following steps: the expulsion of Jews who are not citizens, a prohibition on the immigration of Jews from the East, restrictions on Jews accepting positions of power, etc." [end of clause 7].

Once again—quite childish. The "naturalized Jews" will remain in our midst. A hair will not fall from the head of Rothschild, Bleichröder, and others. Jewish immigration from the *East*—and what of the North, South, and West?—They must be forbidden as well.

The "restriction" on Jews entering "positions of power." This was forbidden *on paper* for more than a thousand years. But "baptism" removes all obstacles. If we relate to the Jewish question as a purely *racial question*—how many thousands of scientific committees, armed with "microscopes" and "chemical scales," would we have to convene in order to clarify where Semitic blood ceases and Aryan blood begins?

For this is one of the *basic principles* of modern anti-Semitism—*racial intermingling* between the Semites and the Aryans always works *"to the disadvantage of the Aryan race."* This is the *principle* which anti-Semites defend with a considerable amount of *inspiration*.

Permit me therefore to declare that I was somewhat surprised when I read the following in the *Anti-Semitic Catechism,* 13th edition, p. 28, under the title "Answers to Everyday Expressions" (against anti-Semitism):

"20: Didn't Spinoza, Mendelssohn, and Heine do a great deal? The renown of these famous Jews was also inflated by means of Jewish publicity. If they had not existed, German science and art would not have missed much.

"Furthermore, it is characteristic of these three that they more or less turned their backs on Judaism, revealing certain improved characteristics which seem to provide *confirmation for the assumption* that they were not *of pure Jewish blood*. What they possess of value must *apparently be credited to a few drops of foreign blood.*

"As is known, the amount of sympathy for Spinoza's ideas was so small among the Jews that they wanted to eliminate the isolated philosopher by the sword and murder." [The emphases are those of Marr.]

Let's talk impartially! How can modern anti-Semitism scientifically denounce the mingling of the races, on the one hand, while—in the same breath—emphasizing its advantages?

There is an explanation for this. Like all abstract parties, modern anti-Semitism also tends towards *current affairs,* i.e., it agrees with everything that suits its interests from today to tomorrow, without considering whether it contradicts itself, from the scientific aspect. As with all the parties, it's also true for the anti-Semites—the interest of the leadership and party officials is the main thing.

I admit that the question of racial intermingling, which is on the agenda of the anti-Semites, is still not completely clear to me; as we have seen above, it has been *removed from the agenda for the present*. I favored the theory [of the intermingling of the races] in my *Der Judenspiegel* (1862). I later retreated from this opinion, in the fervor of the "Jewish war."

I've become suspicious now, after the *Anti-Semitic Catechism* has declared that blood is a "special liquid," and—in self-contradiction—declared that it provides an advantage for the Semites and the Aryans.

The joke is on the members of the anti-Semitic party, *who pretend* that *they believe* in the purity of *the Aryan race. Racial intermingling* is increasingly occurring, thanks to the *means of communication* which are inestimably developed; the dogma of *Aryan blood,* which modern anti-

Semitism "rides" as it would a racehorse, appears to me as ridiculous as the dogma of the "blue blood" of aristocrats from birth. The *natural law* which will transform humanity into a mixed race will not be stopped by the rigid Jewish rabbinate, the heads of the Protestant church, and not even by modern anti-Semitism, either abstract or commercialized, which fishes in troubled waters.

We can't know whether this is good or bad.

But all the academic anti-Semitic casuistries concerning the advantage of one race over another are only *fizzling fireworks,* if not *"commercialized fraud,"* with the aid of which they hunt the fools, throwing them the straw of illusions.

Cancel the steamships, the railroads, the telegraph, the telephone connections, which today are the *matchmakers* of the intermingling of the races! You don't have any hope! (. . .)

And so, gentlemen, the more I ponder the matter, the *"Jewish question"* appears to me to be [nothing] more than a war of mercenaries, between *anti-Semites and Semites,* as I myself was engaged in, to my sorrow, for quite a long time.

I ask the pardon of the Jews and the Christians for permitting myself to be brought fraudulently to this *convenient and vulgar* anti-Semitism.

I therefore announce that I am severing my ties with this anti-Semitic movement, in which the egotistical blabbering person who makes a business of anti-Semitism is not to be distinguished from *the filthiest Leipzig Jew.*

What do I have in common with *those making a business out of anti-Semitism?* What do I have in common with *the Jews?* If I will find among them a person with human *feelings,* that person will be *my friend.*

I can't be, and do not wish to be, a commercialized fraud posing as a world reformer. These viewpoints are what dictated *The Victory of Judaism* to my pen. I declare that the Aryan society is bankrupt, now more than ever, with anti-Semitic *commercialized fraud* presenting itself as the *saviour of the business,* in a manner more Jewish than *the Jews themselves.*

Let's start with ourselves, we Christians and Aryans. Let's "remove Judaism" from ourselves first, and let us not make a group of Jews the scapegoat for our *"self-Judaization."*

That which Christianity and Aryanism claim is an *admission of failure:* an admission of failure which *bears profit* at times for the smart ones who make a business of anti-Semitism.

VII

Anti-Semitism committed a serious tactical error, an error to which I was also party: from the beginning, we adopted a strong position against

Social-Democracy, despite the fact that we had, or could have had, certain points of contact.

In principle, we were correct in our enmity towards the socialists, who were led by *"Jews,"* especially after we saw in 1848 where Jewish rule *in politics* led.

But what was the state of affairs in the *conservative* (= preserver of the state) parties? In the party which supported "throne and altar?" Concerning the leaders of the official and semiofficial press? (. . .) State-wrecking Social Democracy did indeed have its *"Singer,"*[8] but the "order party" had *Bleichröder,* and this semiofficial "order party" acted more through its press and its political activity on behalf of Social Democracy than did Singer, Bebel, and Liebknecht. Anti-Semitism therefore committed a serious *tactical* error by transforming the Jewish question into a *battering ram* against Social Democracy. A Social Democrat was right when he derisively told me, "You anti-Semites should set your own houses in order on the Jewish question before you make demands on others." This error may, however, bear bitter consequences in the future!

There is nothing easier than a rotten social system inciting Social-Democrats and anti-Semites to fight one another in street battles during the period of revolutionary social collapse, which will inevitably come. There is no need to stress who will fish in these troubled waters.

I, who was a party to these erroneous tactics, admit my error: a wedge was driven into the social revolutionary party by anti-Semitism, and this is liable to turn it into a *reform* party. Close study reveals what benefit was gained by these tactics. We served the government (which has a greater Jewish labor force in the press, etc., at its disposal than does Social Democracy) as pawns in a game, which could be used regularly; they took [. . .] such as these, so as not to embarrass the "throne and altar" in places where Sem was of importance. The new "governments" did nothing to protect society from the golden or red Judaization.

We should have aimed the arrows in our struggle *against* the governments, instead of making *Social-Democracy* the (male or female) scapegoat for the Judaization of society. We should have made a *socialist* accounting with the Social-Democrats, and not constantly fling at them the existence of Jews among their ranks, when there are ten times as many Jewish leaders in the party for "throne and altar." Why must we proclaim morning, noon, and night in our newspapers—without being forced to—that we are the true, sole, support of "throne and altar?" This, at a time when we should have noted in the pages of our newspapers the *official* victories of Judaism, where the official statistics showed our downfall beyond the shadow of a doubt! As one who is expert in cultural history, I cannot understand today why anti-Semitism had to necessarily hang onto "throne and altar." (. . .)

[8] Paul Singer (1844–1911), Jewish Social Democrat, the founder of the Social Democrat newspaper *Forwärts.*

But—I'm beating my breast—I cooperated with the folly of this loyalty of the anti-Semites out of honest belief; I'm only expressing *sharp self-criticism* here. I think that my loyalty to the monarchy was unquestioned, after I left my childish revolutionary steps. I cannot, however, *force* myself on a *monarchy* which relates to us, Christians and Aryans, as being of little importance, and even as [. . .] for the benefit of the Jews.

I haven't been a "Jew-baiter" for some time! I even already believe in the secret mission of the mysterious Jewish people. But I'm not so shortsighted and inexperienced *in history* not to know that it was specifically the kings *and their governments* who, for reasons of their own, aided the Chosen People again and again, either actively or passively.

A few statements concerning the Jews made by a few monarchs, such as Friedrich the Great, Napoleon I, etc., do not change anything here. *The Jewish People* knows how to make itself indispensable in the eyes of the "throne and altar" and the nations. There is something *extraordinarily* demonic, if you will, *in this phenomenon!!*

I can no longer blow the *vulgar, childish, anti-Semitic trumpet.*

But I know: the *Jewish question* is the axis around which the wheel of world history revolves. I no longer feel that it is my mission to become entangled in its spokes. I leave this to the bankruptcy of the monarchy, the Church, and Aryanism. I leave it to the *social revolution* to contend with the *chaos* to the best of their comprehension and desire. Our entire society is disintegrating and destroying *itself* and — — —

"Christianity will not help you,
Neither Bavarian nor Prussian."

Do you anti-Semites believe in God?! I put a question mark after this *fine name.* You must accordingly understand that — — —

The ways of the Lord are hidden
and His rules cannot be fathomed

If you are materialists, you must understand that the "Jewish question" is a *chemical distiller* of world history, in which the "elements" and the "substances" implement a chemical process. This is a process which led to results *beneficial* to the Chosen People in the realm of *chemistry,* as in the realm of *"faith."* "Faith" and "science" were not successful during the course of thousands of years in preventing the Jews from being the *"hammer"* on the *"anvil"* of the rest of humanity. It is true that I do not like the Jews, but I bow my head before the *historic mission* which was apparently placed upon them by *"God" and "science."* This is a *mission* against which there is no hope for *practical Christianity, the commercialized fraud* of *vulgar anti-Semitism,* or the foolish attachment of anti-Semitism to the "throne and altar!"

The current *vulgar* anti-Jewish incitement by commercialized anti-Semitism *arouses my revulsion!* Turn please to the *Caesars and kings,* to

Charlemagne and to the governments down to our time, who do not believe, out of *"state logic,"* in their ability to exist *without* the Jews.

Israel would have had to have been more foolish if it had agreed to waive the support of the highest *official authorities* in *its mission.*

No! It is not the Jews who are to blame for the Judaization of the Christian-Aryan society! Don't the princes and their governments who ordered bowing to the Jewish Golden Calf for dynastic and political reasons also bear the guilt?

Doesn't modern anti-Semitism *place itself* at the foot of this "very Christian" royalism? Without paying attention to the *kicks* which it receives in its rear end every day from the official statistics on the Judaization of society?

Business-of-anti-Semitism! [Geschäftsantisemitismus]

VIII

And what is the end of the story?

Our entire period is socialist. The entire world speaks of social questions. According to the principle of making an omelette without breaking the eggs, of course.

Since the Social-Democrats will apparently not join the anti-Semites, the reverse will occur.

The old parties are going bankrupt. Including the anti-Semitic one as well. Social and economic conditions have reached such a state that faith, nationalism, and race will become marginal issues for humans. Tremendous sums are needed today to remain "devout," patriotic and faithful, order loving, etc. Anti-Semites do not have such sums. At best, apathy has spread among them, and they will leave the "minority" of Jews happy, and the Christians to their fate. The anti-Semites are also *exhausted* if they belong to the better conservative circles. They don't care about "the party" any more. They want their comfort. Patriotism, which means "champagne" for the upper-class minority, will be *light beer* or *ersatz-coffee* for patriots of the less fortunate class. The spreading weariness and lethargy have become an epidemic. Only the Jews and the Social-Democrats possess élan (. . .)

The Kaiser and the kings, the priests, advisors, large estate owners, large industrialists, bankers, and other well-to-do people, who think that they have *leased* Christianity and patriotism solely for themselves, will please wage the war against the *red dragon* by themselves. We, the modest patriots, are restrained from taking part in this struggle. We'll live and see how they make out with the *Social-Democracy* which they hate from the bottom of their souls and with the *Jews* under their patronage. This matter no longer touches us. Society is collapsing upon itself. We anti-Semites should certainly not impose *loyal service like stable boys* on behalf of the Judaized status quo. Let's be *fatalists!* We are sinking [untergehen] just like the farmer, the artisan, the citizen from the middle class, and the petit bourgeois are sinking and vanishing. We do not have the spiritual or physical strength, even if we wanted to aid those few who belong to "the top hundred thousand" *in the struggle against the red dragon.* We are *exhausted, replete with battles, and confused.*

I'm forcefully driving the pick deep into the wound of modern *patriotism.* This "patriotism" is only a soap bubble, and I *accuse Kaiser and kings* who still believe in the *circus* which is being prepared for them, and who have not learned from history that the circus-loving masses which call to them *"Hosannah"* today will shout at them tomorrow, with the same passion, *"Crucify him!."*

Circus performances can be very useful in politics, but not without *bread.* The excitement of the *"circus"* wears off very quickly, and then— — the stomach rumbles.

In conclusion: I forego all the *parties,* and therefore also the specialty of anti-Semitism (. . .)

IX

(. . .) In another two years, no one will mention *"Semitism"* or *"anti-Semitism"* (. . .) We are marching towards social chaos, and this will engulf all the old parties, from "altar and throne" to today's social-democratic party (. . .) I don't know what this chaos will bring forth. (. . .) It is for this reason that I am severing myself from the philosophy of modern anti-Semitism, of which I was one of the veterans and earliest pioneers (. . .)

X

(. . .) The present mass migration of Jews from Russia will only lead to their flooding the world with their special characteristics. All the international antipathy will be of no use here. No nation wants them, but every nation wishes them upon its enemies. It is therefore inconceivable that international diplomacy will find a separate place for them to live.

(. . .) We anti-Semites made two severe mistakes. *Firstly*—we emphasized religion (I'm one of the guilty parties here). Christianity must remain outside the rules of the game. It was nevertheless forcefully dragged into the propaganda of the *goyim* [sic], even though it was repeatedly stressed that the Jewish question is *not* a religious question. *Secondly*— (here too, I acknowledge my guilt)—despite all the experience of history, we anticipated deliverance *from above* instead of going down to the *people.*

Yes! I can, am permitted to, and must state this openly: the Social-

Democratic party should have been closer to us than the covert policy of the Wilhemstrasse[9] in Berlin and the conservative synods. There are more influential Jews in Wilhemstrasse than in Social Democracy (. . .)

I am therefore completing what was lacking from my *pessimism* in *The Victory of Judaism over Germanism.* I ask the pardon of the Jews, not for my anti-Semitism, but for the erring ways of anti-Semitism, in which I exceeded the bounds of responsibility which a person with sharp logical comprehension, such as myself, was permitted to take upon himself (. . .) Yes! I bow my head before the *mystery,* before the Sphinx of world history, before *Judaism,* which has succeeded for 4000 years in impressing its unique mark on humanity.

No matter whether Judaism is a "Divine phenomenon" or a "natural phenomenon"—it has been clear for 4000 years that this Judaism was the *principal motif* of the social policy of all peoples. More courtesy must be shown to such a "Divine phenomenon" or "natural phenomenon" than to the *commercialized business of anti-Semitism* which the "leadership" of anti-Semitism tries to adopt for itself.

A small group of *dispersed* Jews, is infused with greater *self-aware-ness* than the Christians and Aryans! Who knows—when Israel attains world rule, matters may improve for the Christian and Aryan proletarians, and the starvation wages, of which those *making a business of modern anti-Semitism* make so much use for their purposes, will not be stolen from the "pale German seamstress."[10]

I must therefore live with the inevitable. All our social, commercial, and industrial developments are built on a Jewish world view, and have always been directed in accordance with this world view. The social order could not exist at all without it. Political means will not rectify this. All of modern humanity has become so *realistic,* so *lacking in ideals,* that our innermost tendency is to return to the crude days during which we walked on all fours in the forests "with bears and apes." Even if this should be the case, the question still remains: Won't *the same* cycle of life and civilization which we know today sprout from this nihilistic-radical state?

The development of industry, commerce, and technical matters is what has made human society what it is, for which the Jews were made a scapegoat. But the sins of the "goats" do not negate our own sins. Even if "we beat to death *all* the Jews"—we will still be permeated with the Jewish "spirit," as the modern business-of-anti-Semitism proves in the most successful manner.

No special Jewish question therefore still exists for me (. . .)

W. Marr
Hamburg, August 5, 1891

[9] Wilhemstrasse—the street on which the government (Chancellory, Foreign Office, Prussian Interior Ministry, etc.) was located.
[10] This paragraph was deleted by Marr in the original text.

Epilogue:

Forward!

This fine word which my pen writes now has only retrospective significance in relation to modern anti-Semitism.

"You broke the ice!" I received many dozens of responses in this spirit orally and in writing, and even in print, after the appearance of my essay which was mentioned so often above. I won't deny that this unexpected success flattered my *craving for honor*. My experience of life still hadn't taught me 12–13 years ago what I know now (. . .) My craving for honor didn't go so far 12 years ago as to have me believe that "I broke the ice." It's impossible to do this with a pamphlet to the "people of patience," the German Michel,[11] not even today, with Aryanism sunken within the morass of materialism.

But, I thought to myself, perhaps you have succeeded in breaking *a hole* in the ice. See, if you will, what is breaking through this hole into the light of day. . . .

Even though I clearly wrote on the title page of the pamphlet that I was dealing with the Jewish question *from a nonreligious viewpoint,* despite this areligious stance apparently being the reason for the wide distribution of the pamphlet, and despite the modern anti-Semites (who were exposed in time for making a business out of anti-Semitism) faithfully stammering after me that the Jewish question is not a religious or reactionary medieval question, ecclesiastical elements appeared in the program[12]—together with other anti-Semitic hoaxes, which fortunately enough were self-defeating from the beginning (. . .)

We anti-Semites are lying to and deceiving ourselves and others by insisting on making the Jewish question the alpha and omega of cultural history. I will present myself from the crudest anti-Semitic viewpoint: *What,* in the final analysis, are those few Jews? (. . .) A small nation, *which will vanish like chaff in the wind* in the future storm of social chaos, like the other nations.

In comparison to the *social deluge* towards which we are progressing, all the revolutions until now will look like weak lemonade, like thrice-brewed tea.

Not Germany, not France, etc.—the entire current society is in distress, is a corpse which they will try in vain to resuscitate with galvanic means.

History had to fulfill itself. *Social elementarism* will sweep all the parties into the whirlwind. Just as the ancient societies committed suicide socially, so will modern society also end its days in social suicide.

"Let the dead bury the dead."

W. M.

---

[11] Michel—an appellation for the German farmer.
[12] Statuten der Anti-Semiten-Liga, Berlin, 1879.

Notes

Chapter 1

1. P. W. Massing, *Rehearsal for Destruction* (New York, 1967), p. 211;
   P. Pulzer, *The Rise of Political Antisemitism in Germany and Austria*
   (New York, 1964), p. 49. These two sources base themselves on Dubnow,
   who called Marr "the son of a Jewish actor, who was christened." S. Dubnow, *Weltgeschichte des jüdischen Volkes* (Berlin, 1929), Bd. V, p. 18;
   Die Neuste Geschichte des jüdischen Volkes (Berlin, 1923), Bd. 3, p. 10.
   Dubnow was the one who gave an academic imprimatur to defining Marr
   as a Jew; he was followed not only by Massing and Pulzer but also by
   anti-Semitic historians or chroniclers. On the other hand, K. Wawrzinek
   (*Die Entstehung der deutschen Antisemitenparteien* [Berlin, 1927]), who
   was the first to systematically treat the history of anti-Semitism, doubted
   Dubnow's version (p. 13).
2. H. Jonak von Freienwald, *Jüdische Bekenntnisse aus allen Zeiten und
   Ländern, Nürnberg* [1941], p. 6.
3. Fritz Zschaek, "War Wilhelm Marr ein Jude," *Weltkampf,* Die Judenfrage
   in Geschichte und Gegenwart, 1944, pp. 94–98.
4. Schröder, H., *Lexicon der hamburgischen Schriftsteller* Bd. 5, pp. 36–39.
5. Paul Alfred Merbach, *Heinrich Marr* (Leipzig, 1929). This author, a clear
   Nazi, was certainly aware of the principle of family racial sin; it is
   doubtful whether he would have dealt with Marr's father if he had suspected the latter of being Jewish.
6. *Hamb. Sch. Lexicon,* Bd. 5, pp. 39–41.
7. Taufregister St. Johannis, Magdeburg Jg. 1819, p. 243, Nr. 214.
8. Nachlass Marr, A 149, W. Marr and H. Marr, June 27, 1843. Heinrich
   Marr's biographer intentionally refrains from dealing with Heinrich's son
   Wilhelm. He does mention, however, that Heinrich married Wilhelm's
   mother, despite his father's displeasure. The biographer does not state the
   reason for this. It is possible that this was due to the bride's being preg-
   nant, not by the man she married. Merbach, *op. cit.,* pp. 32, 38.

9. F. Sailer [Friedrich Israel], *Die Juden und das deutsche Reich. Offener Brief an einer deutschen Frau* (Berlin, Juli 1879), p. 18.
10. *Sieg des Judenthums über das Germanenthum,* Vorwort zur llten Auflage (Bern, 1879), pp. 6–7.
11. *Sigila Veri,* Semi Kürchner (Erfurt, 1931), Bd. 4, p. 345.
12. *Österreichischer Volksfreund.*
13. *Hamburger Fremdenblatt,* 15.4.1893.
14. *Israelitische Wochenschrift. Eine allgemeine Zeitung des Judenthums,* 25.8.1893. This pasage is not to be found, unfortunately, in *Sabbath-Blatt.*
15. See Note 1, above.
16. Nachlass Marr, B V a, *Im Philosemitismus,* p. 51.
17. *Ibid.* There is also a slight possibility that Rabbi Jellinek heard about Marr's revolutionary activity from his brother the revolutionary (who was executed in the 1848 revolution), who had been active in Leipzig and Vienna.

Chapter 2

1. See below, p. 118.
2. Nachlass Marr, B I a, *Memoiren* I (1819–1842), p. 204.
3. *Ibid.,* pp. 249–251.
4. *Ibid.,* p. 362.
5. *Ibid.,* p. 352, *Im Philosemitismus,* S. 47.
6. *Das Junge Deutschland in der Schweiz. Ein Beitrag zur Geschichte der geheimen Verbindungen unserer Tage* (Leipzig, 1846).
7. *Ibid.,* p. 67.
8. *Ibid.,* p. 115.
9. Wilhelm Marr, *Der mensch und die Ehe* (Leipzig, 1848), p. 251.
10. *Ibid.,* p. 261 ff.
11. Nachlass Marr, A 149. W. Marr an H. Marr, June 27, 1843.
12. *Das Junge Deutschland,* p. 53. Marr also mentions another revolutionary, Adolf Follen, the brother of Carl.
13. *Gegenwart und Zukunft* (Schaffhausen, 1843); *Glosse über die Petition der Kölner an den Konig von Preussen* (Strassburg, 1843).
14. *Das Junge Deutschland.*
15. Ernst Barnikol, "B. Bauers Kampf gegen Religion," *Zeitschrift für Kirchengeschichte,* 1928, p. 15f. An attempt was made in this essay to reveal that Marr did write the essay. The author relied on complex comparisons; it would have sufficed, however, to examine the bibliography which Wilhelm Marr himself had prepared in his old age, in order to prove this. Nachlass Marr, B VIII, p. 2.
16. Cf. *Das Junge Deutschland,* p. 131. For the issue of radicalism and its stance on the Jewish issue, see E. Sterling, *Er ist wie Du* (München, 1956), pp. 102–118.
17. *Das Junge Deutschland,* p. 221.
18. *Ibid.,* p. 133.
19. *Ibid.,* p. 79. Marr deleted this passage when he copied the essay into his memoirs. He eliminated his republican-nationalist past from his memoirs

out of loyalty to the Germany of the kaiser, whose colors were black-white-red.

20. *Ibid.*, p. 115.
21. Even though it was specifically the radical revolutionary government which had expelled Marr.
22. *Ibid.*, p. 27.
23. *Ibid.*, p. 344.
24. *Memoiren* II (1842–1845), p. 1311, "Das waren mir selige Tage"; this had appeared previously in 1875 in the Hamburg journal *Reform*.
25. *Memoiren* III (1845–1852), p. 1.
26. *Memoiren* II, p. 1322.
27. *Hamburgs Montags Nachrichten*, Nr. 9, 1869, "Wie man Annexionist wird," Nachlass Marr, A 541: 373 Cap. 5. There were those who claimed, on the other hand, that Marr had betrayed the Association by revealing its secrets.
28. Cf. Y. Toury, *Mehumah u-Mevukhah be-Mahapehat 1848*, pp. 126–130. [Hebrew]

Chapter 3

1. "Zur Charakteristic des deutschen Liberalismus," *Der Mensch und die Ehe*, pp. 288, 296, 330–331.
2. The king of Denmark was also the prince of Schleswig-Holstein. Holstein had a special status as a member of the German Confederation (Bund). The Danish national movement in Schleswig insisted upon the annexation of Schleswig to Denmark. The Germans in Schleswig and Holstein were, of course, against it. The minimal demand of the German nationalists was to sever the connection between Holstein and the Danish crown. The more extreme German nationalists were against the political separation of Holstein and Schleswig, and demanded that both be separated from the Danish crown. Legally this problem was only theoretical as long as the king lived. But as he had no son and as according to the law the heir in Holstein had to be a male, the problem would become acute the moment the Danish king died.
3. *An Schleswig-Holsteins Männer der That* (Hamburg, 1846).
4. "Wie man Annexionist wird." About the journal see also J. Stettenheim, "Aus meinen Jugenderinnerungen," *Allgemeine Zeitung des Judenthums* 22.9.1893, 29.9.1893.
5. *Memoiren* III, p. 12.
6. *Ibid.*, p. 18.
7. *Der Mensch und die Ehe*, pp. 123, 137.
8. *Mephistopheles*, 16.2.1851, p. 3, 13.4.1851; *Herr Heckscher als Agitator, Volksvertreter und Staatsmann* (Hamburg, 1851).
9. *Mephistopheles*, 22.11.1848, "Offener Brief."
10. *Ibid.*, 16.2.1851, 13.4.1851.
11. *Memoiren* III, p. 36.
12. *Ibid.*, p. 39.
13. *Mephistopheles*, 8.10.1848.

14. *Ibid.,* 22.10.1848. The moment he was elected he tried to appease the liberals, promising to carry out their program and not to drift to extremism. He did not keep his promise, and there was no need to, because radicalism was en vogue by then.

15. *Ibid.,* 5.11.1848.

16. *Die Jacobiner in Hamburg* (Hamburg, 1848), p. 4.

17. *Wöchentliche gemeinnützige Nachrichten. Patriot* (Extra-Blatt) 30.10. 1848.

18. *Mephistopheles,* 1.9.1850, 29.9.1850, 6.4.1851, 11.5.1851, 1.6.1851.

19. *Ibid.,* 5.11.1848.

20. *Ibid.,* 24.6.1849.

21. *An Hamburgs Wähler. Ein Wort zur rechten Zeit* (Hamburg, 1849).

22. *Mephistopheles,* 5.11.1848.

23. Riesser, letter to Mrs. Haller, 1.6.1849, in M. Isler, *Gabriel Riessers Leben* (Frankfurt, 1867), Bd. 1.

24. *Mephistopheles,* 2.9.1849.

25. *Ibid.,* 2.9.1849, 9.9.1849, 23.9.1849.

26. *Ibid.,* 5.8.1849; on the other hand, Stettenheim claims that even before that Marr had thrown away his (Stettenheim's) ardent articles against Prussia and in favor of the liberation of Schleswig-Holstein. But Stettenheim does not specify when this incident of "Marr's lack of courage" took place. *Allgemeine Zeitung des Judenthums,* 29.9.1893, p. 467.

27. "Wie man Annexionist wird."

28. *Memoiren* III, p. 75. The police initiated legal procedures against Marr because of an article ("Am 13. August") he published on the first anniversary of the entry of the Prussian army into Hamburg. Marr blamed Prussia for bringing the reaction to Hamburg. *StAH* Polizeibehörde Kriminalwesen C, Serie VI, Lit. W, Nr. 454.

29. *Memoiren* III, p. 80.

30. *Mephistopheles,* 23.12.1849, 27.1.1850.

31. *Ibid.,* 4.2.1850, 24.3.1850, 7.4.1850, 2.5.1850.

32. *Zum Verfassungs-Streit* (Hamburg, 1850), pp. 10–11, 17.

33. Cf. "Die Hamburger Verfassungsfrage," *Mephistopheles,* 27.7.1851.

34. *Ibid.,* 21.1.1850.

35. *Ibid.,* 25.8.1850.

36. *Ibid.,* 27.10.1850.

37. *Ibid.,* 3.11.1850.

38. *Ibid.,* 16.3.1851.

39. *Ibid.,* 21.9.1851.

40. *Ibid.*

41. "Auch ein Wort über Mischehen," *ibid.,* 10.8.1851, 24.8.1851.

42. *Ibid.,* 9.11.1851.

43. *Ibid.,* 20.7.1851.

44. A cartoon representing Riesser exchanging blows with Marr while the Prussian and Austrian armies are closing in. As mentioned above, the events of October 18, 1838, aroused in him the deepest disgust with the guiding spirit of this German holiday.

45. *Ibid.,* 27.6.1852.

46. Nachlass Marr, A 67, Fritsch to Marr, 28.4.1886.

Chapter 4

1. *Reise nach Central-Amerika* (Hamburg, 1863).
2. Marr had explained his ideas in the press of 1853, but he had to do so again after the publication of *The Mirror of the Jews* in 1862. See his letter to the editor of the *Freischütz*, No. 79 (1862, p. 4) and its confirmation in the same paper, No. 86 (19.7.1862) signed by Eduard Delius.
3. H. Laufenberg, *Geschichte der Arbeiterbewegung in Hamburg, Altona und Umgegend* (Hamburg, 1911), Bd. 1, p. 211. Another accusation was that he had sold his immigrants in Cuba instead of Costa Rica, for higher profits. *Freischütz*, 26.12.1863.
4. *Memoiren* VI, p. 201.
5. *Reise*, p. 33.
6. *Memoiren* V, p. 1.
7. *Ibid.*, pp. 2–11.
8. Cf. W. Marr, *Lichtbilder aus der Hamburger Bürgerschaft* (Hamburg, 1860). There he attacks the who's who: Baumeister, Martens, Knaut, Godeffroy, etc.
9. *Hamburger Nachrichten*, June 11, 1861, session no. 21 from June 8.
10. *Ibid.*
11. *Memoiren* V, pp. 63–68.
12. [W. Marr], *Travailler pour le roi de Prusse. Ein Beitrag zur deutschen Flotte* (Hamburg, 1861).
13. L. Feuerbach, *Das Wesen des Judenthums*, Chap. 12.
14. *Der Judenspiegel* (Hamburg, 1862), p. 54.
15. *Memoiren* V, pp. 62–63.
16. *Freischütz*, 22.2.1862.

Chapter 5

1. *Memoiren* V, pp. 69–71. As we know, Heine was referring to a Catholic priest and a Jewish rabbi.
2. The hint is implied in the letter quoted in Note 3: "The extraordinary Jews are not Jewish any longer."
3. Marr's letter to the editor in reply to Dr. Rée. *Freischütz*, 14.8.1862, p. 3.
4. Bruno Bauer, *Die Judenfrage* (Braunschweig, 1843), p. 3.
5. Cf. E. Sterling, *op. cit.*, p. 139 ff.
6. *Freischütz*, Nr. 63, 7.6.1862, p. 3.
7. *Memoiren* V, pp. 72–73.
8. Marr admitted that this man rescued him from prison by paying the bail. Zacharias also confessed to Marr that he had converted to Christianity only to marry a gentile, while deep inside he remained Jewish. *Ibid.*, p. 74.
9. *Ibid.*, pp. 78–79.
10. *Der Judenspiegel*, p. 4.
11. *Ibid.*, pp. 45–46.
12. *Ibid.*, pp. 35, 41.
13. *Ibid.*, p. 54.
14. *Ibid.*, p. 48.
15. *Ibid.*, p. 51.

16. *Ibid.*, p. 52.
17. *Ibid.*, p. 42.
18. *Ibid.*, p. 36.
19. *Ibid.*, p. 38.
20. On p. 49 we find, "We, who are not Jews." If his co-citizens, who knew him well, had considered this a lie, they would have reacted.
21. Leo Baeck Archives, NY, *Memoirs of Sophie Wohlwill*, p. 172. Emil Wohlwill was a Jew who rejected his Judaism (see M. Zimmermann, *Hamburger Patriotismus und deutscher Nationalismus* [Hamburg, 1979], p. 219). Already in November 1861 he came into conflict with Marr, when the latter attacked him for supporting the idea of a German fleet. However, this episode did not prevent their collaboration on the board of the Democratic Association shortly after.
22. Marr claimed during the debate that he had given Dr. Banks a document proving his innocence, but the latter had not brought it with him. *Freischütz*, Nr. 79, 3.3.1862, p. 2.
23. J. Audorf, *Herr Marr und die Arbeiterfrage* (Hamburg, 1863), p. 14.
24. *Der Judenspiegel*, p. 51.
25. Marr was the one who handled the publication of the book in Hamburg that year. Marr would clash with Nordmann again in 15 years' time, after a short period of cooperation in the anti-Semitic organization.
26. *Der Arme Jude, wie ihn der grosse Demokrat Wilhelm Marr besp. beleuchtet von keinem Juden* (Hamburg, 1862), pp. 3, 5, 13.
27. *Ibid.*, p. 11.
28. "Zur Judenfrage," *Freischütz*, 3.7.1862, 5.7.1862. In his memoirs (vol. V, pp. 80–81), Marr claimed that it was he who increased the paper's subscription from 1,800 to 9,000. In the end, Lenz fired him and hired his disciple Stettenheim in his place. Nevertheless the paper closed down after 6 years.
29. *Der Judenspiegel*, p. 3.
30. *Freischütz*, Nr. 79, 3.7.1862, "Eingesandet."
31. E. Salinger, *Hep! Hep! ein Blick in den Judenspiegel* (Hamburg, 1862), pp. 30, 38.
32. J. Stettenheim, *Der Judenfresser. Ein 'Wohl-bekomm's'* (Hamburg, 1862), p. 4; cf. Nachlass Marr, A 254.
33. *Hamburger Nachrichten,* 27.10.1862.

Chapter 6

1. Cf. *Hamburger Schriftsteller-Lexikon,* vol. 5, p. 36.
2. "Zum Verständnis der Nordamerikanischen Wirren," *Freischütz,* 26.2. 1863.
3. Laufenberg, *op. cit.,* pp. 221–223. Cf. also A. Herzig, "The Role of Antisemitism in the Early Years of the German Workers' Movement," *Leo Baeck Yearbook,* XXVI, 1981, pp. 243–259; A. Herzig et al., *Arbeiter in Hamburg* (Hamburg, 1983), pp. 139–176.
4. Cf. H. Rosenberg, *Nationalpolitische Publizistik Deutschlands* (München, 1935), pp. 555–556.
5. J. Audorf, *op. cit.,* p. 1.

6. Ref. the Polish revolt of 1863.
7. Audorf, *op. cit.*, p. 10.
8. *Mephistopheles*, 3.12.1848, 2.9.1849, "Hamburgs Zukunft."
9. W. Marr, *Messias Lassalle und seine Hamburger Junger* (Hamburg, 1863), pp. 5–7.
10. *Ibid.*
11. *Die Nessel*, 7.9.1864.
12. See Chap. 3, p. 21.
13. Cf. Th. Schieder, *Vom deutschen Bund zum deutschen Reich* (München, 1975), p. 15 ff.
14. *Memoiren* V, pp. 85–87.
15. *Ibid.*, p. 102a (while numbering the pages, Marr allotted numbers 101–110 twice. Therefore I refer to them as -a and -b).
16. *Ibid.*, p. 87.
17. *Ibid.*, p. 105a.
18. "Italienische und deutsche Patrioten," *Die Nessel*, 16.4.1864.
19. "Was wir wünschen, was wir können, was wir müssen," *Die Nessel*, 4.6. 1864.
20. "Wie man Annexionist wird," *Hamburgs Montags Nachrichten*, Nr. 10, 1869.
21. "Der Polenprocess in Preussen," *Die Nessel*, 31.8.1864.
22. *Memoiren* V, p. 105a.
23. Otto v. Bismarck, *Gedanken und Erinnerungen* (Berlin, 1919), pp. 337–361.
24. W. Marr, *Selbstständigkeit und Hoheitsrecht der freien Stadt Hamburg sind Anachronismus geworden* (Hamburg, 1866), p. 62.
25. Nachlass Marr, A 228, 12.4.1864.
26. "Für den deutschen National-Verein," *Die Nessel*, 5.10.1864.
27. "Nur keine Illusionen," *Die Nessel*, 3.9.1864.
28. *Ibid.* He attacked Wolffson also for suggesting taxation on property. Marr regarded this proposal as a pretext to discover what assets the public possessed. It is possible that Marr feared the uncovering of his own secret enterprises.
29. *Hannoveraner Courier*, Nr. 2092, 29.2.1864.
30. Nachlass Marr, A 149, August 1864, an Dr. Endrulat.
31. *Ibid.*, A 212, Schernikau: concerns the financial problems connected with this transaction with Ismeyer.
32. Cf. F. R. Bertheau, *Kleine Chronologie zur Geschichte des Zeitungswesens in Hamburg 1616–1913* (Hamburg, 1914), p. 75. This magazine was established in 1850 and continued after Marr quit, but details about this publication are unclear.
33. See Note 24.
34. *Selbstständigkeit*, pp. 55–56.
35. *Ibid.*, p. 16.
36. *Ibid.*, p. 64.
37. *Der Ausschluss Österreichs aus Deutschland ist eine politische Widersinnigkeit* (Hamburg & Leipzig, 1866).
38. Verein für den Anschluss Hamburgs an den Zollverein (Hg.), *Beleuchtung der zwanzig Gutachten der Freihandelspartei* (Hamburg, 1867).

39. W. Marr, *Streifzüge durch das Concilium von Trent* (Hamburg, 1868), pp. 3–4.
40. *Ibid.*, p. 35.
41. *Sieg des Judenthums über das Germanenthum* Vorwort zur llten Auflage, pp. 8–9.
42. *Memoiren* V, pp. 150–157.
43. *Dr. Strousberg und sein Wirken, von ihm selbst geschildert* (Berlin, 1876), pp. 10, 13.
44. "Die Tripelallianz," *Die Nessel*, 12.10.1864.
45. *Die neue Dreeniigkeit* (Hamburg, Richter, 1867). The revue could not be located in any library, but the following document appears to be the synopsis of its contents in French.
46. A. C. F. Beales, *The History of Peace* (London, 1931), pp. 119 ff.
47. Nachlass Marr, B XI, 1 p. 3d.
48. *Ibid.*, p. 4d.
49. *Mephistopheles*, 29.9.1850.
50. *Memoiren* VI, p. 159ff.
51. Cf. *Sieg des Judenthums*, p. 31.
52. "Demokratische Betrachtungen aus der Vogelsperspective," *Politik* (Berlin) 17.12.1873. Was also printed in a Viennese paper. To be found in Nachlass Marr, A 541/373, Cap. 3.
53. *Ibid.*
54. "*Demokratische Betrachtungen*," 1.11.1872 [?], *ibid.*, Cap. 5.
55. *Ibid.*
56. *Ibid.*; Marr represents the Jews as involved in more than finances: "The red revolution is also in Jewish hands, as the head of the International is no other than Karl Marx, the cosmopolitan."
57. *Ibid.*

Chapter 7

1. *Jüdisches Lexikon* (Berlin, 1927), vol. 1 "Antisemitismus"; *Encyclopaedia Judaica* (Berlin, 1928), vol. 2, p. 1019; *Sigila Veri, "Antisemitismus";* P. Massing, *op. cit.,* p. 6; P. Pulzer, *op. cit.,* p. 49; A. Bein, "Der moderne Antisemitismus und seine Bedeutung für die Judenfrage," *Vierteljahreshefte für Zeitgeschichte* (Stuttgart, 1958), S. 346; N. Cohn, *Warrant for Genocide* (New York, 1970), p. 189; J. G. Riquarts, *Der Antisemitismus als politische Partei in Schleswig-Holstein und Hamburg 1871–1914* (Kiel, 1975), p. 38.
2. S. Dubnow, *Neueste Geschichte,* vol. 3 (Berlin, 1923), p. 10.
3. Wawrzinek, *op. cit.,* p. 94; R. Rürup, *Emanzipation und Antisemitismus* (Göttingen, 1975), p. 177; J. Katz, *From Prejudice to Destruction: Anti-Semitism 1700–1933* (Cambridge, Mass., 1982); the last two have corrected the mistake.
4. *Memoiren* VI, pp. 210–212.
5. *Ibid.*, p. 219ff.
6. *Gartenlaube* 1874 Nr. 47, pp. 758–759.
7. *Memoiren* VI, pp. 200–202.
8. *Ibid.*, pp. 239–242.

9. See p. 101, below.
10. "Das Kapital," *Reform* 1872: Nachlass Marr, A 541/373 Cap. 3.
11. *Religiöse Streifzüge eines philosophischen Touristen* (Berlin, 1876), p. 19ff.
12. *Ibid.*, p. 18.
13. Not long before, in 1876, he published a eulogistic poem to the atheist Feuerbach in the Hamburg *Reform*.
14. *Religiöse Streifzüge*, p. 144.
15. *Hamburger Abendblatt.* Cf. *Wählt keinen Juden. Der Weg zum Sieg des Germanenthums über das Judenthum* (Berlin, 1879), p. 11.
16. *Illustriertes Musik- und Theater-Journal*, 16.8.1876.
17. Nachlass Marr, B II c, *Erinnerungen an das erste Bühnenfestpiel in Bayreuth* (1876).
18. *Memoiren* VI, p. 252ff. Marr laments Büllow's retirement from anti-Semitism.
19. J. Scherr, *Deutsche Kultur- und Sittengeschichte* (Leipzig, 1876).
20. *Ibid.*, pp. 570–573.
21. *Ibid.*, p. 598.
22. Cf. *Sieg des Judenthums*, p. 39.
23. *Memoiren* VI, pp. 842–843. Hödel's first attempt on the life of Wilhelm I took place on May 11, 1878.
24. It is not clear whether he was legally wed to his fourth wife at the time.
25. *Ibid.*, p. 243.
26. *Ibid.*, pp. 242–244.
27. Nachlass Marr, A 39, 17.6.1878.
28. *Ibid.*, 1.2.1879.
29. Nachlass Marr, A 212 (Schernikau).
30. Nachlass Marr, A 217 (Schirmer) 1.10.1878.
31. *Schlesische Volkszeitung*, 17.12.1878.
32. Cf. *Sieg des Judenthums* and also *Vom jüdischen Kriegsschauplatz* (Bern, 1879), p. 44. He regarded the Russian nihilism as worse than the German brand and felt that the Russian revolution would be Jewish.
33. *Allgemeine Zeitung des Judenthums*, 18.3.1879, "Gegen W. Marr." In the paper *Ha-Magid*, published in the remote province of East Prussia, Marr was mentioned for the first time in November, in relation with the establishment of the "Antisemiten-Liga," 5.11.1879, p. 331.
34. J. Perinhart, *Die deutschen Juden und Herr W. Marr* (Loebau, 1879), pp. 10–23, 40.
35. Ludwig Stern, *Die Lehrsätze des neugermanischen Judenhasses* (Würzburg, 1879), pp. 27, 32, 45–55, 62–63.
36. Deutsch-Israelitischer Gemeindebund, Session of Dec. 4, 1879; in: *CAHJP* GA M1/8, vol. 1.
37. *Ibid.*, sessions of July 2, 1879, and Oct. 10, 1879; Circular from Nov. 1879; M1/16 Strafanträge in Bekämpfung des Antisemitismus, Korrespondenz mit Stadtgericht Berlin, 17.11.1879, 26.11.1879, 15.1.1880.
38. L. Stern, *op. cit.*, pp. 1–3, 31, 58.
39. F. Sailer [Friedrich Israel], *Die Juden und das deutsche Reich* (Berlin, 1879), pp. 11, 18, 36.
40. "Ein Kuriosum," *Deutsche Wacht*, pp. 164–165.

41. Nachlass Marr, A 125, J. M. Kohn 1.12.1879.
42. Nachlass Marr, A 254.
43. W. von Ernst, *Noch etwas vom besiegten Germanenthum. Offener Brief an die Herren Marr, Perinhart, u.s.w.* (Dresden, 1879), pp. 5, 14.
44. Gustav von Linden, *Der Sieg des Judenthums—eine Widerlegung der W. Marr'schen Polemik,* Leipzig, 1.7.1879.
45. M. Reymond, *Wo steckt der Mauschel, oder: jüdischer Liberalismus und wissenschaftlicher Pessimismus. Ein offener Brief an W. Marr* (Bern, 1879), pp. 6, 17, 48.
46. Paulus Kassel, *Die Antisemiten und die Evangelische Kirche* (Berlin, 1881), pp. 5, 9, 15, 24, 34–39, 41.
47. Nachlass Marr, A 39, 25.7.1879.
48. *Wählt keinen Juden,* pp. 1, 8.
49. *Der Judenspiegel,* 1879, p. 72.
50. *Lessing contra Sem* (Chemnitz, 1883), p. 26.
51. *Der Judenkrieg, seine Fehler und wie er zu organisieren ist* (Chemnitz, 1880), pp. 1, 6.
52. *Ibid.,* pp. 17–19.
53. Nachlass Marr, A 65, Graf von Frankenberg (conservative Landtag member), cf. *Kriegsschauplatz,* p. 20.
54. "Anti-Stoecker," *Deutsche Wacht,* 1879, pp. 81–83; "Die Christlichsoziale Arbeiterpartei," *ibid.,* 1880, pp. 629–648.
55. *Judenkrieg,* pp. 3, 8.
56. *Öffnet die Augen Ihr deutsche Zeitungsleser* (Chemnitz, 1880), pp. 9, 21.
57. *Memoiren* VI, pp. 247–248.
58. Nachlass Marr, A 68 (Froben) 14.8.1879. It appears from this correspondence that ten editions of *The Victory of Judaism over Germanism* sold 16,500 copies (i.e., all 11 editions did not sell as much as 20,000 copies).
59. *Kriegsschauplatz,* pp. 36–37.
60. *Goldene Ratten und rothe Mäuse* (Chemnitz, 1880), p. 4.
61. *Ibid.,* pp. 6–7.
62. *Kriegsschauplatz,* pp. 6–7. One can find similar expressions in Wagner's writings.
63. *Wählt keinen Juden,* pp. 11–12, 42–43.
64. *Ibid.,* p. 41; *Goldene Ratten,* pp. 11, 20ff. In light of the confrontation between Marr and Riesser in 1848, in the 1850's, and in the early 1860's, one should not be surprised by the fact that Marr attacked Riesser again in the late 1870's and even in his memoirs, written three decades after Riesser's death. But here again we are aware of inconsequence on his part: Immediately after Riesser's death in 1863 Marr published a eulogy, "Dem Andenken Dr. Gabriel Riesser's," in his own magazine, *Die Opposition* (Erstes Heft, 1863), pp. 44–46. There he described Riesser as a political enemy, but not as a villain. He even "lowered his flag" before the memory of Riesser the man, and claimed that Riesser was misused by a political party which was his (Marr's) real enemy. It could be that this unique evaluation of Riesser was written not only under the impression of his death but also under the impression of their common and recent political failure in Hamburg, an impression that faded out later.
65. *Judenkrieg,* pp. 10–11.

66. *Öffnet die Augen*, p. 25ff; cartoon *in Mephistopheles*, 3.12.1848.
67. *Goldene Ratten*, p. 30.
68. *Ibid.*, pp. 16–18.
69. *Ibid.*, p. 30.
70. Cf. *Sieg des Judenthums*, p. 46.
71. *Goldene Ratten*, p. 30.
72. *Ibid.*
73. *Der Judenspiegel*, 1862, p. 52.
74. *Lessing contra Sem*, p. 27.
75. *Kriegsschauplatz*, pp. 40–41.
76. *Deutsche Wacht*, 1879, p. 199.
77. *Kriegsschauplatz*, pp. 42–43.
78. *Ibid.*, pp. 38–40.
79. "Palästina und die Juden," *Der Judenspiegel*, 1880, pp. 37–38.
80. "Offenes Schreiben an den Herrn B.A(ron) von Hirsch," *Antisemitische Correspondenz*, 6.1.1889, signed: Jeremias Sauerampfer.
81. Nachlass Marr, B IV 12 p. 196, 10.9.1897.
82. "Der Gesellschaftsvertrag mit den Juden," *Deutsche Wacht*, 1879, p. 68.
83. "Israel droht," *ibid.*, p. 93; "Gesellschaftsvertrag II," *ibid.*, pp. 122–132.
84. *Ibid.*, p. 69.
85. *Kriegsschauplatz*, p. 37; *Judenkrieg*, p. 1; "Offenes Schreiben," *Antisemitische Correspondenz*, 6.1.1889.
86. R. Rürup, *op. cit.*, p. 95, mentions the appearance of the word in Rotteck's *Lexicon* from 1865, but this was only a curiosity. All later publications name Marr as the man who introduced the term into politics: Otto Ladendorf, *Historisches Schlagwörterbuch* (Strassburg & Berlin, 1906), p. 7; *Encyclopaedia Judaica* (Berlin, 1928), vol. 2, p. 1019; S. Dubnow, *Weltgeschichte*, vol. 10, p. 18; A. Bein, *loc. cit.*, p. 341; Chris Cobet, *Wortschatz des Antisemitismus in der Bismarckszeit* (Munchen, 1973), p. 221; R. Rürup, *op. cit.*, p. 177; A. Bein, *Die Judenfrage* (Stuttgart, 1980), vol. 2, p. 163 ff.
87. *Kriegsschauplatz*, 4th ed. (Bern, 1879), p. 34.
88. *Judenkrieg*, p. 6; Nachlass Marr, A 39, 25.7.1879, where Kostenobel refers to the term "anti-Jewish Association" in a letter to Marr.
89. *Allgemeine Zeitung des Judenthums*, 15.10.1879. The organizers of the meeting mistakenly thought that the Jews would be at prayers on the eve of the holiday and were surprised by a group of about ten Jews who attended at least the first part of the meeting (*Germania* Nr. 223, 27.9.1879). According to the *Berliner Börsen-Courier*, the meeting was a total fiasco, but even the anti-Jewish *Germania* admitted that only 40 people were ready to sign their names and that the meeting could only be described as a preliminary one. The formal foundation of the League was postponed for about three weeks.
90. Cf. E. Cramer, *Hitler's Antisemitismus und die Frankfurter Schule* (Düsseldorf, 1979), pp. 89–91.
91. *Judenkrieg*, p. 15.
92. Nachlass Marr, A 39, 25.7.1879.
93. Nachlass Marr, A 82, 20.9.1879. It is difficult to trace the first activities of the Association. Newspaper reports (see Note 89) confirm Marr's

memoirs concerning what took place at the first strange meeting of the
League. Marr also states that the man whom he nicknamed "tapeworm"
(*Bandwurm*) appointed himself president, was dismissed after three
weeks, and only then submitted his position to de Grousillier. But from
de Grousillier's letter to Marr (20.9.1879) it is obvious that the connection
between Marr, de Grousillier, and the League existed before that strange
meeting.

94. H. de Grousillier, *Nathan der Weise und die Antisemiten-Liga* (Berlin,
1880), p. 31.

95. *Ibid.*, p. 32. This religious orientation of the League did not result only
from deliberations that took place between the time of the meeting of
Sept. 26 and the opening ceremony in mid-October. Already the original
invitation to the meeting of Sept. 26 called upon a Christian public to attend ("Christlich gesinnte Männer"), *Vossische Zeitung*, 26.9.1879. Marr's
antireligious intention in inventing the term "anti-Semitism" was literally
nipped in the bud!

96. *Flugblatt II der Antisemiten-Liga* "Die Krumme Art," Berlin [1879].

97. Skizzenbuch der *Wahrheit*, Jahrgang 1880, Berlin 1881, p. 8.

98. Nachlass Marr, B V b *Testament eines Antisemiten*, p. 105.

99. *Ha-Magid*, No. 43, 5.11.1879.

100. This was Marr's fate not only in *Ha-Magid*, but also in the Orthodox
paper *Der Israelit*. In the months of April and May the newspaper reacts
to the *"Risches"* [Jew-hatred] of Henne am Rhyn and not to Marr's *Victory of Judaism* (26.3.1879), and from September on it only mentions
Stoecker's party and never Marr's "Antisemiten-Liga" (30.9.1879).

101. *Berliner Tageblatt,* Nr. 52, 1879.

102. Nachlass Marr, A 149, letters 2–6, Oct.–Nov. 1879. In his memoirs,
Marr states that he did not become a candidate for the presidency because
of his radical past, unsuitable for a man heading a conservative association, and also because as a Hamburg citizen he could not lead a Berlinese
institution. He also claims that the person who "leaked" this information
was no other than the first and dubious president of the league—"Bandwurm."

103. Wawrzinek, *op. cit.*, p. 33.

104. Nachlass Marr, A 256, Nov. 10, 1879. This is the second letter Stoecker
wrote to Marr. Apparently Stoecker forgot about the first one (21.7.
1878). Concerning Stoecker's denial of any connection to Marr, see
D. von Ortzen, *Adolf Stoecker, Lebensbild und Zeitgeschichte* vol. 1
(Berlin, 1910), pp. 210, 225, and Werner Jochmann *et al., Protestantis-
mus und Politik. Werk und Wirkung Adolf Stoeckers* (Hamburg, 1982),
pp. 146–159.

105. Nachlass Marr, A 180, 21.11.1879. It is interesting to note that Pinkert
is too frightened to admit that Waldegg is his pseudonym even in a personal letter. He speaks of Waldegg in the third person, obviously from
fear of a leak.

106. See *Allgemeine Zeitung des Judenthums*, 2.12.1879.

107. *Judenkrieg*, p. 15; *Flugblatt I der Antisemiten-Liga*, Berlin, Oct. 1879.
The joiners were officially assured of secrecy.

108. Marr's intention to publish an anti-Semitic weekly was announced in the

Allgemeine Zeitung des Judenthums of Sept. 2, 1879. Rürup notes that this was the first instance of the term being used in that year! Are we to conclude that the Jews were those who coined the term? It seems to me that we should not attach great importance to the news item, as Marr used the word only three weeks afterwards. I assume that Marr recoursed to the new notion for "Jew hatred" only *after* Stoecker's attack against the Jews on Sept. 19, 1879, and in order to make a clear distinction between Stoecker's anti-Jewish movement and his. There is no evidence that the incidental use of the term by the *AZJ* directly or indirectly influenced Marr.

109. *Neues Statut des Vereins "Antisemiten-Liga,"* revised Jan. 1881, Berlin.
110. *Judenkrieg,* pp. 6–11.
111. *Ibid.,* p. 3.
112. Marr wrote another pamphlet which appeared only in 1883 (and apparently could not be sold—all the copies I found carry the year 1885 on the title page [i.e., after Fritsch bought the whole edition]): *Lessing contra Sem.* This was in fact Marr's answer to de Grousillier's lecture, "Nathan der Weise und die Antisemiten-Liga," from the year 1880. Although Marr made some positive remarks concerning Christianity, the general conclusion is the logical outcome of Marr's radical system, and is compatible with the inner logic of the term "anti-Semitism": The Jewish problem is no longer religious but racial and social (pp. 20–21). It should be noted, that the discussion of *Nathan* is a part of the general debate conducted by Germans and German Jews alike on the occasion of the 100th anniversary of the drama *Nathan der Weise* (1779) and of Lessing's death (1781); cf. M. Zimmermann, "Lessing contra Sem. Literatur im Dienste des Antisemitismus" in S. Moses & A. Schöne (Hg.), *Die Juden in der deutschen Literatur* (Frankfurt, 1986), pp. 179–193.

Chapter 8

1. Nachlass Marr, A 273, 21.7.1879.
2. L. Poliakov, *The History of Antisemitism,* vol. 3 (London, 1974), p. 456.
3. Nachlass Marr, A 180, 14.2.1880.
4. Schmeitzner's *Internationale Monatsschrift. Zeitschrift für die allgemeine Vereinigung zur Bekämpfung des Judenthums* (Chemnitz, vol. 1–1882, vol. 2–1883).
5. "Anti-Stoecker" *loc. cit.,* p. 81 ff.
6. Nachlass Marr, A 256, 3.11.1880, 28.6.1882, 27.7.1882, 30.4.1884.
7. Nachlass Marr, A 7, 28.8.1884.
8. *Der Judenspiegel,* 1880, pp. 13–14.
9. See Chaps. 4–5 above.
10. Nachlass Marr, A 136, 22.12.1879, 11.4.1884, 2.8.1884.
11. Nachless Marr, A 99, 14.3.1881, 28.8.1884.
12. Nachlass Marr, A 67, 1.7.1885.
13. *Ibid.,* 8.5.1884.
14. *Ibid.,* 16.6.1884.
15. *Ibid.,* 7.4.1884.
16. *Ibid.*

17. *Ibid.,* 19.5.1885.
18. *Ibid.,* 16.9.1885.
19. *Ibid.,* 16.10.1885.
20. *Ibid.,* 22.10.1885.
21. "Antisemitische Wucht und Verluste," *Österreichischer Volksfreund* (1891):
    A fragment in the Nachlass.
22. Nachlass Marr, A 67, 26.3.1886.
23. *Ibid.,* 28.4.1886.
24. Nachlass Marr, A 256, 12.11.1886. This is the latter of the two letters.
25. *Testament eines Antisemiten,* pp. 103–104.
26. Nachlass Marr B V a *Im Philosemitismus.*
27. Nachlass Marr, A 67, 14.11.1887.
28. *Thatsachen zur Judenfrage* (Leipzig, 1889).
29. Nachlass Marr, A 67, 12.11.1890, 28.1.1891, 22.4.1891, 16.5.1892.
30. *Antisemitischer Volkskalender* (Leipzig, 1889).
31. J. G. Riquarts, *op. cit.,* p. 66ff.
32. See the *Testament of an Anti-Semite,* p. 145f.
33. "Deutsche und Französische Sozialdemokraten," *Antisemitische Corre-
    spondenz* Nr. 41, 15.12.1888.
34. "Warum die Antisemiten meistens konservativ sind," *ibid.,* Nr. 46, 3.3.
    1889.
35. *Ibid.,* 16.6.1889; in reaction to an article entitled "I am a progressive and
    an Anti-Semite." The only progressive people are the anti-Semites, but this
    as a counterweight to the Jewish anarchy.
36. *Österreichischer Volksfreund,* in *Antisemitische Flugblatter* 17, Fritsch,
    (Leipzig o.D. [1889]).
37. Marr could afford that because he signed his articles in this particular
    paper with the pseudonym Jeremias Sauerampfer.
38. *Ibid.*
39. Nachlass Marr, A 67, 12.11.1890.
40. Cf. D. Trietsch, "Die Gartenstadt," in *Altneuland* Organ der zionistischen
    Kommission zur Erforschung Palästinas (Berlin, 1906), p. 362.
41. "Antisemitische Wucht und Verluste."
42. See p. 140, *Testament.*
43. "Warum blüht der Antisemitismus in Sachsen," *Allgemeine Zeitung des
    Judenthums* 1893, p. 244.
44. Nachlass Marr, A 254.
45. *Testament,* pp. 75–76.
46. *Ibid.,* p. 84.
47. M. Bodenheimer, *Wohin mit den russischen Juden* (Hamburg o.D. [1891]);
    Gustav G. Cohn, *Die Judenfrage und die Zukunft* (Hamburg, 1891).
48. *Testament,* pp. 90, 96.
49. *Hamburger Fremdenblatt Leserbrief,* 15.4.1893.
50. Nachlass Marr, A 254 (Stettenheim).
51. *Enz. Judaica,* "Antisemitismus," p. 1019.
52. Hermann Lucko, *Ein Jahr im Centrum der Deutsch-sozialen Partei* (Leip-
    zig, 1892).
53. *Ibid.,* p. 19.
54. *Ibid.,* p. 21.

55. *Ecce ego* Nachlass Marr, B X c.
56. W. Heyden, *Die Mitglieder der Hamburger Bürgerschaft* (Hamburg, 1909), p. 180.

Epilogue

1. Getreuter Ekkehard, *Ergebnisse einer Forschungsreise in's Gebiet des heutigen religiösen Lebens* (Berlin, 1880), pp. 36, 40, 45, 51–52.
2. "Antisemitische Wucht und Verluste."
3. C. Cobet, *op. cit.*, p. 221.
4. *Antisemitische Correspondenz*, 4.3.1886.
5. *Thatsachen zur Judenfrage*, 1889, p. 97.
6. R. N. Coudenhove-Kalergi, *Wesen des Antisemitismus* (Wien, 1929), p. 55.
7. C. Cobet, *op. cit.*, p. 223; Julius Moses, *Lösung der Judenfrage* Eine Rundfrage (Berlin, 1907), p. 282.
8. *Handbuch der Judenfrage,* 1931, pp. 15, 474, 490.
9. *Handbuch* (33rd ed.), 1933, p. 503; (41st ed.), 1937, pp. 18, 514; (45th ed.), 1939, p. 414.
10. E. Reventlow, *Judas Kampf und Niederlage in Deutschland. 150 Jahre Judenfrage* (Berlin, 1937), p. 338; Hans Günther, *Rassenkunde des jüdischen Volkes* (München, 1930), p. 315.
11. Cf. Th. Nipperdey & R. Rürup, "Antisemitismus," in *Geschichtliche Grundbegriffe* Historisches Lexikon zur politisch-sozialen Sparche in Deutschland. Bd. 1 (Stuttgart, 1972), pp. 151–152.
12. *Handbuch* (49th ed.), 1943, p. 18; (50th ed.), 1944, pp. 18, 542. See also G. Bording Mathieu, "The secret anti-Juden-Sondernummer of 21st May 1943" *Leo Baeck Yearbook* 1981, p. 292.

List of Marr's Works

1. ARCHIVE MATERIAL (selected items)

Staatsarchiv Hamburg 622/1: Nachlass Wilhelm Marr
A. Briefe (307 Korrespondenten)
B.   I—Memoiren, 6 Teile, 1819–1891.
     II—Nachträge zu den Memoiren
     IV—Socialpolitische Rücksichtslosigkeiten, Tagebuchaufzeichnungen eines
       Pessimisten, 14 Teile, 1892–1901
     V—Schriften betr. Judenfrage
       a. Im Philosemitismus, 1887
       b. Testament eines Antisemiten 1891
    X—Ecce ego, 1895

2. PRINTED WORKS

Gegenwart und Zukunft o. 0 1843.
Glosse über die Petition der Kölner an den König von Preussen, Strassburg
   1843
Das entdeckte und das unentdeckte Christenthum, Bern 1843
Dies gehört dem Volke, Bern 1843
Pillen, Bern 1843
Petit mot d'un étranger au peuple Vaudois, Lausanne 1845
L. Feuerbach, die Religion der Zukunft. Für Lesser aus dem Volke bearbeitet,
   Lausanne 1844
Das Junge Deutschland in der Schweiz, Leipzig 1846
Auch eine Adresse an Schleswig-Holsteins Männer der That, Hamburg 1846
Der Mensch und die Ehe vor dem Richtsstuhl der Sittlichkeit, Leipzig 1848
Was ist geschehen? Was muss geschehen? Zwei Fragen, Hamburg 1848
Die Jacobiner in Hamburg, Hamburg 1848
An Hamburgs Wähler. Ein Wort zur rechten Zeit, Wandsbeck 1849
Herr Meyer, Hamburger komischer Kalender, Hamburg 1851, 1852
*Herr Dr. Heckscher als Agitator, Volksvertreter und Staatsmann. Eine politische
   Skizze,* Hamburg 1851
Anarchie oder Autorität, Hamburg 1852

Travailler pour le roi de Prusse, Hamburg 1861
Der Judenspiegel, Hamburg 1862
Messias Lassalle und seine Hamburger Jünger, Hamburg 1863
Reise nach Central-Amerika, Hamburg 1863
Selbständigkeit und Hoheitsrecht der freien Stadt Hamburg sind ein Anachronismus geworden, Hamburg 1866
Der Ausschluss Österreich aus Deutschland ist eine politische Widersinnigkeit, Hamburg & Leipzig 1866
Streifzüge durch das Concilium von Trient, Hamburg 1867
Es muss alles Soldat werden, Hamburg 1867
Die neue Dreieinigkeit, Hamburg 1867
Die Flagge deckt die Ladung, Hamburg 1869
7 Briefe über den "Stein der Weisen," Bern 1869
Religiöse Streifzüge eines philosophischen Touristen, Berlin 1875
Der Sieg des Judenthums über das Germanenthum, Bern 1879
Vom Jüdischen Kriegsschauplatz, Bern 1879
Wählt keinen Juden. Der Weg zum Sieg des Germanenthums über das Judenthum, Berlin 1879
Der Judenkrieg. Seine Fehler und wie er zu organisiren ist, Chemnitz 1880 (Antisemitische Hefte 1)
Goldene Ratten und rote Mäuse, Chemnitz o.D [1880] (Antisemitische Hefte 2)
Öffnet die Augen Ihr deutsche Zeitungsleser Chemnitz 1880 (Antisemitische Hefte 3)
Lessing contra Sem, Chemnitz 1883

3. NEWSPAPERS AND JOURNALS

Blätter der Gegenwart für sociales Leben, Monatshefte Bern 1844–1845 (ed.)*
Mephistopheles, Hamburg 1847–1852 (ed.)
Freischütz, Hamburg 1849–1852, 1860–1863
Die Opposition. Ein Blaubuch für die öffentliche Meinung, Hamburg 1863 (ed.)
Die Nessel. Hamburg 1864–1865 (ed.)
Der Beobachter an der Elbe. Wochenblatt für Schleswig-Holstein und Hamburg, Hamburg 1865–1866 (ed.)
Der Kosmopolit. Ein Sonntagsblatt für Gebildete aller Stände, Hamburg 1866 (ed.)
Die Post, Berlin 1868–1871
Hamburger Montagsnachrichten, 1868–1870
Weimarische Zeitung, 1874–1875
Hamburger Reform, 1872–1874
Gartenlaube, 1874–1875
Deutsche Wacht. Monatsschrift der Anti-jüdischen Vereinigung, Berlin 1879–1880 (Später: *Judenspiegel,* 1880) (ed.)
Österreichischer Volksfreund, Wien 1886–1893
Antisemitische Correspondenz, Dresden 1886–1890

* Marr as editor.

Index

(Because they appear throughout the book, the items "Wilhelm Marr," "Antisemitism," "Hamburg," and "Germany" have not been included in the index.)

ADAV (Allgemeiner deutscher Arbeiterverein), 54–57
Ahlwardt, Hermann, 11
Alexander II, 79
Antisemitic Catechism, 102, 103, 113, 114, 141–144, 148
Antisemitic Congress, Bochum, 105, 145ff
Antisemitic Congress, Dresden, 97, 142
Antisemitic League (Antisemitenliga), 8, 19, 76, 90–95, 98, 112, 155, 165, 167–168
Antisemitic Parties, Germany, 103–111, 113, 145–149
"Antisemitism, Business-of-," XI, 11, 96–111, 136–143, 145, 149, 155
Antisemitism, Historiography, VII–XII, 70
Audorf, Jacob, 54–58, 162
Austria, 3, 4, 30, 33, 38, 63, 66, 67, 131–132. See also Vienna

Balzac, Honoré de, 9
Banks, Dr. E., 162
Bauer, Bruno, 16, 19, 34, 44, 48, 74, 79, 158
Baumeister, Hermann, 24, 25, 161
Bebel, August, 97, 98, 150
Berlin, 25, 54, 61, 72, 75–78, 83, 90–95, 97, 98, 108, 137–140
Berlin, Congress of (1878), 87

Biedermann, Joseph, 123–129
Biedermann, Samuel (Sem), 112, 123–129
Bismarck, Otto von, VIII, 5, 6, 7, 56, 57, 59–63, 86, 95, 112
Blanc, Louis, 23, 33
Blank Benjamin, 119, 120
Bleichroeder, Gerson, 86, 147, 150
Böckel, Otto, 101, 103
Bodenheimer, Max, 109, 170
Börne, Ludwig, 5, 15, 19, 22, 75, 121, 131, 134, 135, 136
Brafman, Jacob, 8
Bras, A., 62
Bremen, 14, 43–45, 48, 116–118, 122
Briman, Aaron, 8
Buchholz, Heinrich, 10
Bülow, Hans von, 75, 165

Callenbach, Wilhelm, 36, 42
Carlsbad Decrees, 3, 21
Cavour, Camillo, 60
Chamberlain, Houston Stewart, VII, 8
Charlemagne, 152
Charles I of England, 38, 39
Christian IX of Denmark, 58
Christlich-Soziale Partei, 76, 92, 112
Civil marriage, 32, 33, 40
Cohen, Gustav G., 109, 170
Cohn, I. M., 81
Cohn, Jonas, 64

Coudenhove-Kalergi, Heinrich, 113, 171
Crémieux, Adolphe, 68
Cumberland, Richard, 12
Customs policy, 82, 85
Customs Union, Prussian, 4, 106

Demokratischer Verein (Hamburg). *See* Radical (Democratic) Party
Denmark, 5, 6, 21, 56, 58, 61, 62, 159
Deutsch-Israelitischer Gemeindebund, 80, 81, 90, 165
Deutsch-Soziale Partei, 145–149
Deutscher Antisemitenverein. See Fritsch
Deutscher Reformverein, 94, 96, 142
Deutscher Verein (Hamburg), 105
Dohm, Ernst, 79
Drumont, Edouard, XI
Dubnow, Simon, 12, 70, 157, 164
Dühring, Eugen, 100, 141, 142
Dulon, Father, 30

Eichmann, Adolf, VII
Eisenmenger, Johann Andreas, 17, 146
Erfurt, Parliament, 29, 31

Feuerbach, Ludwig, 17, 19, 34, 40, 64, 68, 74, 79
Fichte, Johann Gottlieb, 101
Follen, Adolf, 158
Follen, Carl, 158
Förster, Bernhard, 99, 104
Förster, Paul, 105, 114
France, 7, 9, 33, 66, 68, 105, 147
Frankfurt, Parliament (1848), 5, 25, 27, 28, 31. *See also* Revolution of 1848
Frankfurter, Naphtali, 26
Frederick VII of Denmark, 58
Freitag, Gustav, 15
Friedrich I of Prussia, 146
Friedrich II of Prussia, 151
Friedrich III, German Kaiser, 135
Friedrich VII Augustenburg, 58–60
Friedrich Barbarossa, 24
Friedrich Wilhelm IV of Prussia, 27
Fritsch, Theodor, 8, 12, 34, 99–111, 113, 114, 138, 140, 144
Froben, Georg, 84, 96, 166

Gambetta, Leon, 68
German Confederation (*Bund*), 3–7, 37, 58, 61, 158
Germany, Unification, 6, 27, 63, 68, 75. *See also* Nationalism, German
Glagau, Otto, 11, 71, 99, 100, 104, 141, 142
Godeffroy, Peter, 62, 161
Goebbels, Joseph, 114
Goethe, Johann Wolfgang, 9
Gotha, Program (1849), 28–31, 33, 38, 56
Grousillier, Hector de, 90–95, 98, 112, 168
Gutzkow, Karl Friedrich, 15

Haller, N. Ferdinand, 146
Hambach, Festival, 15
Hampden, John, 38, 39
Hannover, 4, 14, 29, 119, 120, 122
Hartmann, 98
Hebbel, Friedrich, 9
Heckscher, Moritz, 24, 25
Heine, Heinrich, 5, 15, 19, 22, 42, 75, 121, 131, 134, 135, 136, 148
Heine, Salomon, 146
Henne-am-Rhyn, Otto, 168
Henrici, Ernst, 98, 99
Hentze, Otto, 84, 85, 94, 96, 99
Hertz, Hartwig Samson, 65
Herweg, Georg, 125
Herzl, Theodor, 7, 87, 115
Hess, Moses, 17
Hirsch, Moritz Baron de, 87, 104, 167
Hitler, Adolf, VII, IX, 8, 114
Hobelmann, 43, 45, 116
Hödel, Max, 165

Israel, Friedrich, 81
Istoczy, Gyösö, 87

Jellinek, Adolf, 11, 12, 158
Jellinek, Georg, 12
Junges Deutschland in der Schweiz (Young Germany), 5, 12, 15–19, 24, 25, 31, 55, 56, 60, 93, 158

Kalisch, David, 79
Karl Alexander of Weimar, 71
Kassel, Paulus, 82, 83

Kostenobel, Rudolf, 77, 78, 84, 91, 96, 133, 141, 167
Kur-Hessen, Constitution of, 37, 38, 40

Lassalle, Ferdinand, 54–58, 64, 73, 74, 80, 134, 136
Lazarus, I., 41, 42
Ledru Rollin, Alexandre-Auguste, 33
Lehman, Joseph, 8
Lemonier, Charles, 66
Lenz, 50
Lessing, Gotthold Ephraim, 91, 93, 169
Liberalism, German, 3–7, 16, 20–34, 38, 49, 55, 58, 78, 81, 82
Liebermann von Sonnenberg, Max, 98, 99, 104, 105
Liebknecht, Wilhelm, 150
Ligue Internationale de la Paix, 66
Liszt, Franz, 71
Loesch, Isak, 129–130
Lucko, Hermann, 110
Ludwig II of Bavaria, 71

Machiavelli, Niccolo, 25, 60
Mann, Thomas, 23
Manteuffel, Erwin von, 61
Marr (Callenbach), Bertha, 36, 70
Marr, Heinrich, 9–13, 15, 119, 133, 157
Marr (Behrend), Helene, 70, 71
Marr (Kornick), Jenni, 72, 73, 101, 103
Marr, Johann Wilhelm, 9
Marr (Becherer), Katharina Henriette, 9, 10
Martens, Joachim Friedrich, 56, 161
Marx, Karl, 16, 17, 23, 47, 73, 74, 134, 136, 164
Mazzini, Giuseppe, IX, 15, 30, 53, 59, 60, 61
Meissner, Otto, 46
Mendelssohn, family, 86
Mendelssohn, Moses, 148
Metternich, Klemens von, 131
Meyer, Isac Salomon (Ismeyer), 60, 63
Montefiore, Moses, 87
Moses, Julius, 114
Mosse, Rudolf, 72, 78, 84, 93

Napoleon I, Napoleonic Wars, 3, 4, 9, 14, 15, 18, 33, 134, 151
Napoleon III, 33

Nationalism, German, 3, 5, 6, 18, 21, 22, 24, 27, 30, 31, 56, 58, 60, 62, 67, 134, 135
National-Socialism, 88, 106, 114, 115
National-Verein (German National Union), 58, 62
Nobilling, Karl Eduard, 79
Nordmann (Naudh), Heinrich, 49, 84, 85, 94, 162

Oliphant, Laurence, 87
Olmütz (1850), 30

Palestine, 48, 81, 86–88, 167
Patriotic Party (Hamburg), 26, 27, 31
Paulsen, 58
Peine, 21
Perinhart, J., 80, 81
Perl, 93
Pinkert (Waldegg), Alexander, 94, 96, 97, 99, 101, 141, 142, 168
Piza, Joseph, 65
Polokovski, G., 76, 137
Proudhon, Pierre Joseph, 16
Prussia, 3–7, 16, 21, 22, 27–33, 35, 38, 39, 54–63, 66, 67, 83, 90, 93, 146, 160

Race, Racism, 8, 13, 14, 45–49, 53, 64–68, 72, 82, 84, 85, 89, 100, 101, 117
Radenshausen, Christian, 104
Radetzky, Joseph Wenzel, 131
Radical (Democratic) Party, 20, 21, 26–32, 43, 46–56, 62, 64, 162
Rée, Anton, 20, 40, 43, 45, 98, 161
Reventlow, Ernst Graf, 114, 171
Revolution of 1848, IX, 5, 6, 20–34, 58, 85, 103, 106
Riege (SPD), 98
Riesser, Gabriel, IX, 21, 24–26, 28, 30–32, 34, 37–43, 45, 48, 50, 52, 85, 160, 166
Rothschild, family, 16, 27, 36, 68, 86, 124, 131, 147
Rotteck, Carl von, 167
Ruge, Arnold, 59, 135
Russia, 7, 66, 79, 87, 88, 108, 165

Sanghelli (Marr), Elisabeth, 9
Sassulitsch, Wera, 79

Schernikau, Wilhelm, 79
Scherr, Johaness, 73, 75, 86, 100, 103, 138
Schiller, Friedrich, 137
Schirmer, Ernst, 79
Schleswig-Holstein, problem of, 5, 21, 24f, 28, 31, 58–63, 66, 86, 159, 160
Schmeitzner, Ernst, 95, 97, 99, 100
Schönerer, Georg von, XI, 104
Schopenhauer, Arthur, 111
Schramm, Rudolf, 61, 62
Schroffenstein, Baron, 32
Schulze-Delitsch, Frank, 55, 75
Singer, Paul, 150
Social-Democracy, German, 7, 74, 75, 77, 80, 82, 97, 98, 105–107, 109, 137, 143, 144, 147, 150, 152–4. *See also* ADAV
Spengler, Oswald, 106
Spinoza, Baruch, 135, 148
Stern, Ludwig, 80, 81
Stettenheim, Julius, 22–24, 46, 51, 108–110, 160, 162
Stoecker, Adolf, 8, 76, 77, 82, 83, 92–100, 103, 104, 112, 137, 141, 142, 168, 169
Strassmann, Wolff, 98
Straus, David, 17
Streicher, Julius, VII
Strousberg, Bethel Henry, 64, 65, 71, 77

Talnay, Maquis de, 33
Tisza-Esler, Blood Libel, 97
Trautmannsdorf, Baron von, 123, 127, 128

Trebitsch, Arthur, 8
Treitschke, Heinrich von, 8, 94, 113
Trepov, General, 79, 88

United States, Civil War, 49, 51, 53, 66

Vienna, 9, 12, 15, 75, 112, 123–133
Vienna, Congress of, 3, 33
Virchow, Rudolf, 62
Voltaire, 64

Wagner, Cosima, 96
Wagner, Richard, VII, XI, 8, 10, 24, 28, 34, 71, 73–75, 95, 96, 100, 134
Weimar, 9, 65, 71, 72, 74
Weitling, Wilhelm, IX, 16, 17
Wertheimstein, Adolph von, 124–131
Wertheimstein, Hermann, 131
Wex, Franz Julius, 46, 62
Wilhelm I, Kaiser of Germany, 165
Wilhelm II, Kaiser of Germany, 7, 105
Wohlwill, Emil, 49
Wolff, Dr. (Berliner Tageblatt), 72
Wolffson, Isaac, 27, 30, 45, 48, 50, 62, 85

Zacharias, 46, 161
Zerbst, 64
Ziller, Rosalie, 36, 132
Ziller, 132, 133
Zimmermann, Oswald, 101, 103
Zionism. *See* Palestine